Laughing Matters

Steven Jacobi was born in Birmingham and educated in Cambridge, Edinburgh and London. He has published two novels and has written for Radio 4 and a number of national newspapers and magazines.

Also by Steven Jacobi

Going Naked is the Best Disguise
A Short Series of Discrete Problems
Acting My Life *with Ian Holm*

Laughing Matters

Steven Jacobi

Century · London

Published by Century in 2005

1 3 5 7 9 10 8 6 4 2

First published in the United Kingdom in 2005 by Century
The Random House Group Limited
20 Vauxhall Bridge Road, London, SW1V 2SA

Random House Australia (Pty) Limited
20 Alfred Street, Milsons Point, Sydney, New South Wales 2061, Australia

Random House New Zealand Limited
18 Poland Road, Glenfield
Auckland 10, New Zealand

Random House (Pty) Limited
Endulini, 5a Jubilee Road, Parktown 2193, South Africa

The Random House Group Limited Reg. No. 954009
www.randomhouse.co.uk

A CIP catalogue record for this book is available from the British Library

Papers used by Random House are natural, recyclable products made from wood grown in sustainable forests. The manufacturing processes conform to the environmental regulations of the country of origin

ISBN 1 8441 3798 8

Typeset by SX Composing DTP, Rayleigh, Essex
Printed and bound in the United Kingdom by
Mackays of Chatham, Plc, Chatham, Kent

For Pippa

Acknowledgements

Many thanks to those who booked me, especially Jim Grant, Toby Hadoke and Jane Hardee. And to those who gave their time to talk about comedy, in particular Tony Allen, Simon Armitage, Barry Cryer, Ken Dodd, Beatie Edney, Terry Jones, Alison Larkin, Ian Marchant, Bernard McKenna, Lavinia Murray, Logan Murray and D. J. Taylor. To Alan Vaughan for an otherwise unacknowledged joke. To Hils Jago for persuading me to take a clowning course. A sincere debt of gratitude to my agent at Curtis Brown, Euan Thorneycroft. To Hannah Black at Century, who kept me in line and got behind the project, even coming to watch me (once). To my parents, for providing the raw material. And finally, to Pippa, probably the funniest person I know.

ONE

Up the Creek

What a wonderful day it was for walking into the theatre in Wimbledon, guessing the average age of the audience, and shouting out, 'Look at me, missus – no dentures.'

Four years ago, I went to see Ken Dodd 'in concert'. Despite having bought two tickets, I went by myself. The person who had originally agreed to accompany me suddenly found he had some important filing to do that night. I tried someone else, a television director, who said, 'Ken Dodd? Er. No thanks.' I then offered the spare, unwanted, increasingly objectionable ticket to several others. I offered it free; with a complimentary drink thrown in; with a drink *and* a meal and, if they wanted, a tickling stick – but no one was interested. To them, it was clear, Dodd was a has-been, a vaguely funny but mostly *un*funny old man who existed in their memories as a sort of television novelty act from the fag end of the sixties, cartoonishly buck-toothed, with cocked, affectedly arthritic fingers, wielding a feather duster, surrounded (and surrounded suspiciously) by a troop of small people known as 'Diddy Men'. At school, sometime in the 1970s, when the surging tide of adolescent sexuality within me and my friends had finally washed ashore, a 'Dicky Mint' was a sort of fond euphemism for the fellatio we dreamt of but never achieved.

Doddy was a part of those long Saturday nights which, for those of us born in or immediately prior to the swinging decade, were spent mostly in front of the television watching some form or other of what was widely termed 'light entertainment' – though to a young boy, what was on offer seemed neither light nor entertaining. People like Simon Dee, Engelbert Humperdinck, Tiny Tim, Bruce Forsyth, Des O'Connor and Val Doonican were some of the other personalities I recall inhabiting this numbing, night-time landscape.

Once, on the *Parkinson* show, Parky asked Eric Morecambe and Ernie Wise what they would have been if they had not become comedians: 'Mike and Bernie Winters,' they replied. And Mike and Bernie were, of course, also a part of the Saturday-night plot, a plot – it seemed – which was designed categorically to redefine comedy as being a style of diversion almost completely devoid of laughter. In fact, the only person who I recall ever finding any of it remotely funny was my mother. Looking back, I now remember my mum's dislike of Dodd – singled out alone, it seemed, for her unsparing contempt – was somehow significant. Like most things to do with my mother, it said more about her. Though he wasn't much suited to television, Dodd was by far the funniest and most talented of the lot, a fact which is now widely recognised.

At least, recognised by me. Or by me and many thousand old-age pensioners. Apart from the empty seat next to me, Wimbledon Theatre was sold out. They had arrived on crutches, in wheelchairs, with sticks, and sometimes on their own two feet, though even then slowly, gingerly, limpingly and, above all, cautiously. Before entering the auditorium, they adjusted hearing aids, adopted or discarded lunettes, made a final teeth check, came to a practical estimation about the state of their bowels, and queued for the toilet. By the time the toilets were clear, the 7.30 start had been put back to 7.45.

During those unscheduled fifteen minutes, I began to panic, to wonder what I was doing in the theatre at all. Why had I come? I knew, for example, that I was not, in a rather perverse way, using Dodd to rekindle my youth or clutch at the lost innocence of childhood. I am not necessarily averse to such things, but generally speaking, they can usually be attained in much more straightforward and efficiently sentimental ways. By listening to the Beatles, for instance, or buying a Mini Cooper, or watching a video of *Born Free*. No, I thought (or at least affected to think) that my attendance was part of an altogether more ambitious enquiry into the very essence of comedy. This interest had been simmering for a while. And now the itch had become so unbearable that it needed a scratch. Dodd represented the first tentative claw of my finger. It's a bit complicated, so let me explain.

After those pre-adolescent Saturday evenings spent in front of the television, comedy became an increasingly important part of my life. I was not a happy teenager. Not only was I not happy, but I was also unattractive. The two are not, of course, unrelated. My nose was too big for my face. My face was too small for my nose. Hair grew on it in patches, in fluffy, unregulated clumps. Shaving, even secret shaving with my father's Philishave, was managed through an acne-strewn minefield. My eyes were narrow and shifty. The nylon shirts my mother insisted I wore to school (two shirts only; one in the wash, one on me) encouraged my body to manufacture a teenage stench of Rabelaisian magnitude. I was ugly and clumsy and gauche and shy and hopeless. The only way that I could make a mark was by making people laugh, either through humour or, more often, by acting the clown. Laughter assuaged my anxiety and was, at least in my mind, a direct consequence of it.

By the time I was eighteen or so, and the Ugly Duckling in me had become if not a swan then at least some other, marginally less repellent bird, my form master Niall Cluely – who used to write rock journalism for *Sight & Sound*, loved the Rolling Stones, and in reply to one critic who said that Keith Richards was the only true musician in the band, replied that actually there were no musicians among the Stones, that was their point – wrote on my report, 'A thoroughly meticulous hard worker whose excellent attitude has always been a superb model to his fellows . . .' Wait a minute. He did say that, but it's not the bit I meant. I just wanted to share it. Here's the appropriate extract: 'I am grateful for all the fine support he has given to school and House over the years and for *his unfailing good humour which has often lightened darker moments*.' My inclination to use humour had, you see, matured into a characteristic.

I am not exactly sure what 'darker moments' could have occurred in a private school in a well-to-do suburb of Birmingham in the 1970s, but there you are. Maybe being the last house in the street to get colour television (the shame), or not having two new cars on the drive (the humiliation). Niall Cluely is still at the school, though now he is the Very Reverend Niall Cluely. And the second comment on my report was actually made by my housemaster Ian Biggs, known as

'Monty' because he was once in the army. He was a lovely man and a brilliant wicket keeper, though now long dead. Niall and Monty. In the end, God got them both.

I mention them here not merely because of the reports they wrote but because, in different ways, they were significant figures in helping me to understand comedy. Niall and Monty both possessed their own distinct senses of humour. I was literally a pupil learning at their feet. The former was sardonically observant and occasionally witty. He had what in the Middle Ages would have been termed a 'melancholic humour', and there was certainly something of the sardonic gargoyle about him. The latter was a Brian Johnston *naïf* with a gentle eye for the absurd and the ridiculous. He was also an infectious and irresistible giggler. Quite often in assembly he would notice or more likely hear something which would start him tittering – usually the horribly off-key singing of Reggie Everett, head of maths, whom school protocol insisted he stood next or near to. On hearing Reggie's bomber-like drone during 'For Those in Peril', Monty would instictively reach for his red-and-white spotted handkerchief (always immaculate in the top pocket of his immaculate blazer) to cover his helpless, cherubic weeping.

I can now pay tribute to these two in helping to steer the frantic, defensive clowning of my early adolescence towards the less troubled waters of early adult comedic appreciation. At any rate, by the time I left school I recognised, for a number of reasons, that I was 'comedy sensitive', and that humour (for me) was always tangled up with the ugliness of life – and never, ever, far from it.

Reviewing the last twenty years or so brings a realisation that an interest, a fascination, with humour has been a constant part of my life. I wrote a doctorate on a 'funny' novelist, Angus Wilson. My two published novels have both been described as dark comedies, which is exactly as I would wish. At university, my only contribution to college drama was to co-write a pantomime and then appear as one of the Ugly Sisters. I should say that I was also cast as Second Knight in a production of Fletcher and Shakespeare's *Two Noble Kinsmen*, but ruined each performance by giggling (with the First Knight) at the sound of rasping Velcro every time I had to remove my purse.

In addition, and without understanding why, I have collected articles, reviews and interviews with and about comedians, apparently for no discernible purpose other than feeling that they were somehow interesting or one day might be so. I now possess fifteen fat wallets of yellowing newsprint devoted to such things as German comedy, the tears of the clown and Bob Monkhouse.

All this says a little about the way that comedy or an interest in humour has shadowed my life, though doesn't necessarily answer the question, 'Why Ken Dodd?' or 'Why Ken Dodd *now*?' The first is easier to answer: I had read an article about Dodd, and then Michael Billington's short, brilliant monograph about him, *How Tickled I Am*, which convinced me that he was a surrealist comic master whose genius had somehow passed me by. I wanted to see for myself. But Dodd was merely a symptom in a suddenly dynamic and compelling urge to come to terms with my broader interest in funniness.

Why was this? It might, I suppose, be something to do with my age (middle-ish) and the subsequent need to come to terms with it. You know the kind of thing – there's suddenly more stuff, more living, behind than in front of you, so what's it all about then, and isn't everything possibly just a bit absurd and odd and, well, *funny*?

I had already done therapy, and had lied or told half-truths during most of the sessions, excepting the one where I dragged dog shit across the oatmeal carpet and Mrs Freud (sadly, not her real name) stared at me for what seemed like several hours before saying, 'You must be terribly embarrassed.' I was, and freely admitted as much.

Though I gave it a pretty good try, I always felt scrutinised and judged by my therapist, and in the attempt to create a good impression, to please her, I came to the conclusion that I ought to sort myself out *before* seeing her. This might be quite common and probably says something unkind about the relationship I have with my mother, but it also meant that therapy could not be of much use to me.

I have a friend who at about the same time convinced himself that the best therapy was to take on an activity at which you were and always had been no good – and conquer it. In his case, it was singing, and he talked a lot about 'mastering' himself and bringing the left- (or was it the right?) hand side of his brain into play. Turning himself from a tone-deaf Reggie Everett into a competent tenor would, he thought, improve his handwriting and allow him to learn foreign languages, both involving skills which had over the years proved spectacularly elusive. He lasted three lessons. His Christmas cards are still illegible and on his last trip to France he went into a *boulangerie* intending to ask for some bread, and instead informing the *boulanger* that his car had broken down.

My friend and I went about things in a different way, but we were essentially after the same thing at the same junction of our lives: self-appraisal, self-knowledge, and the need to understand who we are. After several false starts, I turned to comedy and then, by way of introduction, to Ken Dodd.

Doddy's act lasted for four hours or so. He joked about the audience not getting home until the small hours, about them missing the last bus, and even about them being locked in during the interval. He gave off a fizz of hectoring madness, painting a skewed seaside-picture-postcard view of England which eventually battered people into laughter. He tried everything and anything, from beating a large drum to actually telling some good jokes. Here are my favourites. 'The man who invented the Catseye did so one night while walking down a dark country lane and seeing a cat coming towards him. Had the cat been facing the other way, he would have invented the pencil sharpener.' And: 'Have you heard the one about the female topless ventriloquist? You can't see her lips moving.'

The audience howled. It cried with laughter. Dentures rattled uneasily around gummy cavities. Prostates ached. Varicose veins became sore. Some people quite probably wet themselves. But the most impressive thing about Dodd is that (despite being in his seventies) he is on the road nearly all the time, averaging a gig every two or three days, continually travelling around the country and name-checking places like Rhyl, Truro, Cleethorpes, Skegness, Darlington, Bedworth, Warrington and Torquay. He has single-handedly and obsessively redefined the phrase 'off the beaten track'.

There is a fanatacism about this which set me thinking. I could vaguely identify with what I recognised as a chronic need to make people laugh. I didn't think my need was as overwhelming as his, but it was, I thought, still somewhere inside me – a little muted and repressed and compromised, but definitely *there*. Doddy had hit a nerve.

I spent some time wondering about all this, mooching round the flat, listening to old *Goon Show* tapes, reading a biography of Peter Sellers, and then even starting to write a novel about a comedian, tentatively titled, *On the Fabric of a Funny Man*. The writing of it soon floundered, crawling its way through a miserable first chapter before hitting the buffers around page ten. I had planned to tell the story of a stand-up comedian called Howerd Cooper who is only moderately good until the point at which his personal life begins to disintegrate. At that juncture, he channels his bitterness and disappointment and so on into his comic routine and is suddenly transformed into a very successful comedian.

The writing quickly came to grief on my realisation that at some point the novel would have to 'show' funny. The opening chapter included things like, 'He wondered what made people laugh, and reminded himself that some people couldn't help being funny. If only you could bottle that! His late Uncle Thomas, for instance, had once eaten a squirrel to win a bet and his party trick was to play the opening bars of Mozart's *Eine kleine Nachtmusik* on the violin using a vibrator instead of a bow.' And so on and so forth.

I quickly put the novel out of its misery.

But the bug had bitten. I thought I was on to something. I knew that I needed to know more about comedy and its practitioners, and one night I decided to visit a comedy club. It seemed odd that I had not been in one before. Comedy had been all the rage since the alternative-comedy boom of the 1980s and the foundation of actual clubs had created a new, fashionable kind of social venue. There were, I thought, two main reasons why I had never paid a visit to the Aztec or the Laughing Horse or even the Walrus Maniacts, all quite local to where I lived in London at that time. One was the sheer faddishness of comedy. I tend to react contrarily or slowly to conspicuous trends. Thus, in general, I have expressed little or no interest in any of the crazes that had taken the nation by storm during my lifetime. Gonks, Clackers, Spacehoppers, the 1970 collection of Esso World Cup Coins, chopper bikes and even the Rubik's Cube created not a single ripple of enthusiasm. And during the eighties, I seemed to be the only person I knew *not* making money. Fads? I missed them all.

I liked (at the time) to think all this had something to do with being a singular sort of chap and possessing individuality, my remoteness from the whims of hoi polloi sending out a clear message of feisty independence. Actually – I now understand – it was more to do with cussedness and insecurity and being anti-social. This last came naturally enough as I didn't have many friends with whom to be social. But cussedness? How else could you explain my fine and fastidiously acquired collection of adhesive stickers for oil products when, in 1970, World Cup year, everyone else was swapping silver coins of their favourite players? They had their Bobby Charlton and Brian Labone medallions, while I garnered (some actually quite uncommon) Havoline and Castrol GTX stickers. With advancing age I have come to realise that, in this respect, my early notions of *difference* don't hold water. Never did. My stickers merely revealed me as a different kind of plonker. Different, maybe, but still a plonker.

The second reason was the theoretical problem of the clubs themselves, the very idea of them. I had always assumed that comedy came from life – from unexpected angles, mind, but always from life – and was in some way 'organic'. Without wanting to sound too much like Samuel Beckett, I thought genuine, first-rate comedy was bound up with the muddle and difficulty of existence, as if life offered some kind of punch-line, and the trick was simply in understanding the rest of the joke, in appreciating the feed. There was, in other words, no need for comedy clubs, the existence of which constituted a contradiction in terms.

Although I have laughed during some films and television programmes (think of Albert Steptoe bathing in the kitchen sink; think of Charles Hawtrey announcing that he's going to the pier for a winkle), the suspicion persisted that this was *substitute* comedy – too formal and organised to be properly funny. And comedy *clubs* were even further away from the real thing. They recreated in an even more artificial environment the kind of thing that one could find merely by walking down the street or observing fellow creatures going about their everyday business. They were excuses for comedy.

Besides, there was something self-consciously awkward about the idea of going somewhere and expecting to be provoked into laughter. Self-consciousness was, I thought, the opposite of comedy. The explosive, collusive surprise of being able to respond to *something just happening* seemed infinitely more potent than anything that could be offered by the pre-prepared funny man (or woman). I realise this kind of thinking risks the negation not only of comedy clubs, but also of music hall, variety, popular entertainers, and anyone else who depends on a cocked, primed, prepaying audience to turn up and watch them. But still. I avoided comedy clubs because I felt cussed and because overwhelmingly I anticipated *not* laughing when confronted by a hopeful joker. This reciprocal element of performance demanded from me was too great a burden.

Doddy, however, lit the blue touchpaper. So one cold night

in April, I made my way to a comedy club in Greenwich called Up the Creek. The trip more or less coincided with the writing of my unfinished, almost unstarted novel on Howerd Cooper and could have been filed under 'research'. I had found Up the Creek in the *Time Out* listings section, and was mildly surprised that there seemed to be so few comedy clubs in my part of south London. An anticipation derived, I suspect, from the fact that much of south London is even less picturesque than the Peckham of *Only Fools and Horses* and in need of as much light relief as it can get.

Up the Creek, I discovered, was part owned and compered by a comedian called Malcolm Hardee, a sort of foul-mouthed version of a foul-mouthed Jonathan Meades (though pre-weight loss Meades), or maybe Russell Harty's alter ego. He was known as someone who would do pretty much anything to get a laugh, even (or maybe, especially) take his clothes off. A year or so previously, his autobiography had appeared and was promisingly titled, *I Stole Freddie Mercury's Birthday Cake*. It tells the story of how Hardee torched the Sunday-school piano in order to see the Holy Smoke and, like one of the more eccentric characters from Evelyn Waugh's *Vile Bodies*, once arrived somewhere or other on a stolen white horse to impress a girlfriend. He also did steal Freddie Mercury's birthday cake, though Freddie didn't much notice, let alone care. And at school (I like this a lot) he used to make up his own sick notes, e.g. 'Dear Mr Garrett, I'm sorry Malcolm couldn't come into school, but he's had a dose of leukaemia. Yours faithfully, Mrs J. Hardee.'

Introducing the programme (admission: £6), Hardee delivered a disappointingly tired selection of jokes. Some of these were merely old or oldish (Q: What goes in and out and smells of piss? A: The Queen Mother doing the hokey-cokey), some lewd and oldish ('Go home, wank into your wallet, and tell people you've come into money'), and some moderately witty (the audience was told, at one point, that people wandering to their seats immediately in front of Hardee were 'just going through a stage').

Up the Creek was a compact place comprising a smallish stage bounded on three of its sides by faded, red velveteen chairs that wouldn't have been out of place in a provincial cinema thirty, forty or even fifty years ago. Two Greek-style columns had been placed at the back of the stage, though neither was comprehensively Ionic or Doric. A single microphone stood towards the front. A bar was situated behind the ten rows or so of seating. It sold mostly lager in pint-sized plastic beakers.

The general buzz of good humour from people who were preparing, I supposed, to laugh themselves silly at any moment, reminded me of an old music hall. Though I had never actually been to one, there was something familiar about the atmosphere of faintly civilised though determined, pre-jocular abandon, something which I had seen before in films and television programmes featuring such halls, e.g. the barely restrained, boisterous, rowdy jolliness on *The Good Old Days*. These people were clearly intent on having a good time.

The music hall thing was probably deliberate, despite being undermined by the special-offer Thai food for sale behind the bar. There were also candles, and a wan light glimmered from a few electric 'spots' which were adequate for most activities up to but not inclusive of reading. Music hall, yes, but also, I now thought, shabby Gaumont, and even a bit jazz club. A small mural of a guitar, a tuba and an accordion vaguely in the form of a question mark added to this ambience, as did the muzak, which involved a guitar playing off a saxophone in Pink Pantherish mode. All this – all this sense of nostalgia, I mean – seemed very wise. The gentle though obscure invocation of a bygone era helped to put people in a good or goodish or at least benign mood and offered a seductive alternative to the temptations of late-twentieth-century cynicism, not insignificant if you were hoping to provoke unconfined jollity.

Such was the theory. But did it work? Well, up to a point. The two headline acts I saw certainly got their laughs, though I still felt the audience was chronically predisposed to laugh, or perhaps jeer, but not at any rate to be reasonable about such things. I suspected that so long as the acts weren't actually dull, then they would *do*. They could be good or bad – or good *and* bad – and in any number of ways, but actual dullness would not be tolerated.

And how they tried, those comedians, the experienced pros and the novices alike. The first comic was very fat, very bearded and very sweaty, though fat above all else. His jokes were entirely about himself and his fatness, and almost entirely at his own expense. 'Funny how some clothes make you look fat,' he wheezed. 'I'm in shape now – in the shape of a fucking onion.' Then: 'Slimmer of the Year lost two stone in one week. My first crap of the day weighs more than that.' And: 'I pick up girls by going to the open-air swimming pool and teasing them . . . I can feel them mentally dressing me.' He ended up by exhibiting exemplar pairs of underpants he had worn during his lifetime, each pair being larger and more shapelessly obscene than the last, this virtual history accompanied by strange and mostly unmemorable music.

The second act was even more bizarre though only mildly

less funny. It consisted of a man in outsize sunglasses holding up records (i.e. vinyl records, old thirty-three rpm jobs) and then smashing them with something he called the 'Golden Hammer'. The audience was invited to vote for records it might want to 'save' from destruction. Some records were actually played, on a small plastic record player at the very front of the stage. I recall a disc by the Wombles being saved and going to what the artiste termed 'Record Heaven', though another by Abba was set alight, and a third (by Neil Diamond, I think), was given a fatal karate chop. As the act built towards what in the trade is probably known as a 'crescendo', more and more records were produced and destroyed, the whole event developing into a speedy orgasm of waste and frenzied devastation.

'What the fuck was *that*?!' asked our man after nuking *Katy Lied* by Steely Dan (I nearly said something at this point), thus drawing the audience ever deeper into the carnival of ruin.

During the interval, beyond which I didn't stay, there was something called a 'Guest Spot' which involved comedic hopefuls and upcoming clowns trying out their talents on a group of people which was by now (flogged into frothy, unselfconscious excitement, slightly pissed) more or less looking for an excuse to go for the jugular.

I think it was Adam Philips, the Freudian psychoanalyst, who observed that nothing is more ordinary in children than the desire to be tickled (to and beyond the point of laughter) and the desire for revenge. In *The Merchant of Venice*, Shylock asks to be tickled to prove that he is human, thus representing himself *and* his vengeance as being natural. The point appears to be well made. At Up the Creek – primed, pissed and tickled – the audience quickly turned on the hapless guest spotees.

They had no chance. A snowball in Hell would have been more secure. One guest was reduced to tears, though obviously not of the laughing kind. Another swiftly involved himself in an argument with a particularly foul-mouthed man, and *then* was reduced to tears. The third got halfway through a joke, saw what was coming, and walked off before it arrived. All had permitted noisy and invariably fatal violations of their attempts to sustain impenetrably comic worlds. When Ben Elton started as stand-up in the early eighties, he talked very rapidly precisely because he feared audience invasion; he gave hecklers no time or space in which to interrupt his flow.

I suspect that each of the guests had rehearsed their (about) five-minute routines in front of mirrors and friends and maybe even girlfriends and/or boyfriends – though never, I would guess, parents – and safe in their sitting rooms had become reasonably confident of their material. Within minutes, or usually within seconds, their plans and their hopes lay in ruins, utterly undermined by an audience that was not so much unforgiving as hell-bent on being so.

One strange thing. The audience's glee and delight, its cackling, triumphalist laughter at the carnage it had created, actually seemed more pronounced and enthusiastically granted than the responses provoked by Fat Man or Vinyl Vandal. Here was delight unabashed, glee unrestrained.

Afterwards, I had stumbled into the chilly night air, my mind, as they say, in turmoil. Though I had witnessed some not very funny comedians, who had been followed by some other not very funny comedians, something in me had definitely been stirred. I thought I understood why all of them – Ken Dodd, Fat Man and Guest Spotee – had risked humiliation. Laughter was power. Making people laugh was the most effective way of imposing a kind of authority over them. It not only made you popular, but also clever.

Thus, somewhere in Greenwich, I had an epiphanic moment.

I recalled the lines from the beginning of *Brideshead Revisited* when Charles Ryder said that inside him something long-sickening had died, except that I knew that inside me something long-sickening could be cured. All that defensive humour as an adolescent, the darkly comic novels, the academic interest in the forms of comedy, the three sodding years of it for a doctorate – it must have meant something.

And I thought I knew what it was. Comedy was inside me, a part of my fabric, an ingredient in my DNA, even though it was long-sickening or whatever. I had attempted to suppress it and to articulate myself in other ways – initially through teaching (*teaching!*), and then through writing – but driving back through the soggy suburbs of Lewisham and Catford and Forest Hill, I knew that now was the time to yield to these deep, atavistic instincts. I knew, somehow, that I had to get on stage and express myself through comedy. I had been reading *Germinal* by Zola, and a phrase from it echoed (inaccurately) in my mind. I looked it up when I arrived home: 'He suddenly hears himself talking and because he'd been silenced for so long, he'd forgotten that he had ideas and that he was worth more than just an automaton, and it's wonderful moment of discovery.' That was it. *Exactly* it. Zola and Me. Ken Dodd and Me. I had to become a stand-up comedian and share my strange, darkly comic vision of the world with others. It would be my mission. My new thing. It would release me, allow me to understand and 'realise' myself.

I went to bed feeling quite pleased with myself.

The next morning, of course, I felt rather differently. Against the manic, moment-incited enthusiasm of the previous night I set down a number of sober, sensible rebuttals. One: I was crap on stage. I had always been crap on stage. Two: even answering the phone made me nervous. Three: I couldn't do accents. And four: at moments of slight stress, I developed a lisp, though the lisp only happened because I was afraid that I might stutter. When 'slight stress' became 'stress' I therefore became a lisping stutterer.

No. It wouldn't work. And teaching, I quickly reasoned, was actually all right, wasn't it? Quite enough to be going on with, at any rate.

For the next few days, I once more suppressed what had momentarily welled up within me, gently easing it back to a place deep in the shadows of my mind where it could skulk with other awkward, forgotten emotions like ambition, happiness, passion and love. They were probably having quite a party back there, but as I wasn't invited, I would never know.

Also over the next few days, I started to review the history of comedic potential in my family. What about the *genes*? I thought. What do they say about me? The first joke my father told me was, 'I can row a boat. Canoe?'

Despite this, he does have a good sense of humour, something not at all inherited from *his* father, who although a very nice and occasionally sophisticated man didn't, for much of the time, seem to possess a sense of humour at all. In particular, he hated the Marx Brothers, once explaining to me the reason why they weren't funny: 'It was a film about the war,' he started, 'and one of the them said, "I have news from the front," and one of the others replied, "Why does it always have to be from the front? Why can't it be news from the side or the back?" What's funny about that? Just bloody daft if you ask me.'

Remembering this, I wonder if 'Tatters' (for that was what we called him) would have found anything funny. He didn't even laugh when my father, sometime in the early 1970s, went up to receive an award at the Annual Dinner of Speedway Writers. As usual, he had forgotten to change his shoes, and turned up in a tuxedo but wearing a pair of tartan carpet slippers. He then won the raffle – a gallon of whisky, though not much good to a virtual teetotaller. He padded up to receive the award, ignoring the good-natured catcalls about his footwear, but then, on the return journey to his seat, slipped and dropped the bottle. He ended up in an undignified heap, sharing the floor with shards of glass and a deepish pond of White Horse. Needless to say, my mother – who did like whisky, or was at least looking forward to finding out whether she did – could not find it within herself to offer much sympathy.

The ecstatic hoots and jeers which accompanied my father's fall reminded me that unlike Tatters, who would merely have been concerned, my other grandfather – the German one – would have certainly enjoyed his misfortune. Germany, after all, is responsible for the expression *schadenfreude*, the malicious enjoyment of others' misfortune. And here are some of the things which made *him* laugh: catching flies and placing them in a spider's web, throwing his (beloved) cat Peter into the brook at the end of the garden, setting off his 'Laughing Sack' toy device on the crowded Hamburg underground system, watching *It's an International Knockout* on television and seeing a butcher from Kidderminster fall into a tub of water, winning at cards, and (painful, this) seeing me fall over and lose one of my front teeth.

He wasn't a bad man – it's just that he found misfortune hilarious. I suspect he was drawn more to pleasure or delight than to mere fun (which occupies comparatively harmless, neutral ground), something which my mother inherited from him. She also, for example, liked to catch flies and relished *It's an International Knockout*, though nothing for her was more funny than the sight of my father's balls, red and then white but irresistibly swollen, which had once been trapped in the zip of his dinner-suit trousers.

My German grandfather had good reason to be more interested in pleasure than fun. He had been captured by the Russians during the Second World War, tortured, escaped to the Americans, was handed back to the Russians, tortured again, and then had all his teeth knocked out in clumps of two or three with the butt of a rifle. When he arrived back home in Germany quite a long time after the war had officially ended, my mother walked straight past without recognising him. She found him at home arguing with the cat about some scraps of food in its bowl. In addition, he was a member of the SS, so in many ways had what might be called 'previous' in his odd sense of humour.

On his deathbed, he bequeathed me three items. A small, rectangular tobacco box, crudely fashioned from tin, the size of a cigarette packet, which he had made (secretly) in prison camp. Also, a black leather jacket, in 'as new' condition, which had been issued prior to his posting to the Eastern front. He had left it at home, reasoning that he was bound to be shot at and it was a shame to ruin such a nice garment. He handed it to me with no buttons and the markings removed, though with the SS issue number still sewn into its collar. The third item was a photograph, taken by him, of Adolf Hitler in mufti, sitting on a veranda reading a newspaper. Though my mother is coy about it, the suggestion is that he was at one time a kind of bodyguard to the Führer. Whatever, it is clear that my grandfather's sense of humour was, from a relatively early stage, subject to all manner of strange influence.

Genetically speaking, I saw that I was situated somewhere in the middle of this comedic babble, vulnerable both to a surrealist hilarity in pain and to a more conventional music-hall style of spoken humour. Germany and England. Visual and verbal. Strung out somewhere between the humorous prototypes of my parents.

Though I didn't think I had what constituted a faultless pedigree, I definitely thought there was some bloodline potential here, a strain that at least made me question my initial misgivings about attempting stand-up.

I was still dithering when fate stepped in and presented me with the kind of opportunity that could not be ignored, or not ignored without great difficulty. A pub in the area had decided to open its top room up for comedy every Friday night. It was close by but not quite close enough by for friends (or worse, pupils) to take much notice. The audience would be small and generally well disposed towards the two-minute try-out acts which the new club had invited to perform during its first month.

So I phoned the pub.

'Hello.' A woman's voice. That was good. Somehow, I didn't much want to speak to a man.

'Er . . . hello.'

'Yes?'

'I was . . .'

Actually I was just about to ring off.

'Are you calling about the try-outs?'

'Yes. How did you know?'

'Just something in your voice.'

'You mean the embarrassment and the reluctance?'

'Yes.' She laughed. That made me feel better.

'Well, in that case . . . yes, I have called about the try-outs. Are there any places left?'

'Yes, there are. Would you like to put your name down?'

'Yes, please. Um – does it have to be my, you know, *real* name?'

Pause. I had decided that if she said that, yes, it had to be my real name, then I would ring off. I hoped that this is what she would say. The truth is, I wanted to ring off.

'No. Whatever name you like. What shall I put down?'

There was no turning back. It was like climbing aboard a roller coaster, realising that you don't really fancy it too much after all, but suddenly you're in the seat, the security bar has been locked in place and the carriage is slowly beginning to move.

'Tony Binns.'

'Is that your real name?'

'Yes. No.'

'One *n* or two?'

'One. I mean two.'

'Which one?'

'Two. Definitely two.'

I knew this because Tony Binns is a friend of mine. At the time, we taught together at the same school. And I gave his name not simply because his was the first one that came to mind, but also because I have always felt there is something slightly odd and funny about being called 'Binns'. Names *are* funny things. You sort of grow into them, 'become' them, enter into dialogue with them. Even though initially you are at their mercy, you tame them, gradually transforming their wayward, general suggestiveness into a personal, specific term of clarification. I thought 'Tony Binns' blended just the right amount of ordinary blokeishness ('Tony') with a hint of easy-on-the-ear absurdity ('Binns'). Tony Binns. It was, I felt, a wise and rather brilliant choice. Evocative but anonymous.

'B-I-N-*N*-S?' asked the woman on the phone.

'That's it,' I replied confidently.

'My neighbour's son is taught by a Mr Binns up at the college,' she continued.

'Really?'

'He lost the poor boy's O-level English coursework. Or is it all GCSEs now? Anyway, she wrote a letter to the headmaster. Still, that's not you, is it?'

'No. It's not my real name,' I reminded her.

'Of course not.'

She informed me that the try-outs would take place the following Tuesday, that I wasn't to worry or be nervous, and that it was all a bit of fun. After all, the audience wouldn't be expecting Lenny Henry or Eddie Izzard. The main thing was that I took part, enjoyed myself, and found out whether I had potential.

Over the weekend I began to panic. Though I only had to write two minutes' worth of material, and had assumed because I could talk for several more or less uninterrupted hours about imagery in *Great Expectations* or Browning's use of the dramatic monologue, that things would drop quite smoothly into place. I began by writing down all the good jokes I knew, jokes that had stood the test of time in pubs and dinner parties, but which now, on paper, looked banal and (worse) unfunny. I threw the paper, actually several pieces of paper, into a bin. Then I started to write a sort of monologue, a single-strand story with comic asides, which I felt would at least have the virtue of narrative cohesion. The first one I wrote was about the time I got arrested at Belfast airport, after visiting my girlfriend, for having in my luggage a pair of handcuffs decorated with a pink, fluffy trim. I set about its retelling with gusto, drawing attention to the crowd of people who had gathered around, the three solemn security guards, and the very public declaration I had to read out while surrendering the handcuffs.

Then I threw the paper into a bin.

By Monday evening, and with nothing decided, I was feeling like the man in the P. G. Wodehouse story who is described as being like a young Hindu fakir about to make acquaintance with his first bed of nails, and wearing the expression of someone who was rather beginning to wish that he had chosen one of the easier religions. I smiled at the recollection of this image, and – eureka! – realised that I had stumbled upon my theme. I would talk about Wodehouse, and deliver a sort of compressed comic lecture which, if nothing else, would at least dumbfound and stifle the hecklers, effectively silencing them before they had a chance to get at me. With no specific jokes to deride, and – so long as I kept going – no narrative gaps for them to exploit, I would be home and dry before they realised what was happening.

There was, I supposed, some additional requirement actually to try and make people laugh, so I decided to write a very brief introduction to Wodehouse's life, concentrating at first on his south London associations, then moving swiftly to his capture by the Germans during the Second World War, and the accusations of being a Nazi sympathiser. From there, I would paint in some of my own family background, and sketch a picture of my grandfather (the SS one) reading Wodehouse to me and recalling a (little-known, though fictional) visit that Wodehouse made to Hitler during the time that he was the Führer's bodyguard.

It wasn't very funny, but it was, I thought – if only in a gently surreal manner – *quite* amusing. There were even two or three places where I hoped to get a laugh; chief among these was the moment when the two men discover a mutual liking for dogs, and then a short scene where Hitler asks Wodehouse to teach him some English insults.

I put it all on paper, tried it out in front of a mirror – though, of course, without ever looking at the mirror – edited the piece down to eight minutes, then six, then four, then back up to six, and finally to just over two. What remained was mostly about my grandfather and Wodehouse talking to one another immediately after the audience with Hitler, and the English writer sharing ideas and notes, for future reference, e.g. about the dictator's moustache ('It is like the faint discoloured smear left by a squashed black beetle on the side of a kitchen sink') and his dogs ('The world is divided into those who can stop dogfights and those who cannot'). 'Can you not say anything good about the Führer?' my grandfather asked. Wodehouse considered. And what he considered I cannot now remember, but whatever he said was certainly very funny – you'll have to take my word for it – and would bring my act to its triumphant close.

The next evening, at around seven o'clock, I arrived at the pub with my Wodehouse/Hitler routine polished and memorised. I'd done a bit more work on it and after seven attempts, had clipped it down to a polished and precise two minutes and seventeen seconds. I made my way up to the first floor of the pub where the other would-be comedians were already signing in.

A large, surly man with cropped hair and a clipboard wrinkled his nose at me as if I were a drain that had got out of order.

'Name?'

'Tony Binns,' I chirped.

'Not the tosser at the college who lost my boy's coursework?' he snarled.

'Um . . . no. Wrong man, I'm afraid.'

He grunted and handed me a cloakroom ticket showing the number 305. I gazed at it without emotion. 'You're on second,' he announced.

'Second?!'

'That's right. Alphabetical, isn't it? Alexander. Binns. That's you.'

'No. *Tony* Binns.'

'I know. *Alexander* is the first hopeful. *Tony* Alexander. Then you. *Tony Binns*. You all called Tony or something? Hur-hur. Second. OK?'

I nodded. Perhaps Binns wasn't such a good choice after all. Second. I looked at my watch. Five past seven. In about thirty minutes I would be in front of an audience talking about P.G. Wodehouse, Adolf Hitler and my grandfather. Why had I ever thought it was a good idea? How could I have ever, ever imagined it was funny? The notes in my hand, my 'reminders', suddenly seemed very damp and very useless.

Twenty minutes or so later there were fifteen of us – all men – assembled behind a black curtain. We could hear the audience trooping upstairs from the bar. Apparently, a general invitation had been issued to anyone who happened to be in there having a drink at that time. Of the fifty or so customers, about half had accepted the offer. Number Fifteen, who was nearest the curtain, watched nervously as they started to take their seats.

'Anyone out there pissed?' asked Number Nine.

'No,' said Fifteen, 'but they've all got drinks.'

'Too early for drunks,' said Five, 'that's good,' though he said it with neither pleasure nor conviction. Then I saw that his hands were trembling. My hands seemed quite stable, but my stomach was doing the rounds, moving at will, sometimes journeying to my mouth, most often to my groin, but never where it should have been. I could have risen to my feet and left, but I had decided to see this thing through, though I must have seemed (as Wodehouse once said – since last night I had got to know my Wodehouse very well) a melancholy-looking man, with the appearance of one who has searched for the leak in life's gas pipe with a lighted candle.

The audience settled and the surly man who had dished out the tickets at the door came forward to introduce the evening. He craved the audience's tolerance, emphasising that we were all mere novices, that the 'entertainment' would only last for a little over an hour, and that in any case it was free. 'Let's be having them, then!' someone shouted, and without more ado, Number One, poor Tony Alexander, lurched through the curtains and began his two minutes' worth. The audience gave him almost a full minute before, when he told a joke about someone with a peanut allergy playing Russian roulette with a packet of Revels, someone shouted out, "Heard it before, you twat,' and everyone joined in, callously *oohing* and *aahing* at each one of the mostly unfunny gags which completed his act.

Thin applause. Some indifferent chortling. The surly man again. Then me. 'Good luck,' whispered Number Three, though in a way that suggested he was about to lose his voice or be sick.

I walked out in front of the audience which was, straight away, inquisitively quiet. They looked at me and I looked at them. Do not believe it when people say that at least you can't see your audience; I could distinguish almost every one of them, certainly those in the first three or four rows, and can even now vividly recall the stony set of their faces, the primed indifference that sought some kind of cruel release.

I began to speak, the words pouring out in an uncontrolled surge. At first – and more or less as planned – the audience seemed genuinely bemused by what they were hearing, then a little restless. One or two, however, were quite attentive. A chap with an overbite in the third row was smiling to himself. Smiling inanely, but smiling nonetheless. Someone else coughed, clambered noisily out of his chair, and left. But a third person – glasses, shaved head, jeans – was laughing. Actually chortling. I found myself playing to him, slowing the delivery down and – sort of – feeling in control. Someone near the back said, 'Come on, professor,' but the collective abuse I expected was not forthcoming. Encouraged, or at least not discouraged, I ploughed on, reaching the point of my 'story' where Wodehouse and my grandfather are discussing the meeting with Hitler. As I came to a stop, I counted four distinct laughs – and a guffaw. Nobody jeered. There was what is known as a light scattering of applause. I did something which looked a bit like a bow and plunged back behind the curtain.

'Well done,' said Number Three, still whispering, pushing past me towards the stage, 'that was very average.'

I sat back down in my seat. I felt as if I'd just had a very expensive facial, or the kind of facial I'd heard about, where your skin glows and throbs with a kind of pummelled pleasure. I hadn't been very good. I hadn't even been quite good. But there were moments, arguably only a single moment, when people had laughed and I had succeeded. Something had bloomed inside me. Small, exquisite explosions detonated around my body. It was like no other feeling.

And I wanted more.

TWO

Dead Funny

Well, in a sense I wanted more, though as my little foray on to the stage occurred about three years ago, I can't have 'wanted more' very much, or at least not enough to actually get more. Despite the tingling invigoration I had felt at the small triumph of not being humiliated, of being on stage at all and not making an absolute prat of myself, I did not do anything about it. No developing of material or nurturing of act. No building on the undoubted potential for psychological development. No establishing of useful contacts or building of reputation. No traipsing around other small grubby pubs. And certainly no anticipating the moment when I would be 'spotted' in one of those pubs.

Not even another visit to a comedy club.

Nothing.

Not a sausage.

What happened? Why should I have immediately loosened my grip around even this lowly rung, the same lowly rung of the same small ladder I had previously contemplated with such boundless, self-enquiring enthusiasm?

A number of reasons spring to mind, some of them even quite good reasons. I still had a job, of course. Not only a job, but a demanding, responsible, grown-up sort of job, the kind of full-time job that guzzles hours of your day and leaves you limp and flagging at the end of it. The kind of job that would naturally prohibit any notions I had of cultivating any hobbies, even flippant ones like putting together a comedy routine.

True, it was a teaching job, and I know by heart the jibes about long holidays and short working hours, but the thing is, they just aren't true. Trust me on this, gentle reader. You must believe me when I say that each day's challenges left me wrung out. That holidays were exclusively set aside for recharging batteries, preparing next term's teaching materials and refamiliarising myself with an all-but-forgotten family.

So, the job was one thing.

There was also, I admit, a degree of laziness, or perhaps willed flaccidity, about my comedic limbo. Startled that I had been on stage at all, it already felt to me as if Everest had been climbed and conquered, the Rubicon well and truly crossed. Honour had in some way been satisfied.

Perhaps this needs some elaboration. I was a teacher. A 'head of department at a leading London independent school' kind of teacher since you ask, but a teacher nonetheless, and if that doesn't tell you something about the level at which I set my bar, nothing will. I could never be accused of being overly ambitious. Or even ambitious.

Another thing that held me back (and here I claim the moral high ground) was the birth of a son.

Otto saved the day. The moment he was born I knew – just *knew* – that any activities other than working, trying to sleep, not managing to sleep and occasional dozing, would be wiped from my agenda for months, even years. If I played it right, Otto would become a tangible, organic excuse for not doing much else besides Otto. Obviously, though, the phrase I preferred was 'otherly focused'. Still, I was immediately dubbed 'Papoose Man' by Pippa, my girlfriend, Otto's mum, who quickly recognised the avoidance game I had set my mind on playing.

Otto wasn't planned. He wasn't that much desired, to be honest. But when it became apparent that he wasn't going to disappear of his own volition, we sort of went along with whole thing. Babies are hard work all right, but it's the kind of work that is compulsory, irresistible and, though intellectually undemanding, too knackering to leave much time for anything else. As far as doing more comedy went, as far as doing more anything went, Otto presented a convenient, incontestable barrier.

Perfect.

However, lurking behind these variously reasonable excuses lay the realisation that something else was holding me back. Fear. And this fear arrived in a number of complex forms. The fear, for example, of trying something at which I might, at which I would *in all probability*, fail. And the not unrelated fear that I just wasn't funny. (This, though, I think is different from failing. Many funny people would fail as stand-up comedians, while some very unfunny people manage, against the odds, to be quite successful, if not actually funny. My fear was doubly emphatic: I feared being crap *and* unfunny.)

Now for the more complex version of fear. I was afraid of stepping outside of myself, of becoming someone alien or different to the person I knew. Instinctively disinclined to move beyond the boundaries of my known existence into worlds which were not familiar. I therefore resisted any movement towards any way of life for which I considered myself conditionally and genetically unsuited. Put like that, it seems fair enough. Exhilarating as my brief sally into comedy had been, the thrill had been derived as much from the otherness of the experience as anything else, and this sense of 'alternative' now frightened me.

Here, I felt, was the rub. Thus far, my life had been built around the prosaic certainties of working towards prescribed goals (usually 'exam goals'), and of doing well enough at each hurdle to advance to the next plateau of expectation.

And so on and so forth.

And that's more or less how whole lifetimes can disappear.

A middle-class, Middle England, absolutely middling state of grinding, no-nonsense achievement had been inscribed in me from an early age, and though there were occasional and often feeble attempts to break loose, for the most part I had bought into its values and rewards.

Stay with me on this. Its significance will soon become apparent.

My parents sent me to prep school and then the local independent school, not so much because they believed in education for its own sake, but actually for the precise opposite reason. On the one hand, they believed that such schools were most likely to push me forward and allow me to reach certain goals, or rather the certain respectable goals they assumed I would need in life. They also, I think, saw education as a way of fitting in, somehow joining an exclusive club, the membership of which allowed the bypassing of embarrassment and social awkwardness, things (however) which I never quite eluded despite being educated to the hilt.

Mr Callaghan, who owned Cedarhurst Preparatory School and was also its headmaster, was liked by parents because he instilled a quasi-military sense of disciplined obedience into his pupils, insisting that the boys doffed their caps and the girls curtsied to him whenever he was encountered, even if the encounter was a distant one. The merest glimpse of him, a hundred yards or so across a crowded playground while he was looking through the window of his third-floor office, would initiate an immediate frenzy of lifting and bending.

Parents thought this was the way people acted, or at least the way people ought to act, and that children like me were therefore being properly conditioned for life. Mr Callaghan's aim was to ensure as many of us as possible passed the eleven-plus examination and then the entrance exam into one or other of the area's private schools. Somehow, the doffing and curtsying were connected to this goal. Never a simple matter, learning under Mr Callaghan gradually became a terrifying and eccentric business.

At the end of one term, I remember that no one was allowed to leave school until they had correctly identified and written down with precision the most important pitch positions on a cricket field. On another occasion, we were compelled to hear out Beethoven's Fifth before being allowed home, the entire school sitting cross-legged on the floor while Mr Ross's reel-to-reel tape recorder thundered and swooped in front of us.

Though undoubtedly erratic, over the years I have come to the conclusion that all this has probably proved more valuable than almost anything related to the national curriculum. Extra tuition was ordered (at extra cost) on Saturday mornings for those who looked as though they might be flagging, and for my sister the added embarrassment of tuition with Miss Crossman in her cramped caravan, which was parked ten miles away in Wooton Wawen.

Failure was not a word that the cigar-chewing, E-Type Jag-driving Mr Callaghan was prepared to contemplate.

On the morning that entrance-examination results dropped through the letter box, I can still recall my mother's crestfallen expression as she scrutinised the contents of the buff envelope.

'Oh,' she sighed.

'I've failed . . .' I said, and slumped hopelessly into the blue armchair.

'More or less,' she continued, 'and don't sit there – I've only just puffed the cushions.'

'What do you mean?'

'Well – you got in . . .'

'That's good, isn't it? That's what I was meant to do.'

'Yes. But Isobel Perkins called me a few minutes ago. Mark got a scholarship.'

'What's that?' I asked, already somehow suspecting that one might be worth having.

'It means he won't have to pay any money to go to school.' She dropped the letter and looked directly at me. 'But we will.'

It was much the same several years later when when I passed an exam for Cambridge and she took out a small ad in the *Solihull News* announcing her pride at my achievement in getting to Uxbridge.

Though snatching despair from the jaws of triumph was therefore something of a speciality, the point remains that the legacy of my education (and, presumably, of my parents' aspirations) was a belief in the unswerving, the respectable and the honourably straight-and-narrow. This was the hole into which my parents unwittingly drilled me and, to reinforce the point, home soon became a version of life at school. Meals, for example, were tightly timetabled in the same undeviating way – Mondays was beans on toast, Tuesdays was hot dogs, Wednesdays was mushrooms on toast . . . and so on. Some areas of the house were out of bounds (always the sitting room, for example, frequently the garden and, until protective newspaper was lain down on the swirly yellow lino, the kitchen), and my mother applied a tough disciplinary code while also enforcing a strict 'lights out' regime at the end of the day.

It would be fair to say that I was heavily institutionalised.

Unsurprisingly, my childhood also made impressions on my choices of career, which were not, I now think, 'choices' so much as timid, fearful endorsements of much that had gone on before. Actually, 'foregone conclusions' might be nearer the mark. I lived in fear of not having a 'proper' job because my parents lived the same fear and through my education and upbringing passed it on to me.

Somehow though – deep, deep within me – a battle was being fought. The factors that had propelled me on to a stage for two or three minutes at a not very nice pub in south London still existed. But three years ago they had found a great deal to contend with. Quite quickly, or at any rate quickly enough, they came across those other, more long-lived, inbred, visceral forces I have been describing. Rather than releasing me, my little sortie had actually enslaved me, permitting a brief vision of otherness which frightened the life out of me and from which I immediately shied.

Being shy of something brought back, incidentally, a line my classics master had once used about me in a report: 'He shies from the Latin verb as a horse from the puff adder.' The man was right, of course, unwittingly identifying a lack of bottle which would dog me for years.

But now things would be different. Now, suddenly (and for me quite keenly), I felt the need to try again.

So what had changed?

Otto, of course, who was now three years old and day by day becoming less of an excuse for me not doing very much. He had a nursery to attend and his own interests to pursue. He had made a start on that journey which would eventually lead him from unconditional love of his parents, to amused tolerance, through mere tolerance, then resentment, then virtual ignorance and, finally, years later, back to tolerance. As Jasper Carrott put it when discussing the similarities between teenage children and their grandparents: 'They're both on drugs, they both detest you and neither of them have got a job.'

Whatever. Otto was now less of an excuse.

His second birthday more or less coincided with me leaving my job. I had vague notions of writing full time and turning away, perhaps flinching, from the very things around which my entire upbringing and education had been constructed. When I telephoned my parents to tell them what I was up to, my mother answered and then placed a not very discreet hand over the receiver. 'The bloody fool's gone and done it,' I could hear her muttering to my father, who is deaf and was anyway watching Spanish football on the television. Her reaction reminded me a little of the time when a friend of mine resigned from the Foreign Office only to be scalded by his angry father-in-law, an ex-army man, with, 'What do you think you're buggering around at? Another twenty-five years and you'd have picked up an OBE.'

I doubt I'd have picked up a gong for services to education, but he and my mother were clearly cut from the same cloth.

I didn't therefore resign a job (*and* security *and* a pension) for the sake of comedy, but because I wanted to write about comedy, and doing stand-up seemed to be a Route One way of finding out about it. Other reasons chipped in. My age must have been one of these. Not quite old, not quite young, but old enough to know that I would never be properly young again. I suppose it's called being 'middle-aged', though it's a label I dislike, probably because I'm the sort of middle-aged bloke who doesn't consider himself to be as middle-aged as all the same-aged middle-aged blokes he sees around him.

On the other hand, I do admit to having recently owned a sports car (an avenue of pleasure swiftly blocked by Otto's arrival), still think in terms of pounds, shillings and pence, and boast a Simply Red CD in my collection.

So, middle-aged it is.

Nevertheless, most of my hair was still in place and I was not conspicuously overweight.

Still, there were plenty of other signs that so far as youth was concerned, the game was well and truly up. I had, for example, begun to feel nostalgic for the 1970s. I enjoyed taking Otto to look at the old steam engines on small, privately owned railways. I heard myself tutting about modern architecture and computers. I hardened against binge drinking. And though I don't need glasses, I was beginning to find the *A–Z* a bit tricky. Then the in-laws bought me a trimmer for nasal hair.

I therefore reasoned that the process of life winding down – my life winding down – had already started, and I wasn't sure I wanted to spend the next twenty-odd years of it in schools. That is, another twenty years of listening to a burly man called Mook advising me of the best routes out of north London during the Friday-evening rush hour. Another twenty years listening to Barbara's bleating dismay that she was teaching more periods than the apparently awful Mrs Telfer. Another twenty years of hoping that it would be cheese scones at break time. Another twenty years of hoping for summer storms so that I wouldn't have to umpire the Under 14 Bs against Mill Hill or Epsom or Harrow. Another twenty years fending off a liver-lipped bursar's advice to order a set of 'character-forming thrillers' about mountaineering because they would be 'jolly good fun' for the boys.

In short, I began to wonder what life was for and how much of it was left for me. In this epiphany, teaching didn't seem to cast much light.

There was one more key event which not only made me consider what might be round the next corner, but actually quite distressed me.

This moment may even have been the jump-start that my system needed.

It was the death of Bob Monkhouse.

Bob Monkhouse and I actually go back quite a long way. We have, as they say, a bit of previous. We first came across one another in the 1960s when he was working on a show called *The Golden Shot*. This was something my mother used to watch – I think it was on a Sunday afternoon – a programme that held almost as much of a grip on her as *Crossroads*, *Daktari*, and something called *All Our Yesterdays* which seemed to show little else but the pulverising of German cities by Allied bombers.

I must admit that for me, at that time, *The Golden Shot* seemed impossibly glamorous and sophisticated. At its core was the placing of an arrow or bolt into a crossbow which was apparently mounted on top of a television camera. This was then aimed at a target on the other side of the studio. 'Home' contestants would direct the dramatically blindfolded cameraman's aim with instructions given over the phone, and guide him in the same way that they might have directed a reversing lorry into a smallish parking space: 'Left – right – right a bit more – left a bit – STOP,' until the moment arrived when they felt that camera and target were perfectly aligned. Then they would shout, 'Fire!' At which point the bolt was released. The idea was to hit a small detonator in the centre of an apple which would then explode. The whole process being lent extra drama by the sound of a clock counting down the allotted time for this process. The successful marksmen qualified for a place in the studio the following week, when they would shoot at a more difficult target from a free-standing crossbow. The two with the highest scores would then go on to fire at an even tougher target, this time using a joystick. Finally, the best competitor would have a chance to tackle the 'golden shot' itself, aiming to sever a thin thread which would release a shower of gold coins into a treasure chest.

More significant than any of this, however, was the smiling, benevolent presence of Monkhouse himself, always ready with a quip and a kindly word. Because of black-and-white television, his oft-derided tan was not apparent to us, though even if it had been, I'm not certain I would have taken against him. At that time, tans were a sign of great exoticism, their certain source (according to my mother) being Spain. He seemed like the kindly uncle I never had, and his catchphrase of 'Bernie, the bolt' – uttered at the ritualistic moment when a man apparently called Bernie loaded the crossbow on top of the camera – somehow made him even more endearing and familiar. There were also constant allusions to 'the lovely Anne Aston', a young blonde woman who I didn't then appreciate as being a lovely blonde woman, to whom I assumed he was married or at least engaged. I took this for granted because the programme was made in Birmingham and also because Aston was a suburb of the city; it followed quite naturally that they were a fairy-tale couple and that he was one of us.

My fondness for Bob reached something like fever pitch when Mum spotted an advertisement in the local paper which announced (no – 'proudly' announced) that he would be opening, in person, a carpet showroom in Solihull's new shopping precinct, Mell Square, the following Sunday morning. This was a time when it was still acceptable to leave young children by themselves for an hour or so in a town centre, so Mum dropped my sister and me outside the shop about fifty minutes before Bob was due to make his appearance.

She left us there with copies of *Bunty* and the *Dandy*, and two tubes of Smarties.

There was already a long queue which oozed back beyond Beatties the department store, W.H. Smiths, Sainsbury's, Boots, and Woolies. (Who said that the demolition of a medieval tangle of streets to accommodate commercial behemoths hadn't been worthwhile?)

'I'll be back in about an hour,' my mother said, 'and mind what you're doing with those feet.'

She had only taken possession of her bottle-green Mini two weeks ago, and was still understandably sensitive about the prospect of dirty mats. Then, almost as an afterthought, but only as an afterthought, and said through a hastily wound-down window, 'And don't go straying too far. No further than the post office,' and she stabbed a warning finger back towards the square itself, gesturing at a point just the other side of an ornamental fountain, already the jewel in Mell Square's crown and, I noted, already broken.

My sister and I queued for about forty-five minutes. Eventually, the shop doors were heaved open and the line moved forward in a mild, peristaltic surge. Still no sign of Bob, however. 'Perhaps he's done a bolt,' someone shouted, and shouting it loud enough to let everyone know it was a joke.

Some people even laughed.

'I could murder a Mars bar,' said a fat woman with a hearing aid.

'AnywunwannaWispa?' asked another.

Then it started to rain and a kind of Dunkirk spirit kicked in. Those who had umbrellas put them up. Those who didn't were invited to share. A yellow-fingered woman who looked like a man with a wig opened a bag of liquorice allsorts. She offered us one, but we shook our heads, even though we wanted one, not talking to strangers or taking sweets from them being something that Mr Callaghan and our parents had drummed into us.

'Goo on,' the woman persisted, and rustled the bag invitingly.

My sister and I glanced at one another and slipped our hands into the bag. The woman smiled, displaying a set of alarmingly white teeth.

The new clock on the far side of the square showed it was already five past. 'That's slow,' my sister fussed, checking the dial against her newish Timex, a Christmas present from Auntie Dulcie. Finally, at quarter past, a large black Jaguar drew up in front of the shop. A murmur went around the crowd, then a few mild cheers as Bob finally emerged from the car, waving and smiling. He was wearing an immaculate suit, light in tone so that his tan, a kind of rusty haliborange, glowed the fiercer. (The actress Beryl Reid once commented that the tan would look overdone on lederhosen.)

'That's España for you,' someone observed, 'where all the stars go.'

'Oh yes, but I couldn't be doing with all that squid,' replied her companion.

Years later, I discovered that Bob's permanent tan was not simply due to having a second home in Bermuda (Spain was merely a convenient rumour which fitted with what people wanted to think), but also because he wore make-up to cover the skin condition vitiligo. But at that moment, as he glided from the Jag, faultlessly coiffured, impeccably suited, luminous of hue, he appeared as nothing less than a god.

After a brief, cheery wave, he disappeared into the shop where he took his place behind a medium-sized wooden desk in front of a conspicuously impressive display of Axminsters. Not used to the presence of celebrities, the good folk of Solihull became reverentially hushed, shuffling apologetically forward to get their autographs and shuffling as if they were approaching a communion rail.

My sister and I were almost convulsed with excitement. When, after another ten minutes of jostling, we reached the table, I saw that Bob had a pile of black-and-white photographs beside him, all ready to dispense to his adoring fans. A woman with blonde hair, probably someone big in the carpet business, stood behind him, grinning in an overwrought manner. She couldn't have been more pleased if the Queen had popped in for a cup of tea.

'What's your name?' asked the beaming Bob when I eventually made it to the front of the queue.

'Stephen Max Jacobi,' I replied.

'How long have you been waiting, Stephen?'

I looked imploringly at my sister. She displayed Auntie Dulcie's Timex.

'Seventy-three and a half minutes.'

'That's marvellous,' Bob sparkled, though not looking up as he scrawled, 'To Stephen. Best wishes, Bob Monkhouse!!!' on his likeness.

Afterwards, my sister said, 'He didn't ask my name *and* he didn't write the same on my photograph.'

It was true. Bob had just signed his name on hers. No greeting. No 'best wishes'. Just the name.

I tried to look a bit concerned or disappointed on her behalf, but it was a difficult manoeuvre, and actually, of course, I was delighted.

It had always been thus with my sister. I was the one who got to go on holiday to 'The Imperial' at Torquay with our grandparents and who got the new Mini-Moulton bike. In addition, when Dad had brought back two identical sets of plastic Beatles figurines from a business trip to Liverpool, it was her Ringo and not mine who quickly lost his adhesiveness and slumped awkwardly forward into his drum kit.

After that, and despite clinging possessively to his autographed portrait for several months, Bob virtually dropped out of my life. Though fond memories were occasionally reignited by a glimpse of him on *Celebrity Squares*, *Family Fortunes* and the inevitably named *Bob's Your Uncle*, we more or less became strangers.

Then, early in the nineties, I heard him being interviewed by Dr Anthony Clare for the radio programme *In the Psychiatrist's Chair*. I listened rapt as a clearly emotional Bob revealed some of the less familiar, more tragic details of his life. A seventeen-year estrangement from his mother over his first marriage, the premature death of a disabled son, alcohol problems, and finally a falling-out with his second son who then died early of a heroin overdose. No wonder he called his autobiography *Crying with Laughter*. No mention on the programme, though, of opening a carpet store near Birmingham in the 1960s, an event which clearly didn't loom as large in Bob's mental landscape as it had done in mine.

By this time I was teaching at Dulwich College in south-east London, one of England's oldest public schools. Anthony Clare mentioned that Bob had been educated there. This took me by surprise. The school was usually very quick to trumpet its eminent alumni, though Bob was not on any list of distinguished Old Alleynians that I knew of. This list, by the way, included any number of fuzzy-wuzzy-bashing soldiers and ambitious politicians. In fairness, the heroic explorer Shackleton was also much lauded, as were P.G. Wodehouse and Raymond Chandler, the college's representatives from the arts. However, the great film director Michael Powell, the Roxy Music guitarist Phil Manzanera and Monkhouse himself were more or less ignored. Perhaps they were simply the wrong kind of people (i.e. popular, or rather, the wrong kind of popular), though there was a rumour that Bob had been expelled for wrapping toilet paper round the clock tower. Thus, he once more entered my life, even if only in a small way, suddenly embroidering the misty nostalgia of childhood memory with a sharp sense of here-and-now reality.

Bob had become one of those people who for one reason or another play cameo parts in your existence, a minor but not insignificant presence, somehow punching above its weight.

It was therefore with some regret that I heard the news of his death at the beginning of 2004. I wouldn't quite say it was like losing a member of the family, but it nonetheless had an impact that had been reinforced by the brush of personal contact. I knew that people said he was artificial and smarmy, but somehow it didn't matter. Bob was dead. It was sad news. He was seventy-five, which neatly called into play one of his own jokes: 'I can still enjoy sex at 74 – I live at number 75, so it's no distance.'

I then read a piece in the *Independent* which suggested that Christmas and New Year always seemed to bring its crop of departures. It said: 'Maybe the old hospital wisdom about patients making it through to Christmas on sheer willpower alone has something in it. Or perhaps there isn't much else for newspapers to write about and so deaths that might normally be part of the general landscape of mortality achieve unusual prominence. Whatever the case, you can safely bet your leftover turkey that December will deliver a sheaf of showbiz obituaries. This year, Alan Bates and Bob Monkhouse were the headline acts, with Dinsdale Landen and Patricia Roc posthumously upstaged.'

Neither did Monkhouse's death go unnoticed at Dulwich. The headmaster wrote an appreciation of him in *The Dulwich Yearbook*, saying that 'The College is very proud of Bob's achievements . . . Robert Alan (Bob) Monkhouse was arguably the best-known OA [Old Alleynian] of all time'. He also noted the school stories of him making the life of 'Horsey' Grange a misery and being beaten by Treadgold. So there you go. Fame at last for Bob.

Maybe it was something about this seasonal affective disorder, but Bob's death did trigger something within me, and I found myself thinking back three years to my Hitler/ Wodehouse routine in the south London pub. Maybe it wasn't so much Monkhouse's death as the prospect of death, now brought nearer to home, of life shrinking, which in turn had been prompted by his demise, which affected me.

Whatever, it caused me to think.

And here's what I thought.

I now wondered whether there might be significance in the fact I had just watched an entire series of *Six Feet Under* on DVD. I also noted that my father, whose heart attacks cast a constant shadow over his life, had been joined in death's waiting room by my mother, whose own heart was playing up. She had to go into hospital just before Christmas to have it stopped and then electrically restarted. When I telephoned to ask how the heart restart had gone, my father just said, 'Success – they found one!'

Then, at more or less the same time as Bob Monkhouse was dying, my only living relation in Germany, a great-aunt, passed away. I remember her chiefly for crushing the life out of her favourite pet budgerigar which she accidentally shut in the kitchen door, though she had always been kind to me. 'Tante Walda's dead,' my mother informed me, 'so don't expect your usual twenty pounds this Christmas.'

Unexpectedly, compellingly, a blizzard of dying and an accompanying awareness of death was now swirling around me. And all this somehow joined with comedy in performing a kind of hypnotic dance, with Bob Monkhouse a pivotal, master-of-ceremonies figure. Reading the runes, I launched into my first ever episode of *The Royle Family* and then had my first experience of *The Office*. Someone also gave me Ben Thompson's *Sunshine on Putty*, a book which examined the apparent golden age of British comedy during the 1990s. Death and comedy. Circumstances seemed to be resuscitating my interest in humour, then annexing it to bereavement.

I was also mindful that in a sense I had been down this road only a few days before. At a party a short time after New Year, I met an actress called Beatie Edney who had been in Terry Johnson's play *Dead Funny*, which I saw in 1994, about the same time as Monkhouse's appearance on *In the Psychiatrist's Chair*.

First, a few words about the play. In a collected volume of Johnson's work, the introduction says, 'Each of the plays in this volume has a death at its centre. And in each, a different comedy idiom is provided as "frame".' In *Dead Funny* itself, this frame is the leering, childish and generally reprehensible television comedy of the 1960s. All the characters (bar one) are its fans, only able to exist through dead comedians such as Benny Hill, whose sudden death is announced during the course of the play. Eleanor (the 'bar one') tries to puncture her husband's morbid fascination with Hill which she blames for his inability to have sex with her: 'He's [i.e. Benny] probably watching you now. Sitting on a cloud with a television remote in one hand and his penis in the other. Come on Richard, he's saying. Give her one for me.'

It's all very funny, especially so if you're not approaching or have just approached middle age and aren't feeling a bit unsettled about things.

The great sadness and also the great humour of *Dead Funny* is in watching educated and successful people hiding behind moribund comedy and using it as a substitute for real life. These people collect comedy like other people collect stamps or cigarette cards. Or, if I'm honest, adhesive stickers advertising oil products.

Though if you're English, of course, not much of this is news.

But here's the thing. Meeting Beatie Edney, the death of Bob Monkhouse, *Dead Funny*, Tante Walda, *Six Feet Under*, and my mum's dodgy heart. Everything unconnected suddenly, well, *connected*. Don't you see? Everything sort of coming together. Death nudged me. Comedy pricked me. Death and comedy. Comedy and death. Here was the answer to what I should be doing with my life.

In the tradition of experiencing a great or sudden revelation, I explained to Beatie about going on stage and performing a stand-up routine to find out about comedy and through finding out about comedy and writing about it to find out about myself.

It was a good plan, even if wasn't quite true. Not quite. I hadn't actually made a plan. I had only really just decided, just put all the pieces together. But I had to tell *someone*, and the telling made it seem possible, even real.

She listened politely as I explained how I viewed her presence at the party and the subsequent recalling of *Dead Funny* as a defining moment in my life.

'You should go to clowning school,' she advised, rather coolly.

'Clowning school?' I echoed, thinking of men in large frilly costumes wearing shoes like paddles and sporting red ping-pong balls on the ends of their noses. I reckoned she must have misunderstood.

But she hadn't.

'Go to clowning to find your comic persona,' Beatie confirmed.

This made more sense. I knew that I couldn't just go up on stage and be funny. I couldn't even read a joke out of a

Christmas cracker and be funny. I also understood that I would first have to invent some kind of interface between me and the audience. In fact, a very substantial interface. I had once heard Jack Dee talking about locating an aspect of your personality that you enjoy making people laugh with. 'In my case,' he said, 'you might call it my grumpy side.'

I quite liked Jack Dee. A few years ago someone had told me that Dee and I probably had the same sense of humour. 'What's that?' I asked. 'You're both Eeyores,' came the reply. In other words, killjoys. Spoilsports. Wet blankets.

He was probably right.

The bastard.

I still doubted, however, that Beatie quite appreciated the quasi-religious dimension of my comic quest or knew absolutely what she was talking about. Then she told me about Hugh Grant writing material for her own stand-up act, about Hugh and her being a kind of team, and I assumed she probably did. At least, far more than I did.

I did feel bold enough to tell her my favourite joke, i.e. the most recent one I had heard and therefore the only one I could remember. I noticed her wince when I started. A mild, polite wince, but a wince nonetheless.

'A man goes to his doctor and says, "Doctor, I wonder if you could help me. I think I'm a moth." The doctor replied, "I'm afraid I can't help you. You need a psychiatrist." "I know," said the man, "but I saw your light was on so I came up."'

Beatie smiled, but she didn't actually laugh, and I noted that she took a short backwards step towards the cheese straws as the punchline arrived. Anyway, a short step away from me and my joke. I thought this was significant.

As Frank Carson often said, 'It's the way I tell 'em.'

'Jokes don't work terribly well in stand-up,' she said. 'It's more about creating the right atmosphere for laughter, for letting people know it's OK to laugh. Jokes can be a bit . . . you know, con . . .'

'Conventional?' I offered.

'No . . .'

'Conversational . . .?'

'No . . .'

'Convenient?'

'Confrontational,' she said.

I didn't have any plans to tell the joke on stage, but I still wanted some sign that it was funny. That I was funny.

'Our interests,' the poet Robert Browning wrote, 'are on the dangerous edge of things / The honest thief, the tender murderer / The superstitious atheist.' Characters without contradictions are like eggs without salt. And here, I reflected, was part of my problem. As a stand-up, I would have to – as Jack Dee put it – locate a single aspect of my character and play it for all it was worth. I would have to become radically uncomplicated whereas, like most people, I was full to the brim of contradictions and wrinkles.

I suspected that there were very few comedians who were 'themselves' on stage, or fully themselves. There were possible exceptions. Billy Connolly, for example, who from the outside (at least) always seemed to be having fun, always laughing. Quite the same on stage as he is in real life, people said, almost as if he was just telling stories in the pub. But wait a minute. What about his wife's biography of him and all the stuff about abuse and a life which had its share of pain? Could he not have been adopting a comic persona in the pub and then merely transferring that persona to the stage?

Tricky.

On the one hand, I understood what Dee was saying and appreciated that by shuffling on stage and being 'ordinary' – confused, contrary, inconsistent and irreconcilable – it would be difficult to put together any kind of effective act. On the other . . . adopting a persona, slipping in and out of another, albeit somehow related, character was even more complicated and difficult than I thought.

I managed to think all this and even think it quite lucidly between making a visit to the bathroom and finding the sausage rolls.

Beatie was long gone.

The problem was apparently straightforward. I was too rooted in myself. I was or had become relatively comfortable with my own discrepancies. Being inside your own skin is, I guess, the same as living in your own house. At first, you do all the redecoration and are very aware of how things look. Then, after a while, you get used to stuff and don't much notice the peeling wallpaper and the fading and anyway mismatched cushions. Gradually, you begin to accept what's there and stop hoping for perfection or symmetry.

And inside me, it was much the same story.

So, who cared that I had voted for all three of the main political parties during the last twenty years? Or that I had swung full circle on the question of giving money to beggars but was still inconsistent in how I dealt with each fresh encounter? These folds in my character were what made me who I was. They were also, actually, the reasons why I couldn't act, couldn't sing, couldn't speak a foreign language, couldn't circulate at parties and probably couldn't adopt a comic persona. I was insular and shy and inward-looking. Riven by the sorts of contradiction that could, if I let them, sound interesting. But actually aren't.

Being like this has its merits, but being a natural at going on stage and making people laugh wasn't one of them.

'How would you describe my character?' I had once asked a close friend who had known me since school.

'Difficult. Irreverent. Grudging,' he replied without hesitating, or at least without hesitating enough.

'How about in one word?' I persisted.

'A different one word?'

'If you like. I didn't much like the ones you said.'

'A bit kinder, then?' he chuckled.

'More balanced,' I suggested.

'Funereal,' he said. 'Why do you ask?'

'Just checking,' I said. 'Thought so.'

On reflection, I thought 'funereal' was pretty accurate. Even wise. I quite liked being funereal. I had grown used to being funereal. I doubted I could at this stage in my life be much else, even for a few moments, even on stage. I would be too self-aware and consequently too self-conscious to be anyone else. I could appreciate how people like Barry Humphries *became* Dame Edna or Ken Dodd *became* Doddy (or even how Jack Dee *became* 'Jack Dee'), but I didn't think I was capable of revision. Perhaps I was merely confusing being obdurate with having integrity. Still, I did feel that as far as adopting a comic persona was concerned, I would be unbudgeable.

On the other hand, it might be a good challenge.

All this was racing through my mind as Pippa and I left the party.

In the car, I told her about the conversation with Beatie and my plans to try stand-up again. I explained the reasons why I wanted to do it. I clarified why writing about it would be good for me. Good for us. Good for Otto. It was New Year. She had been drinking. It seemed like a good time to say it.

'Good idea,' she said, 'apart from one small thing.'

'What's that?' I asked.

'You're not funny.'

I had anticipated something like this. I told her that comedians didn't have to be funny in real life. I told her about Jack Dee and grumpiness. I told her about locating that side of me which could make people laugh.

'I know all that,' she said kindly, 'but I'm not sure you have a side that can make people laugh – on or off stage.'

'I make you laugh,' I retorted.

'That's different,' she said.

'In what way "different"?'

'I laugh *at* you.'

'Oh,' I sighed.

'But don't let me put you off. You ought to give it a go if that's what you want.'

'Really?'

'It might be therapeutic.'

'That's what I was hoping . . .' I said eagerly.

'Make you funny. Bring you out of yourself a bit more.'

'Exactly!' I enthused. This was more like it. 'It's about realising my potential as much as anything else. Understanding myself through understanding comedy. What you say is true enough – well, not all of it, but never mind that for now – but I thought I could use that in some way. I haven't really thought it through yet, but I wondered whether I could devise a routine which would somehow reflect who I am. It wouldn't be that funny. More chuckle-inside funny than laugh-out-loud funny.

But funny, or at least *quite* funny. That would be enough. And because it's so, you know, characteristic of me, it would mean that I could get round the adopting a comic persona bit. Sort of bypass it. And I've had this great idea. A routine about death and comedy. You wouldn't believe the number of coincidences which have landed the material in my lap. Literally given it to me on a plate. What do you think? Being funny about bereavement but not so funny that it's in bad taste. Just thought-provoking and amusing. And it would be so "me". It's a good idea. Do you think it would work?'

I glanced hopefully across at Pippa. How could she not respond to my zesty spunk?

In fact, quite easily. She had fallen asleep, and by the look of it, fallen asleep several minutes ago.

THREE

Not Funny

Unbowed by reactions which varied from being ever so slightly interested to being barely suppressed, mirthful disbelief, I set about writing a proper routine, or at least one which I thought would be more substantial than just filling time on stage for around four minutes with the more or less exclusive aim of not being heckled. As Max Miller once said, 'Comedy is the only job you can do really badly and people won't laugh at you.'

Initially, I wanted to do about fifteen minutes of material, not appreciating at the time how difficult it was to generate ten or even five minutes of good stuff. Supposedly, Seinfeld took six months uncovering six minutes of acceptable material when he returned to stand-up. That's six months of writing, rejecting, rewriting and then re-rejecting, not six months of doodling, watching the daytime edition of *Bargain Hunt*, and checking what's inside the fridge.

I had given myself two weeks. Maybe three.

Still, I did at least think I was doing the thing properly. I divided my routine into eight sections, reasoning that an audience would only be able to focus properly on one idea for around ninety seconds before wanting a change of gear.

I don't know how I came up with the 'ninety seconds' idea, or even where it came from. Perhaps it was something to do with football matches lasting ninety minutes. Feasibly, it was connected with part of my new PIN, recently allocated and featuring a '9' and a '0'.

Most likely it was some weird hangover from my days in the classroom. At teacher-training college, we were told that the average adolescent was only able to absorb around eighteen minutes of information in any forty-five-minute lesson. We were told this by a one-armed asthmatic with a limp and a skin condition, and no one found it written in any textbook. But still. He instructed us to bear it in mind when 'delivering the curriculum'.

It was never satisfactorily explained whether the eighteen minutes should arrive in a single pedagogic rush, and if so, at the beginning, the middle or the end. Or whether it should be parcelled up and passed round the allotted time in small nuggets of wisdom, punctuated by jokes and/or diversions and/or appropriate demonstrations of my ability to maintain discipline. And if, indeed, the enlightenment was to arrive in instructive chunks, should *these* come mostly towards the beginning (when the average adolescent is less tired) or the end (when the average adolescent has been eased through the process of educational foreplay)?

I think I plumped mostly for the 'instructive chunks' option, where I calculated that each edifying portion should last about ninety seconds. But here's the thing: is there really much similarity between a classroom full of stroppy, hormonal teenage boys and an alcohol-fuelled audience out for a laugh and a bit of fun.

Put like that, the answer seemed quite straightforward.

Ninety seconds it was.

Ninety seconds per idea. Ninety times eight equals seven hundred and twenty seconds. Or twelve minutes. Allow a minute or so for laughter. Another minute for heckling (mild) or the odd bit of banter with the audience. Add another minute of flexibility for introductions and saying something like, 'Thank you, you've been a great audience' or 'Goodnight and thank you. My name's Tony Binns. If I don't see you next time, I'll see you through the window! Goodnight!'

That was fifteen minutes.

Fifteen minutes.

Piece of cake.

Here's how my comic routine divided up:

- Receiving news of death (links to JFK and my maternal grandmother falling off her bike and dying from heart attack)
- Heart attacks run in the family – examples?
- What happens when the heart stops beating: a medical description
- My father's heart attacks and visiting him in hospital
- The installation of the stairlift and my mother's financial claims (from the council) on becoming 'prime carer'
- Imagining life without my father and the legacy of the dead
- My mother's brain tumour
- The significance (or otherwise) of God

On paper, it doesn't seem very funny. And that was the trouble. It wasn't.

People say that when you write a comic routine your first reaction is to think it is the funniest thing ever created. Then, a short time afterwards, and often a very short time afterwards, you begin to believe it is about as funny as a dose of the clap and probably the unfunniest thing anyone has ever committed to paper.

However, when I finished writing out my routine (in longhand first, like all Proper Writers), I appreciated immediately that it was neither of these. In places (and you'll have to take my word for this) it was reasonably if morbidly funny. At least, it was when I looked at it. Still, I doubted it would ever work on stage. Even the so-called laugh lines – which ground dutifully into action every ninety seconds or so – were not promising.

Somehow I had managed to work in a story about my first erection (while wearing a pair of riding boots belonging to the girl two doors down; I was seven, she was eighteen. It's a long story), and something about my mother instructing an Indian family to leave my stricken father's hospital ward. 'If he's going to die he'll want to it in peace, without all that jabbering,' she reasoned.

Somewhere along the line, though, even the most promising comic material had been neutralised by the way in which it had been packaged. Rather like receiving a potentially OK Christmas present wrapped in newspaper. The element of allure and promise had been taken away.

Another good anecdote about my mother asking my brother-in-law to shave her pubic hair before she went into hospital to have an operation on a brain tumour was more or less thrown away.

Thus, despite containing some promising details, the routine had no hope of recovering from lines like, 'I have a friend who's a doctor. He once told me that if you were to open up someone immediately after he had died of a heart attack, you would find, inside a sack called the pericardium, that the heart was still wriggling. If you put your hand round it, you would find an uncoordinated, irregular squirming – known as ventricular fibrillation – the agonal act of a heart that is becoming reconciled to its eternal rest.' (And here comes the punchline.) 'It's like holding, he said, a wet, jelly-like bagful of hyperactive worms.'

Funny?

No.

Not even the way I tell 'em.

While I was writing this guff, however, I had an idea that I was writing observational comedy, mixing up personal anecdote with reflections on death and mortality, thus producing a heady, potent cocktail of profound laughter – something, I imagined, of a Holy Grail in the world of stand-up comedy. It seemed at the time to be clever, witty, philosophical and entertaining, whereas in fact it was stupid, humourless and dull.

It took a while for me to understand this, or at least to understand the full extent of it. I appreciated immediately that what I had done would not do, but I thought it could be salvaged.

At any rate, I decided to keep my ideas to myself, perhaps suspecting that any sort of exposure would further unveil their ironclad mediocrity. Though another side of me throbbed with purpose, when anyone asked how it was all going, I became evasive and merely replied, 'Fine, thank you. Just a bit of tinkering to do – but basically, it's more or less there.'

Which of course it wasn't.

But the more I looked at the routine, the more convinced I became that although it was indifferent stuff, it was at least fair to middling indifferent, and I could certainly make something workable from the mess. I felt that with a bit of pruning and rejigging, I could get away with it.

For example, I considered how I could present the material and (ominously) my thoughts turned towards appearance and the various ways of disguising myself. I mulled over glasses. I considered a wig. I wondered about a clipboard and white coat, something at least to make me seem more authoritative. If people weren't going to laugh, they could possibly be deceived into believing that they were accepting delivery of useful information. I decided against the white coat/clipboard thing as this, I thought, suggested parody. Actually not a bad move if I wanted laughs, but I hadn't written it as parody, and wasn't yet prepared to concede the point. Also, it was a bit Denis Norden. I determined instead on a sober, dark suit. Respectful and, yes, funereal. That would be right. So – dark suit, open-necked white shirt, smart black shoes and a pair of David Hockney glasses I had found in a charity shop. I ditched the wig.

Then, whenever Pippa was out and while Otto was asleep, an admittedly narrow corridor of opportunity usually occurring between 10 and 11 p.m., I tried out the jiggled-with routine in front of a mirror. Even this relatively straightforward process caused problems.

I am not one of those people who enjoys looking at his image in a mirror. Or on a photograph. Or on a book jacket. Or anywhere, in fact. Shaving, for example, causes me enormous inconvenience.

Is this weird or are most men like that?

I know all the theory about aversion being an inverted form of vanity. Still, it's true. I live in fear of suddenly glimpsing Caliban, so I don't look at all. And when I did look in the full-length mirror at the top of the stairs, it was like reacquainting myself with a lost and unlovely relative. More to the point, I felt ridiculous. The thick glasses and the suit gave the distinct impression that I was a fashionable member of the Jehovah's Witness movement, though a member nonetheless. If I couldn't face up to myself in a mirror, how would I cope when confronted by an audience?

Not to be absolutely deflected, I ran through the material, trying to pace it properly, trying to look at myself, and signalling the seven changes of gear as best I could, keeping my imaginary audience fully involved and engaged. I timed it at fourteen minutes and thirty-five seconds, though this bit of good news had to be judged in the wider context of wondering whether it was actually fourteen minutes and thirty-five seconds of crap.

Still, relatively cheered, I set about finding a venue, this time casting my net a little wider than a manky pub in south London. This would be the real thing. A comedy club. Or at least a designated space for comedy above a pub. And not in south London. In fact, not strictly speaking in London at all. West-west London. I thought this was wise. I would need a more serene and less instinctively impolite lot. A better class of audience. More appreciative of my ambitious material. Less inclined to heckle. *Time Out* described my choice as 'a friendly club' and it was certainly in a nice middle-class area.

I called the manager and explained my needs.

'You can't do more than five minutes,' he said politely, though in a tone that suggested he was neither appreciative nor serene.

'But my material runs for fourteen minutes and thirty five seconds,' I protested.

'That's your problem. You'll have to cut it.'

I said I'd get back to him after I'd looked at my routine to see if a few tactful alterations could be made without ruining the sense.

'It's not exactly Shakespeare, is it?' he chortled.

'How do you know?' I thought of saying, before actually saying, 'No, it's not,' even adding a small, apparently collusive and entirely false laugh. 'I'll talk to you soon, then . . .'

'You do that,' he said, 'and by the way – just so I've got a note – what's your name? I'll put you on file.'

'Binns,' I lied, 'Tony Binns.'

'OK, Mr Binns. You have a think and get back to us when you're ready. Five minutes max, though. Remember that.'

'I will,' I muttered darkly, and the call ended.

That was about the moment when I finally understood what I had written was not good enough. Coming up against obstacles can do that. I mean that hardship can help you to assess what's really important or worthwhile. It was what happened in the war. It's what happens when a relationship breaks down. And it's what happened then. I looked balefully down at the small sheaf of paper in my hand and began to look again, as if for the first time, at the words printed on them. The words that had been carefully typed from the scrawl of my notepad.

They were shit.

I'd have to start again.

The next time Pippa asked me how things were going, I told her that I had put things on hold.

'Why's that?' she asked.

'Er . . . material's not quite right.'

'You mean it's not funny.'

'Not really.'

'Thought not.'

Then she said something, no doubt kindly meant, along the lines of hoping it was the end of all that being funny nonsense even though she applauded the ambition but wouldn't it be better to buy myself a Bullworker or take out health club membership or try yoga if it was only a matter of reinventing myself or whatever it was I was meant to be doing.

I nodded back at her. Nodded a bit, that is. Inside, however, I was secretly more determined than ever. Deep inside the hold, as they say, a fire was raging. It was no longer just about understanding myself through understanding comedy. It was now more about Understanding Comedy. Humour had become a beast that needed to be tamed. If my material wasn't funny, why wasn't it funny? Why had I thought it was funny in the first place? Would anyone else think it was funny? And – crucially – what would it take to be funny? For me to be funny?

Over the next few weeks, I found myself thinking about this quite hard. It wouldn't be an exaggeration to say that the problem haunted me. It became a kind of obsession. A bullet lodged deep down inside me, and one that seemed to have no exit wound. I hallucinated comedy. Was there anything, I wondered, such as the perfect, infallible joke – one that had the potential to make anyone laugh at any time under any circumstances?

I read a short story by Evelyn Waugh called 'Tactical Exercise' and became transfixed by its opening sentence: 'John Verney married Elizabeth in 1938, but it was not until the winter of 1945 that he came to hate her steadily and fiercely.' The question of this sentence's humour (was it funny or sad?) became a kind of fetish.

Was Waugh being funny? Misogyny aside, I thought he probably was. Sometimes the words looked very funny indeed, though occasionally they came across as peevish and hateful. Just changing the words a bit altered the meaning a lot. Thus 'John Verney married Elizabeth in 1938, but by the winter of 1945 he had come to hate her steadily and fiercely' is plain nasty. And 'John Verney married Elizabeth in 1938 though unfortunately by the winter of 1945 he had come to hate her steadily and fiercely' merely suggests domestic disappointment. The original version teases our expectations and then suddenly negates them, and that's more or less what is funny. Or what I found funny.

On the other hand, I couldn't just get up on stage at, say, the Comedy Store and say, 'Ladies and gentlemen, great to be here . . . did you know that John Verney married Elizabeth in 1938, but it was not until the winter of 1945 that he came to hate her steadily and fiercely,' and hope to have the audience rolling around with unbridled mirth.

But it was an intriguing idea and typical of the sort of nonsense that took up space in my head after I had binned the routine about finding comedy in death.

I embarked on a mini-course of 'background reading' and came across one point of view which suggested that English humour veered between innocence and experience, between banana skins and full-blown misanthropy.

I wasn't sure I entirely agreed with this, but it did make me muse about humour and national identity. The English, in particular the English, seem to be very proud of their comedy and their apparently coherent, maybe even systematic, sense of humour. It's the kind of thing that is trotted out whenever the idea of 'national identity' is mooted. As I write this, there are a number of volumes on bookshop shelves with titles like, *British Comedy Greats*, *Great British Humour* and *Great Britain's Funnymen*. Do they have the same sort of thing in France? I wondered. Or Germany!? Do Belarus or Moldavia or Belgium define themselves through comedy?

Miles Kington's introduction to one of these books goes some of the way to answering this. He says, 'There is a theory that humour is international and joins nations together, a theory held mainly by those who have little sense of humour and haven't travelled much . . .'

He's right. Though there are exceptions, comedy does not travel very well. Almost never across the twenty-two miles of the English Channel. Often not even the breadth of the country. Sometimes not from one person to the next.

But when it does, there is a sort of domino effect of almost hedonistic proportions, of a joyous, shared sense of amused communality and festive togetherness. This occurred, for example, with the Goons, Monty Python, and Morecambe and Wise. Though it doesn't quite happen with, say, Bernard Manning or Jasper Carrott. Why not? How not?

And the more I thought about all this, the more bedevilled and gripped I became.

Could there really be anything that bonded together Eddie Izzard with Max Miller, or Pete and Dud with the Two Ronnies?

I had heard that a comedian can only work in one of two ways, either 'with' or 'at' an audience. I knew about and fully appreciated the 'rainbow of comedy' theory, i.e. of laughter and joy being at one end of the spectrum, with the darker hues of satire and irony at the other. I understood how all comedians found their own special places somewhere along these scales.

And I wondered how this kind of diversity could ever be affiliated within an identifiably national 'type' of comedy.

I talked about this with Jo, a friend from university days who had always had a weakness for American comedians. Jo's father had been chairman of the Ford Motor Company and he had spent some of his childhood in America. Some of it must have rubbed off. He was the first person to convince me (a bit) that some Americans do actually possess a sense of humour. At college, he sometimes played me his Tom Lehrer albums. On the other hand, he also made me listen to Genesis and once admitted he had had dinner with Bucks Fizz. Still, Jo was the only person I knew who seemed to understand and appreciate American comedy. He directed me to Bill Hicks and gave me an extract from one of his routines.

'Before you read it,' he said, 'think how you know it's American rather than English.'

'Righto,' I said.

He gave me a book and indicated with quiet solemnity the passage I ought to examine. It was like being back in a practical criticism class with Dr Hartle. At least, the ones I went to.

He observed me as I read.

'"Now we have women priests. What do y'all think of that? Women priests? Yeah. I think it's fine, women priests, you know. So what? Now we got priests of both sexes I don't listen to. Fuck, I don't care. Have one with three balls and eight titties, I don't fuckin' care, you know. Have a hermaphrodite one, I don't, I don't care. Have one with gills and a trunk – I might go to that service".'

At college, Jo and I had been on stage together two or three times. We had been pantomime dames. And it was Jo who had started to giggle uncontrollably during *The Two Noble Kinsmen* whenever his Velcro-attached purse was noisily detached from his woolly tights, making a sort of emphatic farting sound. We could have been good together, Jo and I. As it was, we both ended up as teachers, though he had got there in a more interesting and roundabout way: vacuum-cleaner salesman, Hong Kong civil servant, theatre administrator.

I looked up at him when I'd finished. Over the years, we had spent a lot of time looking at each other. And we always looked at each other in a slightly mournful way, recognising mutual regret, a shared sense of opportunities spurned, life wasted.

This wasn't much different.

'Well . . .?' he asked.

'Something about the language,' I offered, 'all those "y'all"s and "fucks" . . .?'

'Of course the language, Stevie,' he said. 'What else?'

We talked on and decided that it was something to do with the informality of Hicks's language, his complete lack of respect for it and subsequent sense of syncopated abandonment, which somehow made him 'American'. We compared Hicks to something by Frank Skinner, which was every bit as bad-mannered in terms of subject matter, though was in other ways somehow more proper and even buttoned-up.

'It's like he knows he's being naughty,' said Jo. 'There's a bit of tension between his irreverence and the way he says it. Hicks is *all* irreverence. Skinner is quite polite about being insolent.'

'The difference between being insolent and cheeky?'

'Yes. Perhaps.'

Here's the Frank Skinner bit: 'I have to admit, I don't like condoms. I hate that moment, after sex, when you look down at yourself, and there's a pink, wrinkled condom, just hanging there. I hate that. Especially if you weren't actually wearing one when you put it in . . . Oh, it can happen, you know. Those ribbed ones will stay there for months. It's like knocking a fuckin' Rawlplug in.'

I don't think Jo and I were saying anything profound or uncovering some great comic secret. But for good measure, he also pointed out to me that Hicks and Skinner came from different comedic directions. Apparently, Skinner says that he writes comedy because it's funny and says that everything else is incidental. Any attempt to say otherwise is 'bollocks'. On the other hand, Hicks is influenced by the intellectual Noam Chomsky and (like his model) wished to tell the truth and expose lies, along the way communicating the hilarious absurdity of life and making the truth into something funny and cathartic. Jo read out another bit from his Bill Hicks book: '"You have people that want to hear comedy where they don't have to think about anything. To me, they are missing the point."'

'Opposite of Frank,' I said.

'Complete opposite of Frank,' Jo agreed.

'But it doesn't make Frank "English" and Hicks "American", does it?'

'No – but you could say that Frank exhibits a very English fear of appearing to be clever or intellectual.'

'You could say that,' I said.

Standing outside a toilet for three and a half hours on the train journey home, I thought this had been a weekend well spent. If pushed, I would have to say that on the evidence of my (failed) 'comedy in death' routine, I was more with Bill than Frank. Still, I mused, perhaps English comedians don't work on such a large scale as Americans. We have satire all right, but maybe it finds its place in shows like *Spitting Image* and *Have*

I Got News For You rather than in stand-up. Is this separation, if it is a separation, the legacy of music hall in which, on the whole, comic performers just aimed to give everyone a jolly time?

The ghost of music hall recalled my father's first joke. (Remember? 'I can row a boat. Canoe?')

Whimsical. Playful. Harmless. Restrained. Very English. A reserved, discreet watercolour of a joke, in fact, but hardly a rib-tickler. Also like my dad. And containing no sign of 'truth' or other ulterior motives.

Another one of my father's jokes was: 'Give me a sentence using the word "fascinate".' Then, after my boyish self had spent a couple of minutes contorting the English language, he eventually announced the answer: 'The policeman had nine buttons but he could only fasten eight.'

The sad thing is, I still find this quite funny.

Even my mum thought it was funny.

Does that make the joke timeless?

My father was at Dunkirk and used to tell me how, when the time came for him to wade out to one of the little boats, he elected to leave his rifle behind rather than his football. I found this both reassuring and reasonable, and also quite comic. Is it, I now wonder, an illustration of England's so-called 'Dunkirk spirit', i.e. the employment of humour in a mildly ironic and often self-deflating way in order to a) keep spirits up, and b) make light of a particularly tricky situation? Would the Germans, for example, have been so ready to deploy these tactics? Did gallows humour play any part in Hitler's Berlin bunker? How many one-liners did the rounds after Pearl Harbor? And were there Japanese jokes about Hiroshima?

One writer, one English writer I should say, advanced the

theory that Nazism wouldn't have survived if the German high command had spent time at boarding school, playing pranks on one another, making apple turnovers out of their beds, and so on. A good old British sense of humour would have stopped Hitler in his tracks.

A few years ago, my father told me another wartime story, actually his 'other' wartime story. When the British Expeditionary Force arrived back from Dunkirk, those who had actually kept hold of their firearms were ordered to hand them over because there was a shortage among the soldiers defending the south coast, who now suddenly constituted the front line. This seemed reasonable. After all, their need was the greater.

After a few days' rest, my father's company was sent to Dartmoor, a likely drop zone for the German paratroops who were expected to spearhead an invasion. The instructions were issued by a major with a ginger moustache and an obviously public-school accent.

'Your task,' Ginge said solemnly, 'will be to defend England from the marauding Boche in the event that the Nazis launch an invasion.'

My father's company stared at him. Stared quizzically.

'Er, any questions?' asked Ginge.

There was a silence, no doubt an awkward silence, before one of the more confrontational soldiers piped up, 'What are we going to stop them with, sir?'

'What on earth do you mean?' roared Ginge.

'They took our rifles off us when we got back from Dunkirk, sir. What do we use to stop the Germans with if we haven't got rifles?'

The major considered. A smile played across his lips.

'I take it you have transport.'

'Sir?'

'Lorries and suchlike?'

'Sir.'

'Then drive at the Hun, man. Run him over!'

'Sir.'

I always loved this story. It seemed so very English and so very droll. And now, in my general thinking about humour, in the comic medley that was playing through my head, I laughed out loud, which wasn't very English, and apparently at nothing, which perhaps was.

A young bloke with a rucksack who looked like a student, and a baldish man with a can of pissy lager – my companions outside the toilet – looked at me, exchanged the sort of complicit look that strangers give one another when a nutter is in the vicinity, and continued to gaze blankly through the dirty window.

They did quite a lot of gazing. They had to. The train had stopped and was going to be stopped for some time. It was twenty-one minutes before someone (someone who called herself 'the train manager') spoke to us over the intercom and apologised for the delay which, she said, was due 'to factors unknown'. She also announced in a chirpy, metallic voice, that she would of course inform us as soon as she knew what the problem was and when we were likely to start moving again. In the meantime, she reminded us, the buffet car was still open and we could buy some refreshments. Though we couldn't buy a hot drink, because the boiler was buggered.

The baldish man grunted and crumpled the can of lager in a curiously sensitive-looking hand. The student bloke continued to stare out of the window. Perhaps, I thought, he's a philosophy student. In my frame of mind, I could do only one thing – think about movies in which trains played a comic role.

This was more difficult than I thought. The St Trinian's one, obviously. *The Great St Trinian's Train Robbery*, 1966. And *The Titfield Thunderbolt*. *Buster*, but only accidentally funny, and then only because of Phil Collins. There were plenty of other train films, like the GPO documentaries of the 1930s, but none of them comic. And there was the moment in Hitchcock's *North by Northwest* when the train goes through a tunnel at the end, the bit where Cary Grant and Buffet St Marie are taking their honeymoon on board a train. That was quite funny. Come to think of it, Americans tend to be funnier with trains than us. They also have *Planes, Trains and Automobiles* and (I almost forgot) the great Preston Sturges's films, *The Lady Eve* and *The Palm Beach Story*. Long train journeys in them, both of them hilarious. And what about *Some Like It Hot*?

So you see, far from laying my comic bogey to rest, my non-show in west-west London had merely made me more compulsive about humour. I was gripped by it. I still wanted to do stand-up (and still for all the old reasons), but *now* I wanted to do the thing properly and in different parts of the country. I wanted to experience first-hand how humour worked in Manchester or Birmingham or Great Yarmouth. And I wanted to do it as well as I could, rather than just getting away with a few minutes fuelled by nothing much more than adrenalin and the sweet security that I would probably never do it again. I would have to work out a proper routine. I would speak to established comedians. I would talk to Ken Dodd about English humour and for contrast I would fly to New York and watch American comedians. Hell, I would talk to Woody

Allen. I would go to Glastonbury. And Edinburgh. By the end of it – my journey, my *quest* – I would have found some of the answers to the persistent questions that were buzzing inside my head. Why do people laugh? Why do English people laugh? Ha! I would find out. I would know. And in my knowing I would also understand myself through understanding comedy.

There might even be a book in it.

Brilliant.

Well, not quite. First, obviously, I'd have to become a proper stand-up comedian who could do a lot more than merely survive on an obscure stage in front of thirty or so pissed blokes who in any case weren't paying for the doubtful privilege of seeing you and (therefore) weren't too bothered about what you were doing so long as it didn't put them off their ale. So reprising Hitler and Wodehouse was out. So was the comedy-of-death routine. At least, *my* comedy-of-death routine.

I remembered what Beatie had said about clowning school and wondered whether I had been too dismissive. I supposed it might be a route worth exploring. I mused about it for a week, even wondering whether, on the advice of a friend, I should make a call to a university lecturer who claimed that stand-up had been a part of his BA in theatre studies. 'It taught me a lot about mike technique,' he confided.

Well, it would be a start.

I was on the verge of making the call when, by chance, I found something more promising in the *Evening Standard*'s listings magazine, *Metro Life*. It announced in vivid golden letters on the front cover that inside were 'Fifty Things Every Londoner Should Do This Year'. Though I had recently forfeited my right to be called a Londoner (by moving to Gloucestershire), I couldn't resist a look. We're all suckers for lists, and I'm no exception. And there, at number thirteen, wedged between 'Visit the Little Angel Puppet Theatre' and 'See *Harry Potter and the Prisoner of Azkaban* was 'Do a Comedy Course'.

This is what it said: 'Are you ready to unleash your inner David Brent? The Absolute and Almost Beginners Comedy Course, organised by AmusedMoose, will point you in the right direction, whether you want to pursue a career in stand-up or just dazzle your friends with dazzling wit. The course is led by Logan Murray, who doesn't believe comedy can be taught, but over 11 sessions will encourage you to discover your comic persona.' There followed a brief list of graduates from the course who had become comedians and one who had 'actually dated Alan Davies', the shaggy haired comedian-cum-actor. I didn't much want a date with Alan, but the rest sounded good. So I called the number and a nice, sharp, talkative woman answered the phone. She told me her name was Hils Jago.

'H-I-L-L-S?' I asked, wretchedly unable to staunch my pedagogical urges.

'H-I-L-*S*,' Hils replied quite patiently, obviously for the millionth time in her life.

'But J-A-G-O,' I pronounced confidently, suddenly warming to the game.

'Correct,' she snapped back.

I knew all about 'Jago'. At school, it was one of the five houses into which boys were organised. All the names referred to people – I assume 'people' – who were virtually unheard of outside the school gates. I was in 'Shenstone', but I had friends in Jago who were good at cricket though hopeless at rugby. Their head of house was a David Bowie fan who had once organised a sixth form orgy. Jago's colour was blood red, almost maroon, in fact. Shenstone was black. To this day, my favourite colour is black. Sad, isn't it? In case you're interested, Pole was a pale, icy blue; Windsor was royal blue; and Featherstone was yellow.

Yes. I knew all about Jago.

'How can I help you?' Hils Jago was asking.

I explained my wanting to know about becoming a stand-up. I also told her that I might be writing a more general book about comedy.

'I was wondering whether I might talk to you. And Murray Logan.'

'Logan Murray,' Hils said.

'Yes. Sorry. Logan Murray. I thought if I talked to people actually involved in teaching stand-up, maybe even watch a session . . . or two . . . you know . . .'

Hils Jago can be very persuasive. Within three minutes she had signed me up for all eleven sessions and wrested £225 from me. If I was going to allow Logan the opportunity to help me discover my comic persona, I would have to do the thing properly and give him a fighting chance.

'Can I pay by credit card?' I asked.

'No.'

'Cheque?'

'Fine.'

'Right. I'll put it in the post.'

'That's great, Steve. Just one thing . . .'

'Yes?'

'What name do you want to be known by?'

'In what way?' I asked, immediately suspicious.

I had always been wary of names, especially 'other' names or nicknames. Or even names in general. At university, my supervisor of three years never got beyond calling me 'Jacobi'. Even when I broke my wrist and turned up for a supervision, in obvious pain and wearing a cast, he merely turned to his wife, smirked, and said, 'Look, dear. Jacobi's broken a bone.' A parent at one school I taught in always called me 'Jack', which I thought was odd until he addressed his son's absence letter to 'Dr Jack O'Bee'. And then there were the horrors of my childhood. Forced to wear lederhosen until the age of twelve, I became known in Birmingham as 'Plastic Pants' or 'Leather Nicks'. Meanwhile, my mother, the Lederhosen Enforcer, called me 'Stephen' in such a way that I came to think she was referring to someone else. Thereafter, I always insisted on 'Steve', or 'Steven' once I became an author. And at school I was known for a while as 'Wally' merely because I (apparently) waddled like a duck, a legacy of my pigeon-toed childhood – i.e. 'Wally Waddle'.

So I felt within my rights to ask 'In what way?'

'On stage,' Hils said, 'what do you want your *stage name* to be?'

'Steve,' I said.

'Steve what? Or just "Steve"?'

'Steve Jacobi.'

'That's very good.'

'Is it?'

'Oh yes. And distinctive. Any relation to Derek?'

'Distant,' I replied coolly. In fact, I had met the great man at a party in Normandy and we had sort of worked out that our nineteenth-century ancestors came over from the same part of Germany at more or less the same time. Derek and I. Dez. *Uncle* Dez.

'"Steve Jacobi" then,' said Hils, 'sounds good, looks good.'

Thus emboldened, I told Pippa of my enrolment to clowning school.

'A bit like that programme *Faking It*, isn't it?' she said, unimpressed.

'That programme where people try to do something they're genetically disabled from actually accomplishing?'

'Yes,' she said, 'in your case, being funny.'

'That's unfair,' I snorted, 'and anyway, what I'm doing is emphatically not the same as *Faking It*'.

'Isn't it?' she smiled.

'No. For a start, I'm not trying to fool anyone.'

'The audience?'

'Well, yes, but only in a manner of speaking . . .'

'Yourself?'

'What's that supposed to mean.'

'Nothing.'

I explained at some length – explained at some length again – about my interest in comedy, the lack of gimmickry, and the broader dimensions of my enquiry.

She listened politely before saying, 'Well, whatever it is you're up to, I want a seat in the front row when it happens.'

'*You're* not coming!' I roared.

'I am.'

'I won't tell you where I'll be performing. Or when.'

'I'll find out.'

'You won't.'

Then she more or less ignored me and began talking to herself, then chuckling to herself and shaking her head. 'Watching you try to be funny. Now that would be funny.

Our conversation over, I went upstairs, opened the drawer next to the bed, and took out my chequebook. I'll show her, I thought. I'll bloody show her. I'll show the lot of you, I snarled, even though no one else knew apart from Pippa. Oh, and Hils Jago. And possibly Murray Logan. Logan Murray.

Downstairs, the phone was ringing. I heard Pippa answer it. Then I placed the written cheque and a short letter giving my address and contact numbers inside an envelope and sealed it.

Despite what I had said to Hils, for a few moments I'd flirted with the idea of changing 'Steve Jacobi' to 'Geoff Vowden', the name of a Birmingham City midfield player from the 1960s. I got the idea from Frank Skinner, or rather Frank Skinner's autobiography. Frank Skinner's real name isn't Frank Skinner but Christopher Collins, 'Frank Skinner' being the name of a West Bromwich Albion player he remembered from his youth. Anyway, I trifled with 'Geoff Vowden' before thinking it would have made me sound too much like a trades union leader or a plumber from somewhere like Erdington. I also thought, 'No. I must not back away from this. I must face it full on. Be brave! My name is Steve Jacobi. I will be Steve Jacobi. My name is Steve Jacobi. My name is Steve Jacobi. Steve Jacobi. Steve. Jacobi. *Steve* Jacobi. The very funny *Steve* Jacobi. Ladies and gentlemen, I'm very proud and pleased to present a very funny man, Steve Jacobi. Steeeve Jacobeeeeeee!'

Pippa came in. She was holding the phone.

'It's your mother,' she said, 'and she wants a word with you about your new career.'

'You didn't bloody well tell her??!" I snapped, and took the phone. 'Bitch!' I hissed, and pressed the handset to my ear.

No one there. Not a sound.

Nothing.

Not a sausage.

It was dead.

Pippa looked at me. 'It's all in the timing,' she scoffed.

FOUR

AmusedMoose

It was a funny thing to call a comedy course, but then that might have been the idea: 'Stand Up and Deliver Ltd in association with AmusedMooseComedy'. That was what it said at the top of the letter I received from Hils Jago. Why 'AmusedMoose'? I wondered. Maybe it was something to do with the moose not being a notably funny animal and that amusing it and therefore creating an amused moose was somehow remarkable. Or perhaps it was something to do with Canada and that country's supposed dearth of humour. (Right down there with the Belgians, in fact.) Perchance it was a private joke. Then again, Flanders and Swann had made up a gloriously humorous song about a gnu and also done one about a hippopotamus.

So there was obviously gold in them there hills.

Anyway, it was Saturday morning and I was on my way to the AmusedMooseComedy. I caught the 8.37 to Paddington. The train was due in at 10.12. That would leave plenty of time to get across London.

My carriage was packed with football supporters, shoppers

and country folk having a day out in the Big Smoke. But mostly football supporters.

'Ranieri's days are numbered,' said a man with a shaved head. 'You mark my words.'

'He's a cunt,' said one of his mates, also shaven-headed.

'I quite like him,' a third man added, who was more bald than shaven but would probably have been shaven if the opportunity had presented itself. 'It's Abracadabraman or whatever you call you him that I don't like.'

'He's a cunt 'n'all,' observed man number two. Then he paused for reflection. 'They're all cunts.'

The train was late.

Of course it was.

The doors wheezed open and I sprinted towards the Underground. First day at school and late! It occurred to me that I might be able to make a joke about my impending lateness. Remember Reggie Perrin's 'Sorry I'm late . . . badger in the signal box' routine? Maybe I could say something like, 'Sorry I'm late . . . cow on the line at Didcot Parkway.'

Then again, maybe I should just concentrate on being as less late as possible.

I considered my options. Either Circle or District or Hammersmith & City to King's Cross, then change to the Northern and up to Chalk Farm. Or Bakerloo to Oxford Circus, change to the Victoria to Euston, *then* Northern up to Chalk Farm.

I might just make it.

There was a large whiteboard on the concourse which announced that all services today were running well. Apart from the Bakerloo line which was suspended in its entirety, and the Circle and District and Hammersmith & City lines which (due to engineering works) were not running between Baker Street and Aldgate.

In other words, I was fucked.

You know it's not personal, but sometimes it feels like it and feels like it quite a lot.

I boarded a train to Baker Street, resurfaced outside Madame Tussaud's, and began waiting in a queue for the replacement bus service which would get me to King's Cross. One of Red Ken's bendy buses, one of those with a rubbery middle, duly came along and was immediately taken out of service.

'Why?' I asked the driver.

'Engine problems,' he said.

'But you got this far. Couldn't you go just a bit further? Say, to King's Cross?'

''fraid not,' he continued, 'not my decision.'

Then he lit a cigarette.

He's right, I thought, that bloke on the train. They're all cunts. Everyone of them. Everyone is a cunt.

I eventually arrived in Camden at around 11.30, angry, sweating, and not feeling very funny.

The class was being held above the Enterprise, a pub opposite Chalk Farm tube. I scampered across the road and clattered through the double doors.

The first thing you notice about the Enterprise is it's not very clean. That's fine. Some people like dirty pubs. Indeed, think the whole point of pubs is that they're dirty. The second thing to notice is that it's Irish and on the literary side. The walls are covered with framed portraits of people like Joyce and Beckett, and there are posters advertising productions of plays, again, mostly by Irish writers such as Behan and, well, Beckett.

A man with a black T-shirt was sweeping the floor. He had already amassed a small pyramid of fag ends. He looked up as I made my entrance.

'Comedian?' he asked politely.

'Well . . . yes. Sort of,' I replied.

'Upstairs, then,' he smirked.

I took the stairs three at a time, turned sharp right, and pushed through a door into the large room which would be my comedic bosom every Saturday for the next ten weeks or so. There were only four people in the room. One of them was a woman who looked vaguely like a cross between Beryl Bainbridge and Vanessa Redgrave, and who turned out to be Hils Jago.

'Ah!' she said.

'Sorry I'm late,' I wheezed.

A dark-haired man of about my own age smiled and chortled, 'Don't worry. The trains are fucked. Everyone's late.'

I sat down on a stray stool and stared hopelessly at the two people who hadn't spoken.

'Badger in the signal box?' said a tall man with the beginnings of a beard.

The other one, sturdy and agricultural, giggled knowingly.

In the course of time, the room began to fill.

Shortly, there were nineteen of us. And Hils Jago. And Logan Murray, actually (I now discovered) a man of my age. I noted this particular development with dismay. Hils apart, he and I were probably a good ten years older than most of the others.

That made eighteen young, vibrant, confident, self-assured, cockily spirited whippersnappers, not yet ground down by the gross iniquities of life. Probably weren't even aware such things existed.

Plus Logan, who had been doing stand-up for seventeen years.

And me.

Bugger.

I tried to make myself invisible by rooting around in my bag, checking that I had my notebook, spare notebook, pen, spare pen, spare cartridge, Nurofen, train timetable, wallet and mobile phone. Of course I did. I check every five minutes. I'm that kind of bloke.

After a bit, Hils took a roll-call, twisted the 225 quid from those who hadn't yet stumped up the course fees, and left. Logan told us to say goodbye as we wouldn't be seeing her again for a couple of months, if at all. Then he asked us which name we wanted to be known as 'professionally'. 'Keep it as short as possible,' he added, 'because it will appear bigger on posters and flyers.'

Immediately, I was reassured.

You knew you were in the hands of a pro.

Once we were settled and had sorted the bar stools into a circle, Logan gave us a pep talk. 'Don't think about how you feel adults ought to behave or act,' he announced, 'do what *you* want. It's just about fucking around on stage. That's all. If I can do this – and I've done nothing else for seventeen years – then anyone can. There are no tricks, no secrets. Just fucking around. I'm here to help you find a way to do that.'

This was sort of what I didn't want to hear. 'Fucking around' wasn't one of my strong suits. I was good at a small handful of things and maybe quite good at a few more, but 'fucking around' wasn't in either category. Instinctively, I needed and reached for guidelines, targets and procedures. 'Fucking around' sounded like it was the opposite of this.

I wasn't given much time to brood as we then had to stand and introduce ourselves to the rest of the group. Though this felt uncomfortable and a tad AA, there seemed no other remotely efficient way for nineteen strangers to introduce themselves to one another.

We numbered fourteen blokes and five women and though we seemed a pretty disparate lot, there were also points of contact. You wouldn't expect anything else, I suppose, from nineteen people in a comedy class locked in a room above a pub on a Saturday morning, but at the time it seemed serendipitous and oddly comforting.

Many were mildly dissatisfied with their lives or, perhaps more commonly, their jobs, and were looking for some kind of change. Among those looking to improve their lots were a journalist, a banker, an actress, an estate agent and an Australian doctor. The estate agent, Paul, arrived in a suit; I assumed that he had either come straight from work or was maybe going on to complete an afternoon shift or attend a property viewing. But as the suit stayed on him more or less for the rest of the course, I came to think that, actually, it was a part of his act. Moreover, whenever he talked, he rotated his arms in a manically choreographed way and spoke in a sort of hoarse 'you dirtee rat' sort of way, as though his every thought was scripted.

I wondered, as you do when you meet people like Paul, whether he might be one to watch. Or a complete plonker. At the time, it was difficult to tell.

Three or four, including Julie (the actress) and Johnno (a rotund, likeable chap with a dead eye: apparently his mother had told him he'd never get on telly 'with that eye'), had already done some stand-up. They were on the course to refine their performance skills, or in Johnno's case – I later discovered – to recapture his nerve after a bad stage experience in Lewisham.

When it came to my own introduction, I decided to be honest. Honest-ish. 'Hello, I'm Steve,' I said frankly and without equivocation, just about resisting the oddly insistent impulse to wave at everyone. 'I'm here because I want to find out something about myself by doing stand-up, and to learn something about comedy. Also,' I continued sheepishly, 'I want to write a book about it.'

'Thank you, Steve,' said Logan in a tone of voice I hadn't heard for many years. Not, in fact, since my grandfather was dying and we were all being extra nice to him while he lay in a hospital bed, violently pulling tubes and drips from his body and arm, and repeatedly asking the nurses whether Trevor Francis had scored for Birmingham. Logan's voice merely recalled the resigned and terminal pity with which we had spoken to my grandfather.

After the introductions, he instructed us to write down nine important things about performing stand-up. These included practical advice about 'playing the moment' (of which more later), of 'checking in with the audience', and – more prosaically – taping yourself and making sure that your best material was at the beginning and the end of a set. 'Let the middle look after itself,' Logan offered reassuringly.

I wrote all this down, neatly, and even did some underlining. When I got home that evening, I would transfer the details to my special notebook.

So far, so good.

I was good at taking notes and writing things down. It's what school and university are all about. I watched with disdain and no little sense of satisfaction as Johnno searched in vain for his biro, then found it and spent a lot of time shaking it and jabbing the clogged nib on his not-very-nice notepad.

Loser, I thought.

But that, as far as I was concerned, was as good as it got.

The first class was a double session and for the next four hours or so, Logan put us through a series of exercises which seemed specifically designed to humiliate me. Nobody else. Just me. I'd like to say that everyone else must have been thinking much the same, but with the comforting exception of Maria (who gradually made a weird virtue from her discomfort), it wasn't true.

If I spent much of the time paralysed, awkward, embarrassed and pondering my uselessness, it was actually for a very good reason. I was useless.

Chief among the numerous low points of my first session was a role-playing game which involved me having to propose to Natasha, a petite opera singer with a slight but charming speech impediment, who was using the course to help develop her performance skills. The act of proposing was complicated by Logan's instruction that I begin by asking for Natasha's hand in a 'high status' frame of mind, then (as he counted me in) change to 'low status'. Natasha, meanwhile, would be adopting the opposite mind set to my own.

The exercise had a perfectly reasonable and legitimate aim: to make us more flexible and reactive, to enable us to move freely up and down and along distinct emotional scales.

I, however, don't really do emotional scales. I'm just me. All the time.

I watched with horror and mounting dread as the other members of the group set about their own tasks. Johnno was brilliant; unselfconscious, warm, comfortable, emotionally supple and (damn him) funny. And he wasn't the only one.

'I've been thinking about us . . .' I said to Natasha, trying to be as stridently high status as I could.

'What? About you and me?' she replied, very low status, batting my words straight back.

'Um . . . yes,' I stuttered.

'High status, Steve,' Logan shouted, though not unkindly.

'. . . and the thing is,' I persevered.

'High status,' said Logan.

'The thing is *that* . . .' I asserted.

'And, change . . .' Logan instructed. 'Ten . . . nine . . . eight . . .'

'We ought to get married right now,' I announced.

'Seven . . . six . . . low status, Steve . . . five . . . don't forget, low status . . .'

'I wouldn't marry you if you were the last man in the world and anyway I'm allergic to gold so you can put that silly ring away,' said Natasha, suddenly getting into the swing of things.

'Why not?' I asked, opting for something neutral, and anyway having more or less forgotten which end of the status scale I was now supposed to be inhabiting.

'Four . . . three . . . two . . . ONE!' Logan concluded.

'Because I don't like you,' said Natasha, 'you're boring and dull and presumptuous.'

'No, I'm not,' I blurted. 'No. Wait a minute. Yes. Yes, I am. You're right. That's exactly what I am.'

'One . . . two . . . three . . . aaaand, change status . . . four . . . five . . .'

'. . . that's exactly what I am. *Not*,' I improvised, more or less getting my bearings.

I'm sure Logan didn't mean anything by it, but after Natasha and I had finished the exercise, he stepped forward and addressed the whole group.

'Just a few words,' he started, 'though you all did brilliantly. And this is no reflection on Steve or Natasha, both of whom were excellent. But don't *try* to be funny for the first few weeks. Just react. Don't lead. Remember – it's just about fucking around on stage.'

I wondered if he'd spotted the difference between not trying to be funny and not being funny, and trying to be funny and not being funny.

I suspect he had.

There were more exercises designed to make us relax and to be responsive. All of them (it seemed) actually designed to heap further indignity upon embarrassment. Though nothing quite approached the troughs of proposing to Natasha, using a microphone ('mike technique' as we solo comedy performers call it) was also fairly cringe-making. First, we were asked to give someone a big 'Enterprise welcome', and then to say something you didn't mean or about which you weren't sincere.

Maybe, like, I'm enjoying this and it all seems really useful.

But *performance*, you see. Surfing the emotional net.

Logan wrapped up this first session by reiterating the idea of 'living in the moment', which was another way of saying that we should ditch our rigid adult expectations. In fact, he had many different ways of saying this. Clearly it was an important point. 'Get rid of the censor inside your heads,' he exhorted. 'Banish your editor! Don't let him blue-pencil what you really want to say.'

By this time I was happily making notes again, nodding in agreement, and therefore feeling on much safer ground. Then, hang on a minute, I thought. This is all wrong. Or rather, I was all wrong. 'Living in the moment' was, of course, precisely what I was brought up, educated, trained and conditioned *not* to do. Anything but. Generally speaking, I avoided the moment and often took great pains to do so. But here I was cheerfully making notes about it and believing I could manage it, or at least believing it was a possibility.

I looked into my bag. Again. Pens, notepads, etc. All present and correct. I preferred to write in ink and had naturally brought along a spare cartridge. Not only that, but the spare cartridge was wrapped in tissue paper in case it leaked. Then there was another spare cartridge in case the first one had leaked. This one also wrapped in tissue paper in case it leaked. The spare spare. And for some obscure reason, I had also packed a spare piece of tissue paper. Thankfully, no spare spare spare cartridge. But even so. 'Playing the moment'? I think not. Don't make me laugh.

I was cautious, pre-packaged, over-prepared, neurotic, tight, Anti-Moment Man.

I pondered some of this on the trip home.

I liked Logan and thought he was not only correct but also had the authority and the experience to know what he was talking about.

The thing about losing your adult mentality made sense, too. It's not that kids have a better sense of humour than adults – though some have – but they do have the potential to be better. They are born with a capacity to be amused and have an intuitive ability to perceive people and situations in uncluttered, impartially open-minded ways. The sort of ways, in fact, that constitute the opposite of what it is to have become an adult. It's not only your mum and dad who fuck you up. Life also puts the boot in. I supposed Logan wanted us to harness this ingenuousness to our more grown-up powers of communication, without letting the one interfere with the other.

Mind you, the fact that children are so vulnerable to amusement, and therefore embarrassingly ready to laugh at dwarfs, big ears, pimply red noses, disability, or sticky-out teeth, does not mean they have a monopoly on laughter. Most young boys would not, for example, have seen what was funny in Richmal Crompton's story 'Aunt Jane's Treat', from her book *William the Fourth*. William's aunt accompanies him to the fair, and is at first reluctant to join in, though finally she does take a ride on the merry-go-round, mounting (as the author puts it) 'a giant cock. It began. She clung on for dear life. It went faster and faster. There came a gleam into her eyes, a smile of rapture to her lips . . . She seemed to find the circular motion anything but monotonous. It seemed to give her a joy that all her blameless life had so far failed to produce.'

No. Logan was after the childlike dexterity to see around and through life, not to be influenced by what life tells us we *ought* to think.

Like the boy who was asked what the capital of Poland was and replied, 'P'.

In this respect, kids can sometimes be quite brilliant. For instance, I remember taking a group of twelve-year-old boys on a school trip to France. We stopped at a small town and paid a visit to its cathedral, badly damaged during the war but recently restored, and now a gloriously odd mongrel of Gothic and baroque architecture. A book had been placed on a table just inside the doors, which still sported evocative bullet holes and shrapnel scars. Visitors we invited to write down comments and observations about the building.

The boys filed dutifully past, deliberating carefully over what they might write, aware that the task carried a kind of aesthetic obligation. When they had finished, I went over and glanced at their entries. The first few went something like this: 'Harry Grimes, London: very ornate'; 'Nick Partridge; London: very beautiful'; 'Robert Bowen, London: very good at games.'

I knew Robert Bowen pretty well and he wasn't the sharpest tool in the box. Still, it didn't matter whether he intended to be funny or not. Probably not. But it nevertheless makes Logan's point about shaking yourself loose from the squat toad of maturity. There was great comic potential in being able to stare at life without blinkers.

Though none of this was actually much help to me. Quite the reverse, in fact. I began to appreciate that I was probably more unsuited to stand-up than I thought. Even more unsuited.

The next two or three sessions followed a similar pattern to the first. And like a trip to the dentist, the wait between each lesson merely intensified my anxieties. Logan was convinced that the best way to become a comedian was to 'let your mind go'. Being funny was as much a state of mind as anything else. You should never be thinking 'How can I please an audience?' Instead, you should impose yourself and believe what you want to say *is funny*.

'It's fucking about on stage,' he said yet again. 'The audience wants to be entertained. They're on your side. Well, they are when you start.'

In different ways, each session focused on providing a series of helpful exercises designed to aid us in releasing our minds, playing the moment and (a new phrase this, and one I rather liked), 'accessing the psychotic inside you'. To this end, we devised and performed spoof poems, gave one another glitzy showbiz introductions, improvised around a 'thank-you' list, played the part of a suicide case chatting with someone who was trying to talk you out of it, and developed a hate list.

There were so many different ways for me to mess up that I began to develop a peculiar siege mentality. At one point I imagined Logan as chief of a tribe of Indians which had surrounded my wagon. He and they circled it again and again, probing for a point of access, trying to find a way in, seeking to break down my character. And against the odds, my plucky, stubborn little wagon consistently repelled them and remained firmly unentered.

Some exercises worked better than others, though my rare moments of progress were usually slapped back into reality by a disastrous or dim-witted performance in a subsequent drill.

I felt reasonably comfortable while reading out my list of hates (which included rhubarb, lederhosen, PINs and 'train managers'), and even quite relaxed when Logan asked us to hurl insults at other individuals in the group. Being nasty was easier than being nice. Perhaps that was what he meant about accessing the psychotic. But any sense of well-being I might have gained from such drills was swiftly extinguished by subsequently feeble attempts to follow a positive thought with a negative afterthought, or play around with the idea of wanting something but then estimating what you might settle for and eventually admitting what you actually have.

It was terribly distressing.

Another exercise involved standing in the middle of the group which formed itself in an enclosing circle. Holding in your mind a secret category or question, you would then gesture or point at each individual and say whether or not he or she satisfied your covert criterion. Usually a simple 'yes' or 'no' did the trick, though occasionally a slight variation was permitted. The intention was to improvise around the quite straightforward act of gesturing at someone and assigning them a positive or a negative. Without being aware of the criterion by which you were being judged, it was impossible to know how complimentary (or critical) someone was being.

Logan started us off, reeling off a series of snap estimations, all with a slightly different emphasis. Each 'yes' and every 'no' expressed something cryptically dissimilar. What though? When he came to me, Logan smiled broadly, nodded emphatically, smiled, pointed a finger and said, 'Definitely, yes!'

It felt good to be so heartily endorsed.

'What was your criterion?' I asked him during the short break which followed the exercise. He was tucking into one of the several fruit salads he always seemed to bring with him.

'Likely to go grey in the next few years,' he replied.

I sighed, grimaced a bit, and joined the others downstairs. Some had gone outside for a smoke, even though it seemed to me the kind of pub where smoking was compulsory. Others were busy getting their notebooks up to date, especially Nat, who appeared to be making a frighteningly thorough and forensic study of each session. A few us went next door to grab a coffee. I waited with John and Jim while a sullen East European-looking girl wrestled with the coffee-maker. Naturally, we were all keen to know about each other's categories.

'Whether or not you'd ever been taken up the arse,' said John.

I couldn't remember what he'd said about me. Yes or no? It was the kind of thing you wanted to know, so I asked him.

'Maybe,' he snorted.

'Well, I haven't,' I replied.

'But have you ever given it?' asked Jim.

'Why, was that your question?' John asked.

Notwithstanding all this, I found the 'yes/no' game to be one of the less intimidating exercises. And why was this? I wondered. Probably something to do with the fact that in the role of judge I was in a position of power. I could effectively exercise a sort of command over the rest of the group simply through the withholding of information. Then there was the element of performance, in this instance necessarily limited to a brisk 'yes' or 'no'. The limited demands of the acting and the inherent granting of control had, I decided, allowed me to 'play the moment' if only in the smallest way. So small, in fact, that I didn't notice it had happened until after it had, er, happened. For a few moments, confidently and even unselfconsciously, and entirely insulated by the nature of the exercise, I had been myself. If I wasn't quite accessing the psychotic, I was at least accessing someone familiar.

And all because I had felt secure. Protected. The nature of the exercise made it almost impossible to fail.

My criterion was people who dried the dishes immediately after they had washed them. I felt I was something of a connoisseur on the subject.

'Yes.'

'Absolutely not.'

'Yes.'

'Certainly.'

'No.'

'Oh . . . no.'

'Maybe.'

Piece of cake. I had even enjoyed it.

It felt good or goodish.

Well. It was a start.

Something to build on.

Back when I was a teacher, it was much the same. Crowd control was the key. If you felt safe, unassailable, then by and large you were. Your own aura of confident impregnability would emanate from the front of a classroom and radiate to all parts. That being the case, you could get away with any old rubbish. You really could, as Logan said, simply fuck about.

Once, while I was teaching in Singapore, I shared a GCSE set with an Australian (let's call him Martin) who was very pleasant and extremely handsome. He stood over six feet tall and carried with him an air of insouciant charm. Martin was also a model and pictures of him in shirts or underpants would often decorate pages of the *Straits Times*, Singapore's finest and only daily paper. He exuded the sort of confident ease most of us could only dream of. The pupils he taught, especially the girls (though also the envious boys), hung on his every word.

The problem with Martin from a teaching point of view was that he knew bugger all about English literature. We shared an examination class and it was his task to teach *Brideshead Revisited.* He seemed fine about this until halfway through a lesson – and a good three or four weeks into the term – he stumbled into my adjacent classroom. I could tell by the look of blank horror on his face that someone must have asked him a tough question and he needed to know the answer.

'Steve . . .' he hissed.

'Martin – is there a problem?' I said.

'Evelyn Waugh. He is a man, isn't he?'

No doubt he returned to his pupils with this nugget of

information safely lodged inside his head, and continued to wing it, much as he had always done. Despite his lack of basic knowledge, I suspect Martin never lost his audience. He was always in control, or always seemed to be in control, which amounts to much the same thing.

This, in vivid contrast to my own experiences, and one episode in particular, now burned into my memory. This one came right at the beginning of my teaching career, while I was doing teaching practice at a state school just outside Edinburgh. It's a ghastly example of losing an audience, of the combative relationship that exists between crowd and performer, and of paying the price for not being able to 'play the moment'.

The journey to this school was always very pleasant and involved a short though spectacular train ride across the Forth Rail Bridge. Maybe because I'd seen Peter Purves scale it on *Blue Peter* and Richard Hannay hide on it in Hitchcock's film of *The 39 Steps*, the bridge had become one of my favourite pieces of architecture. The reason I mention this is that when I first arrived for my teaching placement, fresh from the romantic journey, I was actually in rather a good mood. The train, the bridge, my own callow idealism, the sense of making one's way, of doing something worthwhile – all bollocks, of course, though all contributing to a mood of eager contentedness.

On arrival at the school, there were already a few warning signs. My chaperone, Jim, a homely middle-aged man who had also been a boy at the school and therefore seen it all before, pulled no punches.

'It's not a bad school,' he said, 'but made worse by all the posh kids they've started taking from north Edinburgh.'

'Why's that?' I asked, assuming that more posh kids meant better behaviour, decent manners, nice middle-class values and such like.

'This is really a mining community,' my mentor explained, 'and a bit rough. The local authority thought the working-class kids could be smoothed out a bit if they had the right kind of influence around them.'

'Peer pressure,' I chirped, parroting my sociology notes. 'Did it work?'

'Er, no. The working-class kids and the middle-class kids are at war with one another. They fight on the buses, they fight on the trains and they fight when they're at school.' He was starting to sound a bit Churchillian.

'I expect the middle-class kids didn't know what hit them,' I laughed.

'Actually, the opposite,' said Jim. 'They're better organised and can afford better weapons.'

'Weapons?!' I blanched. 'What kind of weapons?'

'Nothing much. You won't see them. Not unless you're very unlucky. Oh – except last week there was a touring production of *Merchant of Venice* and Shylock was felled in the first act by a stone from a catapult. Hit him smack between the eyes. Actually, a good shot. It was an awful bloody mess, though.' Jim stroked his stubble wistfully. 'We never did find the catapult.'

'Ah,' I said, already beginning to feel my idealism draining away, 'anything else I should know?'

'Yes,' Jim replied, 'you'll have to do toilet duty at lunchtimes.'

'To stop them smoking?'

'No, no. We turn a blind eye to that. Have done for years.

No – in case a fight breaks out. Fags are expensive . . . the boys in particular think it's worth a brawl to get their hands on a packet of Rothmans. But don't go into the toilets unless you're with another member of the staff. We do toilet duty in pairs.'

'Righto,' I said.

Later that morning, already nervous, I made my way to the first lesson I was scheduled to teach. The second half of a GCSE English language class. I would be relieving the usual teacher, a young, squat man with a Bay City Rollers' haircut, bad breath and a pronounced underbite. As I approached the classroom, I could hear that things weren't going well. In fact, they sounded as if they'd got completely out of hand.

As I entered the room, poor old Neanderthal Man scampered past me wearing an expression of infinite gratitude. 'The Seventh Cavalry,' he croaked. 'The bastards are all yours.'

The bastards, however, seemed surprisingly quiet and attentive. I talked about something or other not very interesting for ten minutes or so and nobody said a word.

Easy-peasy-Japanesee, I thought. That other bloke obviously hasn't got what it takes. Unlike me. Then I set some written work which they started without so much as a murmur.

I sat down behind my desk in triumph. I knew they were sizing me up, but clearly I had gained the upper hand. What was it, I wondered, in that moment of self-aggrandising pomposity, that distinguished me from old Fishbreath?

I looked up to absorb the studious atmosphere and probably to wallow in my triumph, though maybe suspicious that things were a little too quiet. Everyone was still writing and most heads were down, though down (I observed) without giving much sense of concentration. Still. Down, nonetheless.

Then, at the very back of the class, a quite pretty girl with dirty blonde hair got to her feet and walked slowly to the front along the aisle between the desks. She was clearly on her way to my desk.

As she advanced, the class held its breath. I sensed I was about to be tested in some obscure and as yet unannounced way. I steeled myself. Inside the desk was a 'Lochgelly', a leather strap. At that time it was still used to administer punishment in Scottish schools. I didn't intend to use it, and didn't even know how to use it. But it was there, and just knowing that was strangely comforting.

The girl reached the front. She perched on the side of the desk so that I could see her anyway short skirt becoming even shorter. Already, I was staring at a comely leg.

I looked up, then looked up at her sweet face and into her heavily made-up eyes, fearing the worst, already at a disadvantage.

'For twenty quid you can fuck me,' she said, loudly enough to ensure that everyone else heard. Despite what was being said, this was not designed to be an intimate encounter.

'Ah, well . . . ,' I spluttered, 'I'm sorry, I can't. Thank you, anyway. But I'm afraid I'm . . . ah . . . doing something tonight. Some marking. Yes. Marking . . .'

The girl smiled, walked back to her seat and sat down. The rest of the class erupted with jeers and hoots and whistles. I was lost. Hopelessly, emphatically and conclusively lost. They had me exactly where they wanted. I was never again able to exert any kind of control or influence over them. In future, every minute of each lesson would be a torturous and useless struggle to make myself heard. A struggle and, of course, a noisy, blush-inducing riot.

I'm sure Logan would have told me I missed a good

opportunity to play the moment. Even to ride the audience.

And, bless him, he would have been right.

Out of all the things I could have said, I chose the one which maimed me for ever. Weak. Hopeless. Vulnerable. 'Low status'.

And now, after four sessions and approaching the halfway point in 'The Absolute and Almost Beginners' Comedy Course' I had learned a number of useful things, though very few of them had actually enabled me to be funny.

I didn't know whether it was the same for the others (for robust Jim or confident Julie or likeable Johnno or cynical Dan), but I was certain that the most important thing for me was fear of the audience. That and my inability to govern it. Although I had eventually become a good teacher, the memory of that day in a school outside Edinburgh always haunts me whenever I feel nervous in front of a crowd. And for the moment at least, that memory was constantly with me. My chronic inability to let myself go, to fuck around on stage, stemmed directly and absolutely from this fear, which asphyxiated anything of worth I might have to say.

Satisfying a comedy audience's expectations – it does, after all, expect to laugh – is one of life's more daunting tasks. And every time I was placed in front of one the full weight of this anticipation stifled me. That was the problem. Given time, it might work itself out. But for the moment, it was going to take a massive amount of will-power to change things round. In effect, I would have to become someone else, a different 'Steve Jacobi', or at least a different version of him.

And I'd spent such a long time learning how to be this one.

That school has a lot to answer for. Sometimes, though not often, I wonder what the girl with the comely legs is doing now. I can even imagine a scenario where I would be doing a five-minute spot in a small comedy club in Lancaster or somewhere. Things would be going pretty well until someone shouted out, 'Oi! You can fuck me for twenty quid if you like!' And then things would go downhill, I'd have a kind of seizure, and end up heavily medicated and in therapy.

The 18.27 train from Paddington to Moreton on Saturday evenings is as good a place as any to ponder these things. It was the kind of nonsense I thought about most times I returned home from the course.

How could I become better? What *stopped* me getting better?

They're maudlin thoughts but I suspect most comedians have them. Certainly most aspiring comedians.

You can stare out of the windows and, as the train pulls away further from London and rattles through the gently rolling Oxfordshire countryside, you can peer into the darkness and imagine you're having a meaningful, existential-type moment. You try to lend a bit of dignity to your neuroses. You can even imagine you're Samuel Beckett. Well, in some ways you can. For instance, in *Endgame*, Nell says, 'Nothing is funnier than unhappiness.' But then you think, 'Hang on a minute! That can't be right.'

Then you think again, and you realise that he probably *is* right. So, finally, you think even more specifically about your own unhappiness, why it is there at all, and how pathetically unimportant it all is. Like at the end of Chaucer's *Troilus and Criseyde*, where en route to heaven the dead Troilus sees earth disappearing far below him, the same earth where he had experienced such intense sorrow when his beloved Criseyde left him for another man. But from his new perspective, it all looks so trivial, so silly. So what does he do? He starts laughing, of course.

So now you also start laughing – to yourself. Small chuckles at first, which soon develop into reluctant and discreet but nonetheless quite throaty guffaws.

Then someone looks up and says, 'What's that cunt laughing at?' and for a moment you do wonder what you look like. Then you realise. Like an amused moose. You're laughing like an amused moose.

FIVE

Showtime!

I was getting used to my Saturday ritual – the train journey, the out-of-town Chelsea fans, the Heath Robinson dashes across London to Chalk Farm, and of course the three hours or so of comedy class at the Enterprise. I was telling our neighbour Debs about it, over coffee, actually a latte, and actually also a thick slice of teacake, in Murray's, a rather chic deli/café miraculously located in the heart of the Cotswold countryside.

'Where are the classes held?' she asked.

'Camden,' I answered.

'*Chipping* Campden?' she enquired, doubtfully, 'I didn't know there was a comedy club there.'

We laughed – Debs laughed – at her error, though it did burst a bubble and make me wonder what I was doing every Saturday, or how what I was doing must look to other people. 'You mean you take all day getting to and from London to spend three hours inside a small, grubby room so that you can try to learn about something which you're really crap at?'

That was about the size of it. It had been said before and would doubtless be said again.

For a moment, I felt like one of those commuters, a comedy commuter, who boarded trains they didn't want to catch to travel to somewhere they didn't want to go in order to do something they didn't want to do. The difference was, they got paid for it.

We had reached a point in the course when this reality was starting to bite. Logan, bless him, had seen it all before and knew how to respond. He was now doing his level best to perk us up and instil an invigorated sense of purpose into the exercises.

'A joke is like a Chinese puzzle box,' he explained on one particularly grey, wet day towards the end of March. 'It has infinite openings and you can keep finding new ways to open it.'

Though this brought a welcome touch of the Orient to the classes, we were soon back to moving around the room a bit and portraying various obscure emotions, doing it badly but at least achieving a kind of group solidarity, i.e. we were all dismal together. Logan, who usually erred on the generous side, declared we were the worst group he had ever seen at these exercises. So we must have been bad.

Well, it was something.

Still, I knew what he was after. The greater the range of emotions you were able to express, the more emotion you could show on your face to emphasise a line or embellish a joke. The visual accentuating the linguistic, as it were. The trouble was, I still couldn't accentuate the linguistic through the linguistic, let alone the visual. The visual was a foreign country. On the other hand, Julie was quite good at the visual, but then she was an actress. And Laurence, I thought, though perhaps that was just because he was very tall and rather aristocratic.

In less than a month, when the course ended, we would be split into three groups and showcase our achievements in front of a live audience over three separate Sunday evenings.

I was beginning to feel pretty miserable about the whole thing, the worst I've felt since I cheated in a music test at school and as an unforeseen consequence had to learn the violin. I should have learned my lesson then. Square pegs do not go into round holes.

Not only was I coming up against my own inadequacies as a performer, actually my genetically inherent, hard-wired resistance to put on any kind of show or make any sort of exhibition of myself, but my isolation from London and thus from the rest of the group was also beginning to play on my mind.

At one point, though she made the remark jovially and in passing, Viv said, 'You're not taking this very seriously, are you?' Meaning, I think, you're not one of us, you're not part of the gang that goes out and watches comedy in the throbbing metropolis, that you're not giving this comedy thing your full attention.

To compensate, I really needed to experience some kind of success in class, rather than the dismal repetition of awkwardly embarrassed uselessness which had become something of a trademark. As I've already suggested, Beckett was mostly right about failure and unhappiness being such huge fun, though the fun (of course) was mostly for the benefit of other people.

Then, I did achieve a breakthrough – a minor, even minuscule breakthrough, and one that didn't have the hoped-for consequences of liberation and comic lift-off, but a qualified breakthrough nonetheless.

We were playing something called the Hitch-hiking Game

(seasoned television watchers might remember it or something similar on the Channel 4 improvisation programme, *Whose Line Is It Anyway?*), which Logan described as a 'turning-on-a-sixpence exercise'. Actually, he'd already said this about a number of other relatively dissimilar exercises, so the assumption was that although turning on a sixpence was clearly important, we hadn't yet managed to do it. Anyway, we were divided into groups of four, one of whom would be 'the driver'. At intervals, the other three (the hitch-hikers) would then clamber into the pretend car, in this case represented by a simple arrangement of bar stools. Each hitch-hiker was associated with a specific emotion. As each one of us got in, the driver and the passengers would adopt that emotion. Then, the last passenger would leave and the group would revert to the emotion of the previous passenger. Finally, we were told not to 'lead, but react'.

I recognised this as being another way of somehow prodding us into the ability to move rapidly between different sentiments. Low or high status. Love or hate. Kindness or cruelty. It didn't much matter so long as we could get quickly from one to the next.

I recall being the first hitch-hiker into the third car, and I think I was supposed to embody something like affability or kindness. South African Stuart, a journalist in real life, was the next one in, and he must have been anger or rage; some sort of unpleasantness at any rate. I can't remember who the third passenger was, but we went up and down the assigned scales with a weary but reasonably competent dullness, representing rather than actually inhabiting the emotions. I was experiencing my usual sensations of mediocrity when – and I still don't know quite what happened, but it was like the satisfying 'plunk' of a coin hitting the bottom of a well – something just 'clicked'. I remember thinking, I can't do much worse, but I could do a lot better. I'd already spent a number of weeks feeling embarrassed and awkward without remotely being able to do the things which I'd assumed were the causes of me being embarrassed and awkward, so why shouldn't I *really* try to do them? If I was going to have those feelings I might as well get what snooker commentators these days call 'value for the shot'.

By the time I realised this ('plunk'), only Stuart and I were left in the car. From mild complaining I moved up tentatively to abuse and from there, less tentatively, to loud abuse. And from there, to even louder, incoherent shouted abuse.

'Call that driving,' I said to the driver.

'Tosser,' added Stuart.

'Tosser?' I enquired. 'He's a cunt!'

'Yes. Cunt,' said Stuart.

'Cunt! Cunt!' I ranted, not really enjoying myself but feeling slightly light of head, perhaps even on the verge of being 'liberated'.

Though I could never free myself entirely from the shackles of self-consciousness, I was at least throwing myself at the exercise with gusto. Falling with style, as Buzz Lightyear says.

'You're the cunt,' said Stuart, his accent suddenly imposing itself a little more forcefully.

'Cunt yourself,' I shrieked, 'fucking wanking buggering cunt.'

'And . . . out you get, Stuart,' Logan instructed, this also being the signal for me to become Mr Nice again.

For a moment, but only for a moment, I was lost in the role. I was playing the moment. God knows, I was *in* the moment.

Perhaps I was even accessing the psychotic. Then, I turned on the proverbial sixpence.

'Cunt! Cunt!' I screeched, and then as Stuart climbed out, and with perfect timing, in the same breath, and with an instinctive, unpremeditated, virtually unselfconscious softening of tone, I turned to the driver and said, 'Lovely bloke. Really super.'

Well, perhaps you had to be there.

But people laughed.

Logan was right. It is a good feeling.

Afterwards, I experienced a kind of dizziness, strung out between the shock of this minor breakthrough, the surprise of success and a kind of hallucinatory strangeness. It was the kind of feeling I associated with being drunk or of smoking dope (twice), even of smoking cigarettes, I suppose of losing control. It also reminded me how intensely I disliked it. Perhaps I just have a very low threshold for this kind of thing. So from being a bit chuffed, I suddenly became a lot more upset at being stranded, as it were, so far from familiar territory. It felt a bit like being in Australia: quite nice when you arrive, but quickly followed by panic at realising how far you are from anywhere else, or at least anywhere else that makes sense.

What I called my 'Cunt Breakthrough' worked on me in an odd and ultimately revealing, even defining, way. True, I had to a limited degree shown that I was capable of turning on a sixpence. On the other hand, I knew deep inside me that this was an alien experience. Body and soul fought against it. To do it again and to keep doing it would either tear me apart or change me completely. Though I wasn't necessarily all that keen on myself, I was reasonably comfortable with what I had got, the person I had become. Time, habit and no doubt many other things had moulded me into an unsatisfactory but relatively workable human being. Besides, I was too old to start changing on such a grand scale or, in the voguish way people have of talking these days, of 'reinventing' myself.

It left me with two choices: either plunge into the unknown and end up goodness knows where, or take the triumph as a kind of warning, and fall back on what I knew.

Is that what Americans call a 'no-brainer'?

So guess what I did?

I fell back. Of course I did.

After all, Logan had told us to inhabit the comic persona with whom we felt most at ease. And I reasoned that if I couldn't consistently be funny or turn on a sixpence, I could at least be comfortable.

Once this idea had lodged itself, I noticed that (actually) other people were doing much the same. Nat, for example, had developed an anxiety-strewn Jewish character who wasn't too far removed from his own, well, anxiety-strewn Jewishness. And Jim, burly Jim, was beginning to use his bluff northern manner (Stoke, in fact, but northern-ish) to good effect. In addition, Dan's confident, slick cynicism was becoming the mainstay of his stage persona, as was Paul's muddled mania, Nick's Rigsby-esque neurosis, Viv's affable grumpiness about men, and Laurence's aloof, slightly dry take on the world.

So where did that leave me? I wasn't exactly sure, but I knew it wasn't so far off the radar.

The trouble was, although Logan had indeed told us to find a familiar and/or comfortable stage persona, he had also at some point said that nobody in the audience cares what you do, so his other advice would be to just go for it. 'If you start caring too much,' he said, 'you're sunk.'

The actor Simon Callow once told a story about playing a character who was beside himself with jealous rage. The director of the play wasn't convinced by any of Callow's efforts to 'act' the emotion, until the moment when he suddenly lost control, picked up a chair and threw it at the wall. 'Good!' said the director.

Here was my dilemma: I felt most comfortable when I cared. Neurosis to me was what daffodils were to Wordsworth, to rephrase Philip Larkin.

I wanted to talk to Logan about the apparent contradiction between throwing caution to the wind and staying closer to home, so we arranged to meet out of class one day during the week.

He's an engaging character, is Logan, and he arrived precisely on time at Liverpool Street station, perky and busy, carrying some kind of shoulder bag which probably contained his gear for that night's gig and, no doubt, a few pots of fruit salad. Though we were of similar ages, could both remember Peter Glaze in *Crackerjack!*, and were on the whole quite balanced and rational people, there was still an element of 'meeting teacher out of class' about it.

Comedy clubs tend to use old photographs of Logan on their flyers. In these, he is leaning back slightly and has a bouffant of thick black hair piled on top of a roundish but cheeky face that seems vaguely Mediterranean. There's also some kind of medallion hanging around his neck. It looks as though his chest might be very hairy. He could be an amiable pimp or a congenial Italian-American character actor, perhaps filling one of the minor roles in *The Godfather* movies. Now though, his hair is cropped short and spiky, and a set of sharp, meticulously grooved sideburns are burrowing their way down and slightly across his face.

A few minutes later, we are in Starbucks, which I thought he would object to but clearly doesn't. His choice, in fact. In my usual wishy-washy way, I sort of do, object I mean, though don't quite know why this should be so, and in any case drink their milky coffee by the bucketload. Shame on me. Anyway, Logan buys the drinks and I think I remember squeezing a muffin out of him. He tells me that he trained as an actor and only nudged towards comedy when he performed poems such as 'Ode to Torvill and Dean' as part of a musical act.

When we get down to talking about my confusion between being liberated and, er, not being liberated, he said the two positions were in fact quite compatible. I looked doubtful, but was too busy with the muffin to look as doubtful as I felt.

He explained that getting into 'the zone' while on stage was liberating and even permitted a sense of the ridiculous. This, I gathered, was something very different to any sense I might have of my own *ridiculousness*. I did say, however, that I was in any case plagued by a constant sense of the ridiculous and didn't necessarily need to go into 'the zone' to find it.

'My point exactly,' said Logan mysteriously. 'If you don't have to travel far to find, the journey isn't worth making. Some people feel more at home with themselves when they are freed from their usual lives. You don't. And that's fine.'

I think I got the gist of what he was saying, i.e. that due to an individual quirk of character I was able to perceive absurdity without straying too far from home, or entering 'the zone', and (therefore) I should make that my comedic centre of operations.

I ran this by Logan and he nodded. I noticed at this point that he was drinking herbal tea.

'Most comics are white, middle-class blokes with arrested development as children,' he continued.

'That's me,' I sniggered.

There's a passage in Kingsley Amis's last novel, *The Biographer's Moustache*, which I like very much. It may have some bearing on all this. It goes: 'Consistency of virtue, logical behaviour, reliability, sense of duty, however admirable and however resolutely pursued, were middle-class virtues and to some extent under the control of the will, became moral qualities and as such imposed restraints on freedom.'

Perhaps this is why white middle-class English people need a bit of comic liberation? Either that or going on the piss at the weekend and chucking up in the back of taxis and/or getting into fights with strangers. Because every other aspect of their admirable, praiseworthy lives is clad in inhibited moderation.

Anyway, after we'd sorted out my persona problem, we were able to talk more widely about comedy. Logan proved himself very adept with the telling cultural reference. 'There's a need for laughter,' he said, 'it's like in Huxley's *Island* – Utopia doesn't exist, so we need hilarity to make things bearable.'

He also talked of the low animal cunning of the comedian in keeping one step ahead of the audience, and what he termed the 'venal process of comedy', implying it was a kind of trick.

I felt I was beginning to get the hang of Logan by this time. He enjoyed taking apparently antithetical positions and finding ways to mesh them together: comedy as metaphysical necessity *and* as mere opportunism; the ideal stage persona as addictively liberated *and* as soberingly familiar; his own character suspended between serious intent ('the devil hates laughter') *and* insouciant chirpiness ('What's the point if you don't have a laugh?'). The whole point of Logan was that there was no single point, and laughter was the means by which he acknowledged and either celebrated or grieved his understanding of this position.

The next class was only a couple of days after this. It was quite poorly attended and some of those that did attend were late. Maria had disappeared. Johnno had been struck down by a virus and would not appear at any more sessions. Though he was a good bloke, part of me was relieved at his absence; after all, he was a pretty useful comedian. Another John, Irish John, had just melted away. And Mick, the Arsenal fan, had to transfer courses because of a change in work shifts.

Clearly Logan was annoyed at the lateness. When he ticked us off, there wasn't even the hint of an afterthought, so we knew he was serious. He was right to be annoyed – there were only a handful of classes before the first showcase. The prospect of 'fucking around' for real began to concentrate our minds.

Even coffee breaks became forums for discussing, say, the significance of performance over material, or the virtues of the topical gag. Would a rigidly discharged script, for instance, hinder the possibility of giving a performance? Should we simply go on stage with a rough idea of what we wanted to say and then take it from there? Or what? I discussed some of this with Dan. To my dismay, I learned that he had already completed a couple of gigs. He reckoned that with his newly acquired experience he could be pretty flexible. Damn him. He was also intrigued by the feeling that he got more laughs from his improvised material than he did from a carefully honed script. Double damn him.

As we trooped back into the Enterprise after one of these breaks, listening to Logan telling us that now was the time to decide that we had 'to go for it' and 'find liberation as comics', I made a decision. Actually quite an important decision. It went something like this: I couldn't wing it or give a performance. That much was fact. The only thing I knew I could manage was a tight script, perhaps even quite a funny tight script. And the only style of liberation I felt at ease with was liberation from liberation. Thus, I would not devise a stage presence at all but merely trust the material and be me. Organic Steve. 'The very organic Steve Jacobi.'

Though I expected this cunning strategy might work in a damage limitation sort of way, its immediate effect was to make me feel even more isolated from the others, who were still developing their masks. Even though I saw that these disguises were versions of themselves, they were at least still *versions* or variations. Whereas mine as not.

I kept this resolution to myself, even throwing caution to the wind in a few class exercises as a way of concealing my non-performing intentions which seemed somehow shameful, even ungrateful and against the spirit of the thing. The only time that my strategy came unstuck was when we were asked to present a party trick. Amid the slick card tricks and the clever juggling and the zany harmonica playing, the best I could manage was to simulate putting a chair in a trance. In this instance, there was simply no way of camouflaging my inexpert performance skills by making an energetic show of things. On the other hand, it was such an odd thing to do that the general consensus was that I was being ironic or interesting. In reality, it was my best shot.

The sense of being in quarantine and my own gloomy presentiment of approaching disaster intensified while I was away on holiday. For a start, I would be missing a class and –

worse – I found it impossible to avoid eavesdropping on the communal emails and discovering what everyone was up to. 'Sunday night I was helping out at the Enterprise and got to see the showcase for half of the course ahead of us,' said Viv. 'Well done, Nat, an excellent start to your career,' announced Dan, presumably after Nat *had* made an excellent start to his career at some club or other. Everyone apart from me was either gigging or watching other people gig, or gigging *and* watching other people gig. It sounded as if I was missing a comedic orgy. Then Rigsby Nick cheerfully admitted to being 'torn apart by the crowd at the Wibbly Wobbly. Oh yes, hecklers galore,' he chortled.

Hecklers. That was something else to consider. Logan had advised us to deal with them firmly but not in a way that would lose an audience's sympathy. Confronted by a crowd of jeering pests, I suspected I would do one of two things: either agree with them absolutely and slink apologetically off the stage, or take such personal exception to what was being said that I would at once launch into an aggressive and quite possibly violent counter-attack. Bob Monkhouse, I recalled, had once punched a heckler unconscious, though afterwards he had no memory of actually doing it.

Not quite what Logan had in mind, but it would make me feel better.

A friend of mine, an occasional comedian called Ian, reassured me, no doubt with the best of intentions, that being greeted by silence and then jeered is not as bad as it sounds. 'At first I was devastated,' he told me, 'but then I thought, "I'm still alive. Nothing's changed. I'm still here," and things were OK.'

Apart from the bits of comedy over the years, Ian's mostly a very good writer, and has also been a bookseller, a singer, a songwriter, a cabaret performer, and the bloke who manages the Arvon Writing Foundation at Totleigh Barton. His stand-up act is built around a persona, a poet called Hilary Spume, though he's also talked about material which includes a banjo, a strange version of 'Bohemian Rhapsody', and possibly a ukelele. Being ridiculed, you might think, is the least of his problems.

Anyway, Rigsby Nick's mention of hecklers merely escalated my own sensation of exiled hopelessness.

Another day, Viv circulated lesson notes for the session I had missed. Much of it consisted of Logan giving very specific practical advice on how to deliver a stand-up routine. It was precisely the kind of thing I needed and had now missed. Not so much of the 'fucking around' now, eh, I mused bitterly. Instead, there were tips about making an immediate connection with the audience, making eye contact with them, developing afterthoughts, opening up to audience by admitting something shameful or embarrassing (what, like being on stage and not being funny? I thought) and something called 'The Rule of Three'.

The Rule of Three is a joke-deliverance strategy, and not something from *The Matrix* film or a book about Chinese philosophy. Apparently, it percolates quite happily through most jokes and even surfaces readily in advertising slogans. The Rule of Three is: ESTABLISH, REINFORCE, SURPRISE! For example: 'He gave me chocolates, flowers and multiple bruising,' which was used in an advertising campaign for a woman's refuge. Here's another one: 'My hobbies are drink, drugs and keep-fit.' For some reason, three is the magic number, the one and only number. Not two. Not four. And never five. (See. It works.) There's a story doing the rounds that

Neil Kinnock was perceived as a blathering gasbag because he always used five and sometimes even six – and never with a surprise at the end.

Meanwhile, back in Chalk Farm, everyone was also practising microphone technique and learning how to perform 'worry lists'. Progress reports arrived via the loop of anxious but supportive emails which were circulating around the group.

The apparent advances didn't play well with my own insecurities.

'I thought the lists went well,' crowed Viv.

'The purpose of this exercise was that for the *first time* [my italics. Obviously.] we were to try and be funny and incorporate the lessons we had learned in the previous sessions,' she continued.

'A five-minute set is a huge leap . . .' someone else gloated.

Fuck and wank to them all, I thought.

Even worse, an email arrived from burly Jim of Stoke, thanking everyone (except me, natch) who had turned up to his first gig. 'It was good to get the first gig under the belt,' he sighed, 'and I recommend that anyone who hasn't done a gig should do one.'

Do you, Jim? Do you really?

Less than a week to the first showcase and I hadn't so much as sniffed a worry list or a Rule of Three. I hadn't been through five minutes of continuous material on a stage. In fact, I hadn't properly been on a stage. And I didn't have five minutes of material.

Apart from this, it was all fine.

So, I made another decision. Effectively my third. The best way to get back in the loop, I reasoned, was to write a worry list. Even though there was no chance of performing it in front of

Logan, it would at least give me something in common with the others. I would do this while still on holiday. At the time, I was on board a cruise ship following the England cricket team around the Caribbean. Technically, it was work. Of a kind. But, heck, someone's got to do it. It was also, as you can imagine, an unlikely place in which to construct a worry list.

Eventually, I came up with a phobia for public toilets. Not quite up there with anxiety about, say, global warming or terrorism, but at least it was based on fact and constituted a very personal sort of worry.

The genesis of my aversion is not especially dramatic or appalling. It was not sparked into life, for instance, through torrid memories of being fiddled with by a kindly stranger sporting a mac who might have followed me into the public loos next to my prep school. Afraid not. It's more prosaic than that and it begins with my mother's mania for cleanliness in the bathroom, where she set standards (alas, since lapsed) for disinfected purity that could not be replicated anywhere else on the planet. My reluctance to do the business anywhere other than home was consolidated by childhood visits to West Germany where toilets were, perhaps still are, constructed with a sort of viewing platform which 'presents' the excrement for inspection and allows people, should they be in the mood, to run an inquisitive, self-congratulatory eye over their handiwork before finally flushing it down the pan.

Visits to Germany were also associated with my grandfather's thunderbox, an outside loo which was really just a hole in the ground covered by a wooden lid. It gave off a rancorous odour as soon as this was lifted. Once a year my grandfather would scoop out the accreted contents and make merry with them on his strawberry patch.

My fear of visiting public lavatories, in fact any lavatory other than my own, was further inflamed by the fear of invaded privacy. Which also has its origins in Germany.

Come to think of it, Germany has a lot to answer for.

At that time, public conveniences in the Fatherland were routinely policed by stout, unsmiling matrons in white tunics (think *One Flew Over the Cuckoo's Nest*). These harridans guarded their premises with clinical ferocity and wouldn't think twice about forcing their way into your locked cubicle and asking whether you wanted the seat wiped. As a young boy, the threat of being intruded upon in the middle of a poo by a Winston Churchill lookalike in a tunic was truly terrifying. Not to mention being bad manners, running very much against the grain of embarrassed English propriety in such matters. Thus, issues of privacy and contamination, both associated with the real and symbolic threat of invasion, instilled in me a lifelong worry about public toilets.

All this would find its way on to my worry list, actually being its first and only entry. The worry about the prospect of having to enter a public toilet would be there, as would its origins, but so would the network of London hotels I had established *just in case* I was caught short in the Big Smoke. I had divided the city into eight areas and nominated an emergency hotel loo for each one – that is, eight hotels in west, south-west, north, north-west, east, City, central London and the South Bank. No loo is more than twelve minutes away by tube.

In case you think I'm making this up, please try, for example, the toilets in the Garden House Hotel in Kensington High Street, my preferred refuge for London, west. Only a minute's walk from the Underground, its spacious basement loo is private, clean and luxurious. It boasts an array of soaps and perfumes, and has a good range of drying gear. (And if you get there early enough, you can also nick a newspaper from outside one of the first-floor rooms.) Even for me, the trip can be a reasonably pleasant experience. There is no higher recommendation.

I was quite pleased with my 'list'. It seemed (to me) to be quite funny in an oddball sort of way, and it satisfied my own requirements of straight, close-to-home integrity. It also seemed to tick one of Logan's criteria, the one about admitting something embarrassing or shameful. Most important, the writing of it somehow *felt* right; the words flowed, and the material came together organically.

Some of the other passengers found out what I was up to and every now and then would nudge me and say something like, 'Here's good one for your routine. There was a Yorkshireman, an Irishman and . . . er, no, that's wrong . . . it was a bloke from Kent and a Scotsman . . .' Either that or they would tell me the ship's resident comedian Des Cherry was actually very good – a bit like Tommy Cooper without the conjuring – and that I really ought to watch him as I might pick up some tips. It was all meant well enough, though wouldn't have been much use to me. And I couldn't help wondering what, for example, a holidaying dentist might have said if I told him to take a look at Mrs So-and-so's teeth because he would get some good ideas about bridging.

Anyway, I arrived back in England, the Body Beautiful tanned and lithe, with only two weeks or so before my own showcase, the third of three. I felt good about the untried, unpresented, unproven worry list. I felt good about the holiday. In short, I felt relaxed and poised. I therefore resolved that any material I wrote should follow a similar route and concern itself with mild domestic revelation. Not only would it tie in with with my other resolution about not bothering with a stage persona, or at least working hard to find one, but it would also mean I would have plenty of material to work with.

Before putting pen to paper, I glanced at Logan's reading list for the course – did I not tell you there was a reading list? – and saw that it included a book by Arthur Koestler titled *The Act of Creation*. Being a bit of a swot, I thought I'd better hunt a copy down and have a look at it. I was also in the business of creation, and well . . . you just never knew.

I knew Koestler from his novel *Darkness at Noon*, which I recalled being about an old Russian soldier who was a victim of one of Stalin's purges, but nonetheless found some sort of liberation in destruction. I had also read, or half read, a great slab of a book called *The Sleepwalkers*, about which I could remember very little other than it being about states of consciousness – or maybe it was states of unconsciousness. I had come across it many years ago, probably during my Herman Hesse phase. Anyway, I was intrigued to know what this apparently gloomy, introverted, possibly damaged man had to say about comedy.

And the answer, unfortunately, is 'quite a lot'. *The Act of Creation* weighs in at a robust 751 pages. It was originally published in 1964, and advances the theory that 'all creative activities – the conscious and unconscious processes underlying artistic originality, scientific discovery and comic inspiration – have a basic pattern in common'. Koestler calls this pattern, 'bisociative thinking'. That tells you more or less all you need to know, though one sentence in particular did interest me. It identified laughter as a 'luxury reflex which could arise only in a creature whose reason had gained a degree of autonomy from the urges of emotion, and enables him to perceive his own emotion as redundant – to realise that he has been fooled'.

In one sense, I supposed this was just another way of saying that humans are the only species on earth that have a sense of humour, even though that would also be to underestimate the complexity of emotions. But I liked the suggestion that laughter was a 'luxury'. I also liked the idea that being fooled or deceived could be cause for laughter, or rather that an appreciation of emotion's double-dealing was. The sort of taunting, mocking laughter directed at someone who intended to exert influence over you but who had at the last moment been triumphantly thwarted. It was mildly subversive and destabilised the populist association between laughter and happiness. I liked that a lot.

A few years ago, an American film called *Happiness* made sharp observations about several suburban families whose lives exuded anything but happiness. It included a sympathetic though very guilty paedophile and a dog who lapped up a young boy's masturbatory spunk. It was also very funny, though the laughter it stimulated was of the knowingly appalled, relieved, there-but-for-the-Grace-of-God-go-I variety.

And in a similarly cognizant vein, Philip Larkin once wrote a collection of poems titled, *The Less Deceived*. I remember this very well because many years ago my tutor at university had plonked Larkin's volume down in front of me and asked where the title came from. I had only been at university three weeks. I didn't know titles 'came' from anywhere. I looked blank. Hopelessly blank.

'Shall I give you a clue, Jacobi?' he said.

I nodded.

'*Hamlet*,' he said, then sat back and folded his arms.

I had done *Hamlet* for A level. I knew he knew that. I also knew he knew that I knew he knew that. The only thing I didn't know was the answer.

We sat there in silence for several minutes. An awkward situation developed, awkward at least for me. Though I wouldn't have known it at the time, it was like being in therapy.

Eventually, he relented. 'Hamlet tells Ophelia that if she thought he loved her then she was the more deceived. By turning the phrase around – into the *less* deceived – Larkin is announcing himself as someone who is emphatically *not* going to be deluded or beguiled by his emotions. You see that, don't you, Jacobi? You probably knew it all the time.'

I grinned a thin grin. But here was method in my tutor's madness, to throw another bit of *Hamlet* into the pot, because here I am twenty years later, and I can still remember what he said. Larkin's grim humour, a self-indulgent, almost negative, perhaps not strictly appropriate bit of chortling. The realisation that even though he might be a failure, he is at least a failure on his own terms, having gained through his sneering a reprieve from other people's absurdity or self-deception. Inessential laughter, hence luxurious.

Koestler's words also implied that comedy was an unneeded treat, a present if you like. And the best presents (I thought) were doled out with care and an unselfish, considerate thoughtfulness. Thanks and self-gratification weren't uppermost in the minds of their givers. Quite often, proper appreciation only arrived years afterwards. I thought, for example, of Uncle Luigi (not a real uncle, obviously) who had unaccountably given me a pair of cuff links when I was only seven. I was eighteen before I realised their worth and was able to thank him properly.

This outlook, I knew, would be the trigger for my own

material. I would write something carefully crafted and intriguing. I hoped it would be funny – but it wouldn't be shamelessly so. Not 'lowest common denominator' funny. It would also enable me to push aside the considerable doubts I still had about my ability actually to make people laugh. And it would provide me with a fall-back position. Derisive, wry laughter. If my comedy was a gift, it would be the kind of gift I'd like to buy for myself. Like a good book or a decent DVD with lots of extras. Surely I could do no better.

Emboldened by the unlikely Koestler-*Happiness*-Larkin axis, I set about writing my knowingly domestic persona-lite routine. I reduced certain moments of my life to six or seven minutes of continuous narrative, also trying to bear in mind Logan's Top Tips. I wrote and edited, then rewrote and re-edited, before recording the words on to a microcassette-recorder, and then accomplishing what I thought would be a final rewrite but of course wasn't.

I've included a transcript of these words at the back of this book, in the appendix. I've always wanted to write a book with an appendix. Please have a look at it. It will help you to follow the next few pages. Don't feel you have to laugh. Writing comedy that will appeal to a room full of strangers is a daunting task. You tell me – what do *you* think would make fifty very different people all laugh at the same thing at the same time? Tricky, eh? So, and there's no harm in repeating it, please don't feel you have to laugh.

I tried chunks of the material out on Pippa after I'd finished. I think she was still smarting from my cruise holiday, so I expected a bit of resentful carping. I did the opening two minutes and watched carefully as she didn't laugh. Her chuckle muscles were unmoved.

'You're trying to be too clever,' she said.

'As opposed to what?'

'As opposed to being funny . . .'

'That's because I think I can be *quite* clever though not necessarily *very* funny.'

'There you go again.'

'What?'

'Trying to be too clever. Can't you do both?'

'How do you mean?'

'Be clever and funny . . . ?'

'I thought I was being both,' I sighed, 'well, more of one than the other, obviously, but still more or less both.'

'Tragic.'

'You're not exactly a pillar of strength.'

'How can I be a pillar of strength by lying?'

'You don't have to lie – just massage the truth a bit.'

'I said it was quite clever.'

'You said it was *too* clever.'

'I *said* you were trying to be too clever. That doesn't necessarily mean you weren't also being quite clever. Big difference.'

I tried to look very crestfallen.

'So it's no good . . .'

'I didn't say that either . . . God, I don't know. Do you want me to come and watch?'

'No. Absolutely no.'

'That's good, because I can't. But you know I'll be thinking of you.'

'Do I?'

'Yes. Of course.'

'What will you be thinking?'

'I dread to think.'

There was more of this over the next few days, but less as the feared showcase weekend arrived.

I was simply too nervous to waste any more energy on arguments about the material. Just saying all the words in the right order had become the priority, no matter about the quality of those words.

Saturday arrived. The day before it went all went off. I caught the afternoon train to London (no football fans, but many, many noisy children) because Logan was running a special class for the last remaining showcasers to run through their material. That was, estate agent Paul, Australian Eva, amiably acerbic Viv, South African Stuart, Little Tom, Big Rich and me.

I had expected to practise with a microphone and had come to a decision about the way I would hold it. This may not sound a big deal to those non-microphone users among you, but to us performers it's a weighty matter. Especially if holding one was still unfamiliar territory, as unnatural as holding a largish cucumber vertical in front of you for five or six minutes.

Though you understand all the guff about the need to make yourself heard, it still feels odd and unnecessary. Though obviously it's not. But you really only discover that when you're put in front of an audience – not until then, of course.

Anyway, I'd decided to go for a firm clamping technique. This meant holding the thing flush against my chest so that it looked a bit like an enormous tiepin. If I knew it was there – immobile, reassuringly steadfast – then I could just forget about it instead of being tempted to wave it around or, worse, trying to do something clever like produce a special effect. On television, I had seen a music hall master of ceremonies do much the same and was impressed by his aura of impenetrable confidence. That would do for me, I thought. I'll copy him. It's what we comedians call 'a homage'.

None of this was much use, however, because no microphone was available. Five of us spluttered through our unamplified routines while Logan looked on making encouraging noises and giving out helpful notes. Having spent two days memorising my material, nerves overtook me and I promptly forgot it, remembered it again, let it slip once more, and then finally got back on track, though in a toneless, dreary way that was mostly devoid of anything that you could reasonably identify as 'humour'.

'Very good, Steve,' Logan smiled, 'a nice suave energy.'

It had been a long time since anyone had called me 'suave'. Never, in fact.

'Really?' I said, rather doubtfully.

'All the gags worked really well – perhaps make more of the link between James Bond and your dad. Otherwise, all good. I won't be worried about you tomorrow.'

I didn't quite believe him, but then Eva gave me a matey 'thumbs up' so I thought, bugger it – they might just be being nice but being nice is fine and I need all the nice I can get.

I said that only five of us spluttered through rehearsals. That was because Stuart didn't splutter, he positively soared. The bastard had been gigging on the quiet and knew how to deliver his material. He *knew*. And Viv had to do her rehearsal on the pavement as we were turfed out of our upstairs room to make way for a different, clashing event. Probably a comedy event, I thought.

Nick and Lissy, whose flat I was staying in overnight, had left out some curry and I devoured it greedily, having not eaten much all day. By the time I fell into bed, I was exhausted and bloated, though all things considered, I slept pretty well. I finally woke at 7.45, odd bits from the routine surging through my brain, though surging in a kind of *Groundhog Day* nightmare. I always stalled at and then forgot the line, 'At this moment in time'. No matter how hard I tried, and despite making it through to, 'And I hate people who say "At the end of the day"', there was nothing after that. Not a sausage.

Not too worried about this early-morning block, I trudged off to the bathroom. Very unusually for me, a man of scrupulously regular habits, I found that I couldn't go to the toilet. Next, I dropped my toothbrush into the loo. Then, I absent-mindedly allowed my towel to fall into the bath.

Cutting my losses, I ventured out for a coffee and to read a newspaper. Disastrously, and perhaps inevitably, my roguish bowels then started to misbehave and I suddenly needed a toilet. Though, of course, not any toilet. This being High Street Ken, however, I was able to make it to the Garden House in good time. Exiting the hotel soon after, I walked through Kensington Gardens, past Kensington Palace, and along towards Knightsbridge, going over my lines again and again, though always equivocating on 'At this moment in time'. I wondered whether I should just cut the line altogether, but then I started to worry about rhythm and timing.

Then, rather than merely running through the words, I thought it might help if I spoke them aloud, tasted them on my lips. As I passed by other people, eyes glazed and muttering nonsense, they clearly thought another dribbling nutter had been cut prematurely loose from the system. Generally, they gave me a polite wide berth, though a friendly Indian man carrying a pair of Rollerblades did say, 'Pardon?' as he picked up the words, 'How does Mr Whippy do a poo?', originally the joke which ended my routine.

I caught the number 9 bus, or perhaps it was the 59, to Trafalgar Square. I sat right at the front of the top deck, something I'd always enjoyed since childhood. It was a beautiful, early summer sort of day. Warm, sunny, optimistic. I visited a couple of exhibitions, which took me through to midday. Then I caught a bus to the Albert Hall and began another muttering walk through Kensington Gardens. I arrived back at Nick and Lissy's in time for lunch.

'Nervous?' asked Nick.

'A bit,' I lied.

'So brave of you,' he said earnestly, one of the few times I had ever heard him be earnest. Nick is Pippa's brother and like the rest of the family, he has a jolly time taking the piss out of me. He was by nature an ironist, so I had always been good target practice. 'I couldn't do it,' he continued. It felt disconcerting to be out of the firing line. Another of life's certainties gone.

'I'm not sure *I* can,' I grinned feebly, hungrily eying a slab of pâté, though the chances of being able to eat and properly digest it was remote.

I mooched around the flat for a bit, then rewrote my material in tiny, neurotic spidery handwriting on a single sheet of A4. By this time, it was still only two o'clock. Nearly six hours to go. Seeking a film to divert me, I looked in *Time Out* and found myself looking at the comedy section. My eye went straight to 'Logan Murray (as grumpy old charmer Ronnie Rigsby) hosts a show featuring new comics from the Absolute and Almost Beginners course here'.

And there was a charge. Four quid and a pound for membership. A fiver! Surely, I thought, people will have better things to do than fork out the price of a packet of fags or a Travelcard for the likes of us? For £4.99 in Virgin, they could buy a DVD of the film *Lenny*, starring Dustin Hoffman. For £4.99, they could watch a proper comedian at work.

I found the film I was looking for, the re-released *Performance*. It was showing at the Renoir, from where it would be an easy ride to Chalk Farm. I had seen the movie in the 1970s, perhaps in my first year at university, possibly earlier, when sneaking into the balcony of my local cinema where the usher was an elderly and easily distracted man who smoked a pipe. I'd not really understood it, in fact not understood it at all, but had anyway and for years faked a gushing appreciation, in public at least, and pronounced it a classic. Its theme, that of performance (obviously) and identity, also seemed to be appropriate to my circumstances.

The cinema is situated in a curiously modern shopping complex which doesn't really work and never seems to have any actual shoppers. Apparently, it's a listed environment, though for my money you could cheerfully pull the whole lot down and start again. I paid for my ticket and made my way down to the screen. By this time, I was beginning to feel hungry and foolishly treated myself to a cup of strong filter coffee and a modest square of carrot cake. Foolish, because about halfway through the film, at about the moment when James Fox asks Mick Jagger what he thinks he will look like when he's fifty, and for the second catastrophic time that day, my bowels began to misbehave.

The nearest designated place of sanctuary would most often have been the loos in the Marlborough Hotel in Gower Street, but this was an emergency. I lurched from my seat, out of the screening room, and into the toilets, wondering if God was playing some cruel but actually quite funny joke on me.

Afterwards, I caught the tube to Camden and walked to Chalk Farm, running through my lines for a final time. When I arrived at the Enterprise, the other six were already there, pacing around the pavement a bit and talking to and at one another with obvious, speedy distress. Though I held back for a few nerveless moments, I was soon drawn into the hullabaloo.

After a bit, we trudged upstairs to practise with the microphone. I seemed to have reached this point several times already, though I still hadn't actually held a mike. But there it was, atop a rudimentary stage supported at each corner by a beer crate. I saw that Hils Jago was also there. She was organising the event.

Now, Hils is a promoter and probably a very good one. She is also, I don't doubt, kind to animals, generous to a fault and an all-round wonderful human being. What she is not very good at, however, is putting seven very nervous comedians at their ease. Already afflicted by tidal waves of anxiety and apprehensive to the point of being physically sick, she quickly set about dismantling any hopes we might have had about finding a few undisturbed moments in which we might come to terms with impending doom.

While demonstrating the microphone, one of us looked away for a few no doubt fretful nanoseconds, and she wasted no time in shouting, 'Look at me when I'm talking!' This was followed by words to the effect that if we didn't look directly at her while she was talking, we would run the risk of letting down ourselves, Logan, her, the club, the art of comedy, all comics everywhere in the world, all dead comedians, the Pope, Mother Teresa and probably the innocent people of Iraq as well for all I knew.

Who would guess she used to be a teacher?

When it was my turn to try the microphone, which I did using my specially devised chest-clamping grip, she shrieked, 'Can't hear you! Where's your mouth? WHERE'S YOUR MOUTH!?'

I hadn't been spoken to like that since I was at nursery school. I wanted to say, 'You know, Hils, I was at Cambridge and the whereabouts of one's mouth was the first thing they taught us.' Instead, I asked, 'Can everyone hear me OK?' There was some polite and sheepish nodding, so I said, 'Thank you. 'Fraid you're outvoted, Hils.'

Back on the pavement a few minutes later, Viv said, 'You won't be getting any gigs after that.'

I said something to the effect that I wouldn't want a gig if it involved being shouted at.

At the same time, we watched people starting to arrive. They stumped up their fivers and we thought, bugger, they're coming to see us. They really are. This is it.

We made our way up the stairs again, now bound together by Hils's insensitivity. My mind was popping with random lines from the routine and, though I knew it was in there somewhere, 'At this moment in time' was still horrifyingly absent.

The seven of us were instructed to stand at the very back of the room, behind the audience, about sixty in all; no talking, no whispering, no communication with one another while the show was on. Logan would introduce us when it was our turn. Then, and only then, we could move forward ready to gain the stage.

As we sorted ourselves out, I remembered the last time I had been lined up like this: Prize-giving and Speech Day for

Cedarhurst School, held at the civic hall in Solihull in July 1969. I had won two prizes that year. An illustrated edition of *The Golden Fleece* and a novel called *The Pillar Box Thieves* by Henry Treece. One was for games, the other (I think) for essay writing. During the proceedings, Mr Callaghan, our ferocious cigar-chomping E-Type-driving headmaster had fallen off the back of the stage, hurt his back and ended up in hospital.

I was due on after the interval. After Paul, in fact, who was still dressed in his estate agent's suit, though to mark the occasion, he'd now topped it off with a mac. His parents were in the audience, flanking a boy of eleven or so who was, I think, his nephew.

When I'd spoken to my own father earlier that day, he'd asked whether I was doing anything 'special'. This was what he always asked, a sly, enquiring habit borne out of his hope that my life was reassuringly mundane and I wasn't in fact doing anything 'special', or anything so special that it might end with me in the soup.

'No,' I replied, 'just sorting some things out in London.'

What would they have thought, my parents, if they'd known about the pickle I was in? Not much, I don't think. My mother would have assumed I was clad in a tuxedo and about to tell oily old-fashioned jokes with tame punchlines. Come to think of it, she wouldn't have been far wrong.

I was glad to be on after Paul, not because his nerdy persona was much or any worse than anything I might do, but because his all-action, arms-flailing weirdness was so distinct from my own style, if 'style' was what it was. At least there would be the sensation of change, of variety, when I arrived on stage.

A large black sheet hung behind the stage. It depicted a moose's head, the moose having crazed, Crumb-bloodshot eyes which formed the double 'o' of the word 'Moose'. Now, suddenly and annoyingly, another oblique comic reference to the beast occurred to me. It's in Wodehouse, somewhere.

'Life,' said Charlotte coldly, 'is not all gnus.'

'You imply that there are also wapiti, moose, zebus and mountain-goats?' said Sir Francis. 'Well, maybe you're right.'

Advocating, I suppose, that life is not wholly good or wholly bad, but a bit of a mix.

Well, it was something to take on board. Though not right now.

Just after eight, Logan entered as 'Ron', a clubbable, leering character, who is part wicked pastiche of a children's television presenter, part goblin, part variety artiste, and his most recognisable stage persona. He was wearing a Father Christmas hat, a pair of glasses, a tartan smoking jacket and an affable though still grumpy frown. Immediately, he set about making Paul's nephew feel at home and apologised in advance for any bad language that would certainly be coming his way.

Then he swore.

I admired Logan's rapid comic liverishness. He teased the audience, picked on a bloke from Wales, and skilfully incorporated an array of props, including a bunny pop-up book and an animal that squeaked when you pressed its tummy.

Gradually, you could feel heat rising from the gently warmed audience. At one point, I glanced to my left and observed Hils's grinning face, now magically transformed from its ferret sharpness into something less guarded and more generously open. It was an agreeable, even heart-warming sight.

'Slick as buggery, I am,' said Ron, and she smiled, not quite beatifically, but smiled enough to make me see at least some of the point of laughter.

Some, though not all, of the audience were supporters of the seven novice comics. On the whole, they were predisposed to be kind. I appreciated this was not a 'normal' gig in front of possibly hostile, probably tanked-up strangers on the razzle and looking for a bit of fun, but it still felt harrowing enough.

Strands of material were by this time looping around inside my head, suddenly appearing and then vanishing in loud, haphazard gusts of Technicolor. I seemed to have no control over what was happening and became convinced that everything was more or less out of my hands.

Tall Laurence had given me some advice about remaining calm, and now I took it, crouching slightly and staring at the floor. After attending the course only fitfully, Laurence had turned out to be a bit of a dark horse. Apparently a revelation in last week's showcase, he had also stumped up a few thousand quid and booked a room in Edinburgh, for the festival, where he was going to perform an hour-long one-man show called, *The Nine Lives of Laurence K.* So Laurence obviously knew what he was talking about. I took his advice and stared.

From what I could hear, everyone seemed to have tightened their acts since yesterday, changing or even ditching bits which didn't work. I may have been mistaken, but I thought I also detected a general domesticating of persona. Stuart, Eva, Tom and Paul were more distinctly themselves, intuitively tapping what Logan would have called their own particular energies. Perhaps the fact of being on stage was reining them in. Maybe the slight moderating of performance had been compensated for by an increased if unconscious exploiting of self. Possibly I was talking bollocks, but I did sense it, this fall-back position.

As I waited for Paul to finish his hyperactive, gag-led routine, I realised that there was nothing inside my head. No material. No Technicolor. Nothing. Well, not quite nothing. Now all I could remember was, 'At this moment in time,' though nothing else besides.

Through sheer will-power, I tried to recall my first line. What was it? 'Good evening, ladies and gentlemen.'

That was it. Or close to.

Then what? Oh yes. 'My name's Steve Jacobi.' So far so good.

Paul came off to enthusiastic applause and I instinctively patted him on the shoulder, perhaps even gripping it, and said, 'Well done.' I wanted to embrace him and not let go. For a few moments, we were unlikely bedfellows. Fellow passengers on the *Titanic* clinging to the wreckage. Or comradely mountaineers roped together for safety.

I heard Logan joshing the audience, waiting to introduce me. I cleared my throat. I cleared it again. It seemed the only remotely accomplishable thing at that moment.

'I know you'll love him,' said Logan, 'so let's give a big hand for – the suave, the sophisticated, the slightly overweight . . . no, he isn't, he's not at all overweight – the very urbane, Steeeve Jack-o-beeeeee . . .'

And I thought, how nice of you, Logan; you ruined a perfectly good Rule of Three (the suave–the sophisticated–the slightly overweight) just to spare my feelings. You couldn't help going there, but then at the last moment, a little angel whispered in your ear and you broke your rhythm. You pulled back. Sweet.

I bounded on to the stage, even though I'd decided that bounding would be out of character. Terrible things, adrenalin rushes. I pulled the microphone out of its stand, pushed the stand slightly to the side and behind me, though of course immediately forgetting to clamp it tightly to my chest – in fact, waving it around in front of me like a Ken Dodd tickling stick. If I'd started talking at that moment, my voice would have oscillated between being gratingly loud or being virtually non-existent, as the microphone swayed drunkenly close to my face.

As it was I didn't start talking. Not immediately. I was planning on it. Just picking my moment. Imposing myself, you see.

And getting the microphone under control.

Then it began. I made it through the first thirty seconds or so before realising that I wasn't making eye contact, so I fixed the third and fourth rows with a beady stare. This only had the effect of making me forget a key line about my grandfather being in the SS during the war. Without this reference, much or at least some of what followed would not have made sense. So I stalled, wondered whether I ought to go back or forward, and quickly understood what happens when you stall in this way. You don't go anywhere. Furthermore, you come over as a pitiful prat. I gawped at the audience and for some reason saw Stuart's face. Triumphant South African Stuart, who had been on first, done very well, and was now sitting down with a pint and looking very pleased with himself. He was looking back at me with a sort of fearful pleading in his eyes which I interpreted as him willing me back into the groove. I cleared my throat again. I was getting good at it.

Where was I 'at this moment in time'? I wondered. Not there, for starters. Back a bit. Back a lot.

I got myself together and relaxed. Crisis over. The audience also relaxed. Funny how that works, the thing between performer and audience. Symbiosis, you see.

I tried a few more lines. Then, and I can't remember when

it occurred, something miraculous happened. People laughed. Not one of your small, sympathetic, consolation laughs, but a proper one, a collusive reflex among strangers who had decided, after all and against the odds, that they were going to enjoy themselves.

I was unprepared for this and even more so for the next wave of merriment. Without thinking, and I still don't know where it came from – possibly a residual trace from teaching or a peripheral memory of Larry Grayson – I've never said it again before or since – I said, 'Settle down, now.' More laughter.

And away I went.

SIX

Beside the Seaside

It sort of went reasonably well. After the relief had finally drained from my troubled soul, and when I came to consider things in the cold light of day, I realised two things. Number one: that I already knew how unlikely it was that I would become addicted to stand-up, or develop an ambition to become one, or even enjoy very much the attempt to become one. I was neither hopeless nor good, merely marooned in mediocrity. Even the laughter, when it arrived, hadn't made me feel as good about myself as people had predicted it might. I felt either negative – which was most of the time, actually like I feel just before going to the dentist; not exactly nervous but just dull and anaesthetised by foreboding dread – or neutral. Neutral was what happened when people laughed. There was no 'positive', merely a sense of being reprieved. That I was getting away with things.

Number two: that I had absolutely no idea how I came across to an audience. What I looked like and how I 'seemed' remained ineffable mysteries. By giving a resolutely unflinching non-performance, it was difficult to know who I had been.

Naturally, I was intrigued. So I plunged into the communal email pool and asked the others for their candid opinions. I was careful to stress that I was neither fishing for compliments nor inviting fierce criticism, both of which I would in any case have been unable to handle. Well, maybe not the criticism. At least that had the virtue of confirming expectations. No, I convinced myself, this was about my stage persona. Not about me. No siree.

The results were, as they say, interesting.

I'll give them to you unvarnished and anonymous.

'I think you've got a real John Le Mesurier feel to your act. A kind of knowledge that you're superior to the audience but you're far too polite to mention it.'

'. . . you have a very conversational and understated style, which works really well for you. That is, you sound posh and have a James Bond air about you . . .'

'You remind me of a Polite Pirate . . . slightly roguish, but in a good way.'

'You speak softly, but people listen to you because you are so interesting . . .'

'. . . for my money you're like a mysterious James Bond figure suffused with irony . . . I imagine you live by your credit cards, never carry luggage and enjoy the company of beautiful women with exotic accents.'

'A brilliant and witty performer who makes absolutely the most of some sensational material'.

Not really. That last one was made up. But you get the idea.

So, I was an ageing, debt-ridden debauchee. It wasn't quite a majority decision, though there was certainly a consensus. I didn't quite know what to make of it all and sent back an email to everyone reassuring them that my parents lived in an undesirable area of Birmingham and my sister was dead common. I wasn't necessarily taken aback or appalled by who I seemed to be, merely ruminative.

One of the emailers had suggested I look up one of the so-called 'gentleman comedians' on the Net. So I did. He's called Miles Jupp and there was even a picture of him looking tweedy, sporting a red waistcoat, and with a giveaway Earl Spencer hairdo. I haven't seen Miles, or indeed know anything about him, but he won the 2001 'So You Think You're Funny' new act competition. He'd also been nominated for a Perrier Best Newcomer Award for his show, *Gentlemen Prefer Brogues*. Miles had started out as a double act with someone called George who has since joined the police force. Apparently, the posh bits in his act emerged from material he used to do which compared living above a deli to living above a chip shop. Then, his stand-up shifted into him playing a mildly offensive upper-class snob.

Obviously I had mixed feelings about all of this. Was I really mildly offensive, or close to? It was difficult for someone like me, who didn't think of himself as being posh, to be compared with someone who was not only posh but actually accentuated it for his act and played it for laughs. ('It's a very slight reflection of myself,' Hampstead-bred Windsor chorister Miles disclosed.) The effect was to make me wonder whether I would now become self-conscious about 'being me' rather than just being me and being self-conscious about everything else.

Getting into the swing of my comedic journey, I had already booked another gig in Manchester, with the vague intention of using it to have a think about humour in the north. It was a pre-Miles booking, and crippled by my new sense of poshness, I suddenly began to fear for myself. Despite my uneasiness, however, a number of things pushed me on: the remote sense that as I improved, I might actually enjoy being on stage; not wanting to waste the work I'd done on the course; stubbornness in seeing something through; and, of course, the original curiosity – about comedy, about myself – which had not yet been satisfied. Not by a long chalk.

For the moment, there was still plenty to play for.

Of course there was.

So, on I went.

The north has always been a foreign country for southern comics. In the old days, before television made us indistinct clones of each other, they could not go further up the country than Hatfield. People didn't take to them. When Max Miller, the cheeky-chapped epitome of smart-alec southern impudence, was asked if he wanted to perform in Glasgow, he replied, 'I'm a comedian, not a missionary.'

For the moment, I didn't want to think about this too much and decided to spend a day at the seaside. Weston-super-Mare to be precise, to attend the National Music Hall and Variety Festival. While in London, I had picked up a leaflet for this at a bookshop in Cecil Court called something like Of Past Times which specialises in, well, books obviously, but books and memorabilia specifically about comedy, the stage, music hall and variety. (Where else, for example, could you ask for a copy of Ted Ray's 1963 classic *My Turn Next!* or a copy of Eric Morecambe's only novel, *Mr Lonely*? And like all the best shops, it doesn't have any truck with credit cards, seems disorderly but isn't and keeps unfathomably irregular hours. In fact, there's not even a sign on the door to say when the owner Mr Drummond is likely to be around.)

Anyway, the leaflet promised all kinds of events and

performances spread over six days. I couldn't go for the duration but I could certainly go for a day. In fact, I felt I *ought* to go for a day. It would be a good excuse to bone up on the origins of stand-up and perhaps add a bit of historical lustre to my enquiry. There was even an outside chance of picking up a few hints. Maybe there would be a posh comedian I could watch.

When I set off it was one of those gloriously peculiar days that you only seem to get in England. It was sunny and cold, meaning that I was resigned to a day of for ever taking off and then redonning my fleece. I decided to drive, not merely because it was easier than catching a train but because I reckoned it would be a potentially more pleasant journey.

And so it proved. I bypassed Cheltenham and Gloucester (the places, not the building society) before forking north and driving along the Welsh side of the River Severn. I don't think I'd been this way since I was a small boy when, for reasons still veiled in obscurity, Mum and Dad took us for the occasional Sunday jaunt to Hay-on-Wye. It's still one of the only things I can remember us doing as a family, singing 'One Man Went to Mow a Meadow' and 'Ten Green Bottles', falling asleep in the back on the homeward journey, and eating lots of ice cream. Magic. And Dad's feeble Frank Spencerish attempts to row a boat in what must have been some kind of lake have long since passed into family lore.

It was a glorious drive. All the towns and villages were pretty and looked as if they had local bobbies, proper communities where it was frowned upon to lock your car at night, and greengrocers in long brown coats who still sold bananas by the pound. It was exactly the right way to go for a music hall festival.

And on I went, through Newnham, Blakeney and Chepstow, until I came to the Severn Bridge, which I'd never crossed before. I'm still a sucker for things like this and drove across quite slowly, looking both ways at the same time to get the view, only remotely aware of the slight buffeting my car was getting from the fresh crosswinds. The car swayed a little. In truth, I was driving badly, my mind not on the job. I wondered what the statistics were for accidents near to famous sights. Had there been an increase, for example, on that stretch of the A1 which passes by Antony Gormley's *Angel of the North*?

After this, Weston-super-Mare was a disappointment. Perhaps inevitably so. On first impressions, it wasn't quite as dire as the grim and wholly concretised seaside town they used for the film *Last Resort*, though it still seemed a pretty cheerless place.

I parked up in a multi-storey and made my way to the Winter Gardens. Around town, there was nothing to advertise the festival apart from a larger version of Mr Drummond's leaflet, fading and torn, rudely wrapped round an advertising column. The Winter Gardens seemed a good place to start, and so it proved. Even then, if I'd hoped to see evidence of something happening, like the specially commissioned oil paintings of music hall scenes or the gallery of original variety posters and handbills, even the stall selling an array of entertainment ephemera – all of which were advertised on the leaflet – I was frustrated.

There didn't seem to be much of anything going on, so I asked the lady at the box office where I could find the exhibitions and the traders.

'You don't mean "where",' she replied.

'Don't I?'

'You mean *when*.'

'Do I?'

'It's not happening today.'

'Isn't it?'

'Not till Saturday. We're setting up just now. For tomorrow.'

'It is happening today,' I growled, and held up my leaflet.

'Yes, well. Some of it is.'

'What is?'

She consulted a list. '*Hiss and Boo Music Hall Show*. The Playhouse. Matinée and evening.'

'What time this afternoon?' I asked, giving my leaflet a look of intense malice.

'Two thirty.'

'Can I buy a ticket?'

'Yes, of course.'

'That's good. Can I–'

'Not here. At the Playhouse. You have to buy the ticket at the Playhouse.'

I considered. Two thirty. It was now just after ten. Four hours, give or take. Four hours spent in Weston-super-Mare. I'd just have to make the most of it. The lady in the box office noted my disgruntlement.

'The Beverley Sisters are top of the bill,' she said cheerfully.

I smiled thinly, bought a brochure for £5 and wandered over to the Playhouse to buy a ticket for the matinée. That cost £8.50. Then I cheered myself up with a large coffee and Danish, flicked through the programme, and prepared myself for a bit of mooching around town.

I started off with the Grand Pier, one of the last great pleasure piers to have been built, actually in 1904. That it happened so late was because the other and older pier,

Birnbeck, was too far from the centre of town to be of much use. At the time, large numbers of visitors were coming to Weston so it seemed obvious that another pier was the right thing to do. Still, there's something horribly British about all this; one pier was built at the right time but in the wrong place, while the other was built at the wrong time in the right place. By 1904, seaside towns hadn't quite gone into terminal resort tailspin, but they were getting there. Result: two useless piers.

One of Weston's features is that the sea goes out a considerable distance at low tide. It had always been a popular joke that it used to go out so far that it was debatable as to whether it would actually return.

Well, I guess you had to be in the right mood.

The deal was that while the Grand Pier became home to opera, music hall, stage plays, ballet and even boxing, the Birnbeck would provide the bulk of the rides and amusements. As happens to most piers, the Grand was destroyed by fire. Then it was rebuilt and gradually became tacky.

That also happens to most piers.

Having said that, the Grand looked in pretty good nick. Even the outside of the pavilion looked nice enough – though inside it was a different story. The interior has been gutted and now houses an enormous amusement area crammed with slot machines and cheap arcade games designed to wring a few pennies out of you. And that's the saddest thing – the amounts of money asked for and no doubt acquired are so fucking *small*. The other disheartening thing is that the place is empty apart from three old-age pensioners, scattered around, seated at one kind of machine or another, carefully placing their ten-pence pieces in the slots, and maybe hoping for a windfall of *two or three quid*!

Cast down, I went for a walk along the sands. I was alone apart from an old lady with a couple of poodles. It wasn't much of a walk. There were a few stagnant-looking pools of water and the sand was damp and unappetising. I spent most of my time there brooding about Manchester and running through my routine, just for something to do. Then, disappointed and empty, I headed back towards the town centre.

It was even more ugly than I remembered from only an hour or so previously. Admittedly it was in a state of anticipation, waiting for the start of the summer season. Many of the shops were congested with as yet unopened boxes of candyfloss, ice-cream cones, and the sort of useless tat you can only buy in English seaside towns. In between, though generally hidden by the more recent concrete, you could occasionally make out the more pleasing shapes of Victorian and Edwardian buildings, and yet you couldn't help thinking that the place had been wrecked by ugliness and bad planning.

'Faded grandeur' is a much overused phrase, but it seems no other will do. Again and again, I saw evidence of spoiled elegance abutting seafront dereliction. This was the same place where popular culture, from Victorian gaiety and music hall to the accentuated fantasies of mass consumerism, had played for many of the last hundred years or more. Now, the past merely whispered through the sense of ruin.

After lunch – an enormous prawn sandwich smeared with mayonnaise and including some kind of side salad – I walked around the other parts of Weston. I found an old, ramshackle bookshop and bought Bob Monkhouse's autobiography (Vol. 2) and a copy of George Melly's *Don't Tell Sybil*, both for under a tenner. The old bloke who ran the shop had very yellow teeth and a pair of glasses with the strongest lenses I'd ever seen. His eyes looked like a couple of under-poached eggs. Also, he didn't take credit cards thereby putting under strain my theory about good bookshops.

'No problem,' I said, 'I'll just pop to the nearest cashpoint.'

'No hurry. I could keep them for you overnight,' the man offered.

'I don't think I'll be staying overnight.'

'Don't blame you. Bit of a lad, wasn't he?'

'Who?'

'Monkhouse,' he said, waving the book at me. 'Settled down later though, like a good 'un. Mind you, we all do. In the end.' And then he winked, his outsize lens making the poached, winking eye look as if, in a single greedy gulp, it was suddenly being consumed by its socket. 'Funny man, he was. Funny funny, not funny peculiar, if you get my drift. Unfairly derided I should say. I remember seeing him at Bristol once.' And that was it for the next ten minutes as data about Bob Monkhouse poured from the old man.

At least now I felt my theory about bookshops had been triumphantly vindicated.

Even after this and *even* after I'd been to get the money and paid for the books, it still left me with well over an hour to kill. One thing I did want to buy was a saucy seaside postcard, maybe a dozen or so. At least I had time to track them down.

Buying cards of this nature is an obligation when visiting any English seaside town, like buying images of the Eiffel Tower in France or Trafalgar Square in London. Picture cards in general had become very popular at the beginning of the twentieth century when restrictions about writing on them were lifted and our postal system could cope with three deliveries every day. And, no, that's not a misprint. *Three*. It was quite common to post an invitation to someone by first post and then to receive a reply later in the day.

My favourite saucy card shows a smartly dressed girl walking past two men who remark, 'She's a nice girl, doesn't drink or smoke and only swears when it slips out.' This particular card was banned and stocks were destroyed in twenty towns. At one point, Eastbourne banned outright the work of Donald McGill, the doyen of the saucy card. In 1953, in Brighton, there was even a bonfire of the offending cards. All this seemed unnecessarily harsh treatment of a bloke who merely traded on harmless innuendo and had in any case lost his foot in a rugby accident at school. Surely, I thought, people could have been more tolerant and less outraged.

But could I find a single card? Could I buggery. Maybe the shops were awaiting delivery of the summer stock or maybe it was now a fact that cards of Lady Di or whatever sold more units with the consequence that they were now officially 'out of fashion'. For the third time that day I became mildly depressed, though on this occasion I counter-attacked by eating a Twix.

Time was getting on and I made my way to the Playhouse. Even though I arrived in plenty of time the queue I encountered made me wonder whether I had in fact left things a bit late. It was lengthy and moving so slowly that I doubted we would all be inside by two thirty. This was not for the usual overcrowding reasons but because many of those trying to get in were elderly and were either having trouble with the steps and/or (though mostly 'and') difficulties with the wheelchair access.

The Playhouse is a typically utilitarian example of the 1960s, when the original building was destroyed by fire and rebuilt in characteristically brutal manner. If I wanted chandeliers and ornate mouldings, I'd come to the wrong place. On the other hand, the Knightstone Theatre, situated on the edge of the bay, would probably have been more like it. This had been built in 1902 and was a regular venue for all the big music hall stars like Max Miller and Wilson, Keppel and Betty. If you Google it, this is what you get: '. . . the building has a towered Italianate façade and a long rectangular hall which originally had a flat floor'. The accompanying photo shows a building which wouldn't have looked out of place in the Wild West. Unfortunately, Google also says, with unsentimental understatement, 'DEMOLISHED', though not when. Or why, come to think of it. But you can guess, of course, and the guessing would be all about money.

Meanwhile, back at the Playhouse, the queue had spurted forward and I'd actually got in with time to spare. There was still a bit of a kerfuffle at the foot of the stairs leading up to the balcony and the stairlift was doing overtime, but everything seemed to be more or less under control. I must have been the youngest person in the building. It was a moment to savour.

I celebrated by finding the bar and ordering a Diet Coke and a packet of Mini Cheddars. Then, thinking I ought to do a bit of research, I looked round for a likely researchee, someone who looked as if they might know a bit about music hall. I spied a likely-looking suspect and then did something totally out of character; I introduced myself to a strange man in a bar.

After I'd explained a bit about my comedic journey, the stranger told me his name was Peter Aynge and he was a member of the Somerset and West Music Hall Society. Though initially very nervous of me, it was soon clear that Peter really knew his onions. I couldn't have made a better choice. Apparently, he'd been in Oxford quite recently advising people on music they might use in a variety show. Peter was quite but not very old, though he did seem a little fragile. Still, he seemed keen enough to talk. I wanted to ask him about modern comedians, though before I got too far down this line of enquiry, there was a sharp intake of breath and he said, 'Don't like them, I'm afraid.'

'You don't like *any* modern comedians?'

Peter considered or at least gave the impression of considering.

'No.'

'Why not?

'Language,' he rapped back.

'Bad language?'

He nodded. 'That's right. Unnecessary.'

'Is there no one you like – even a bit?'

Peter furrowed his brows.

'At one time I had high hopes for Billy Connolly, but then . . .'

'Language?' I offered.

Peter nodded. 'Promise unfulfilled. And now he's all language. Nothing but language from what I can make out.'

'So what do you like about the older music hall comedians?'

'Their style. Their craft, honed to perfection over several decades. The ability to relate to an audience, to really work it and communicate.'

I didn't think this was the time to him tell about my own styleless, craftless, uncommunicatively reserved routine.

He took a birdlike sip of his drink, I think water or maybe flattish lemonade.

'I expect you're wondering how I got this bruise,' Peter said, indicating a faint purpling on the side of his face.

I wasn't, hadn't in fact noticed it before, but now that it had been pointed out, I couldn't very well not be interested.

'I did wonder,' I smiled.

'Fell down ten days ago,' he explained, 'heart attack. Intensive care for a week. Just got out of hospital. Well, couldn't miss the Bevs, could I?'

'Wouldn't have thought so,' I empathised.

A few minutes later I was in my seat. Front row of the balcony, right in the middle. For the first time, I began to wonder what I could expect from the *Hiss and Boo Music Hall.* My only experience of the genre was watching *The Good Old Days* on television in the good old days of the 1970s. Its guest stars performed music-hall acts and dressed for the part in 1890s costumes. This seemed fair enough, though the audience was similarly dressed, which possibly wasn't. And this, I suspect, had been at the root of my adolescent sneering – seeing grown men and women donning false sideburns (well, the men) and frilly hats (well, the women), joining in, singing along and waving handkerchiefs.

I was glad to be in the balcony. Not many of us had made it up the stairs, but I felt safe from any of that joining-in tosh, which I knew I would recoil from, even in my new public jesting guise. I was also glad that nobody in the Playhouse had dressed up for the occasion. Though of a certain vintage, what people wore was merely nondescript and old rather than ostentatious and antique.

By the time the chairman or master of ceremonies took to the stage, I was even looking forward to the afternoon's entertainment. Then I saw something which warmed my cockles. He was holding his microphone in the prescribed manner, i.e. tightly against his chest, absolutely in the style I aspired to but as yet hadn't quite mastered. He promised to transport us back to 'the good old days' and this is precisely what he did, though not me, obviously, because my good old days would have involved Monty Python, Status Quo, and Roy Wood singing 'Ballpark Incident'.

Still, I quite enjoyed watching the parade of seaside Pierrots, the 'Daisy, Daisy' singalong, and even the nostalgic Piccadilly Circus backcloth with its advertisements for Bovril, Lipton's Tea, Wrigley's, and Fry's Chocolate, admittedly still familiar names though not these days familiar in Piccadilly Circus.

Then a comedian called Jimmy Casey came on accompanied by an angular and exceptionally tall piece of human Meccano called Eli Woods. Together with the chairman, they performed Jimmy James's famous 'Animals in the box' sketch, so famous that even I seemed to know it pretty well. Perhaps my dad had told me about it or I had heard it on the radio. It's a miniature masterpiece of constructed timing. Here's the opening: a man holds a box under his arm. He seems very protective of it. He has just returned from the unlikely post of Colonial Secretary in Egypt where he has been presented with two man-eating lions:

JIMMY: Where do you keep them?
CHAIRMAN (*as Colonial Secretary*): In this box.
JIMMY: I thought I heard a rustling!

Jimmy James was a master at making careful attention to detail look and sound completely untheatrical and carefree. Nowhere was this more explicit than in his drunken stage persona, all precarious swagger and drooping fag. Apparently, he could get massive laughs from merely stamping out a cigarette, succeeding because he always gave the impression he was doing it without knowing he was doing it. In real life, he was actually a teetotaller. But that's what a persona is, I suppose. And it's also, I now appreciated, or appreciated again, one of the reasons why I would never be any good as a comedian.

When I checked the programme I saw that Jimmy Casey was in fact Jimmy James's son. Casey was actually Jimmy James's real name, so he was really Jimmy Casey, like his son. Clearly, all his creative juices were exhausted in producing comic material with none left over for names. Another thing; Eli was his nephew. And Eli's real name was Jack. Jack Casey. At one time, many others, including Roy Castle and Larry Grayson, also played parts in the 'Animals in the box' sketch. I liked the idea that not only was the sketch 'in the family' in a very literal way, but that it had also reached out to a broader comedic family.

In another sketch, not performed here, Jimmy James introduces the improbable Eli as a daredevil parachutist. The plan was for Eli to jump out of an aeroplane 20,000 feet above the theatre, plummet through the roof, and not pull the ripcord until he was only ten feet above the stalls:

ELI: But what if the parachute doesn't open?
JIMMY: You can jump ten feet, can't you?

Critics have said that Jimmy James's dialogue is manically surreal and yet imaginatively concise, calling to mind Pinter and Beckett. To these I would add the Goons, Peter Cook and Dudley Moore, Monty Python and Eddie Izzard, among others. I really did cherish this sense of ongoing continuity, of comedy and comedians sparking and nourishing one another, all plugging into an assumed national psyche.

The last and climactic act of the afternoon was the Beverley Sisters, who must have been well into their seventies, yet wore short spangly dresses and still moved with a willing if occasionally cautious energy. They worked the audience into a kind of maudlin frenzy, stringing together old favourites like 'The Old Bull and Bush' and even 'Hang out the washing on the old Siegfried Line'. They also had plenty to say about how much better life used to be.

'Remember when you could walk home at night and not be worried about being attacked?' asked Joy Beverley, who was married to the late English football captain Billy Wright. They were the Posh and Becks of the 1950s except, obviously, that Joy can sing.

'Yes,' sighed the audience in mournful agreement.

'And when being British was something to be proud of?' said Babs.

Much nodding of heads and another melancholy, almost whispered agreement.

Except for the bloke sitting next to me, who had fallen asleep. Not, I don't think, because he was bored, but simply because it was the time of day when he'd normally have had a nap anyway.

I stayed right to the end, even finding myself nodding along with the Bevs' propagandist lullabies. By the time they came off stage, I really was beginning to believe they don't make them as lovely as 'my Billy' any more, that the past was a better country, and everyone who fought in the war was a bloomin' hero.

On the way out of the Playhouse, I saw Peter Aynge and nodded to him, though like many of the audience he had overdosed on nostalgia and was still in a dewy-eyed trance of extreme mushiness. But then, why they shouldn't they be sentimental? Many of them had probably fought in the last war or made sacrifices during those years. They undoubtedly felt betrayed and believed that in all sorts of ways England had let them down.

Oh well.

Weston-super-Mare, probably no more or less than other seaside towns like Morecambe, Frinton, Margate, Worthing or Formby, had become perhaps the ultimate expression of Englishness and its plaintive requiem. Though the photographer Martin Parr has made use of their collective demise in order to claim them as objects of refined kitsch, the perception of tackiness depends to an extent on the frustrated desire to restore the history and romance to their archaically modern Englishness.

No doubt the laughter of the audience (for Jimmy and Eli and the others) was a kind of cosy restorative, much in the same way that people now watch DVDs of, say, old *Morecambe and Wise* shows or ancient episodes of *Steptoe and Son*. In the future, the sharp, cutting-edged youth of today will probably be doing the same with people like Eddie Izzard and Jimmy Carr. It's already happened with *The Fast Show.* They'll bounce doting grandchildren on their laps and say things like, 'Of course, today's comedians aren't a patch on Eddie. He had craft, you see. You don't get that any more. Just language.' The 'Reassurance of the Familiar' as opposed to the 'Shock of the New'.

The history of music hall suggests this kind of continuity will occur, that in the end we're drawing from a single, affiliated well of comedy where everyone and everything is somehow associated. So what do you call it? Not a common language, I don't think. Maybe a collective or popular understanding, though possibly an understanding which also concedes difference.

The need to be amused is and always has been an important part of our national psyche, irrepressible and persistent. History says as much. The music halls provide the crucial link between the old fairs and circuses that toured England hundreds of years ago and – eventually – today's stand-up comedians. It was during Elizabeth I's reign that being a 'showman' was first recognised as a profession in its own right. This eventually drove many performers into 'musick houses' and taverns. By the 1830s, the acts had become as popular as the drinking, so larger pubs appeared to cope with the demand. These were often sited along workers' routes into town for social get-togethers after work. The entertainer was an important element of their attraction to a largely working-class public.

A publican called Charles Morton (now commonly referred to as 'the father of music hall') became the first to spot the potential of such amusements and he acquired the Canterbury at 143 Westminster Bridge Road in Lambeth as a place of entertainment. Encouraged by the success of his venture, Morton rebuilt the Canterbury several times so that eventually it could hold about 1,500 customers. For 6d, you could expect either a pint of bitter or a large gin, a cigar and top-drawer entertainment. Not bad.

Crucially, Morton could also spot talent. One of his finds was Joe Saunders, a mechanic from the Midlands, whom he saw performing in a sleazy Whitechapel tavern. Morton brought him to the Canterbury, changed his name to George Leybourne, and so introduced a completely new type of turn to the music hall stage. Leybourne's chief rival was the Great Vance. In addition to being entertainers, both were gargantuan drinkers and died in their forties.

These *lions comiques*, in embryo, were the forerunners of today's comedians. They were hard-drinking swells who could woo an audience into frenzy through a mixture of song and side-splitting patter. A whole generation of smart young men desired to be likewise. Maurice Willson Disher, the legendary authority on clowns and showmen, wrote, 'Here at last was an amusement not to be mocked. What fairs were to the Restoration, what musick-houses were to the Georgians, what the circus was to Regency bucks, the music hall was to Victorian mashers. It multiplied everywhere by thousands.'

It's not stretching a point to say that today's stand-ups, especially those still plying their trade in the pubs and clubs, away from the voracious, flattening scrutiny of the media, are part of this harmless, healthily vulgar tradition. The very names of the 'Glee' and 'Jongleurs' clubs are a nodding acknowledgement to their showmen ancestors in fairs, circuses and music halls. Without Vance or Leybourne there would have been no Dan Leno, now recognised as the archetype of the modern stand-up comedian.

The reciprocal relationship between audience and performer, the collaborative, communal urgings to laughter, are part of the legacy which music-hall performers have handed down. The drinking, the laughter, the after-work shedding of inhibition, the smoky and hypnotic security of being in an anonymous throng, are common to both. 'You would hardly appreciate the comic if you felt isolated from others,' remarked Henri Bergson in *Laughter*. 'Laughter appears to stand in need of an echo.'

On the way back to the car I passed a W.H. Smith's and picked up a Ross Noble CD, I was in a buying mood and would probably have bought *The Very Best of the Beverley Sisters* or even their intriguingly titled *Sassy . . . but Classy* if only I could have found them. Modern performers wouldn't have missed such a trick, I thought – they'd have had a stall set out at the front of the Playhouse with CDs, scarves, keyrings, Beverley Sisters' bomber jackets, and probably even photos of Billy Wright.

My mobile rang. It was Pippa.

'How did it go?'

'Fine. I saw the Beverley Sisters.'

'Lucky you.'

'We sang "Down at the Old Bull and Bush."'

'That's nice. Did you get any tips for your act?'

'Not really. Unless you count the realisation that I'm no good and probably won't ever be.'

'I could have told you that.'

'You did.'

'Did you buy any books?'

'No,' I lied. Buying books was something of an issue between us, the issue being that I bought too many.

'Don't believe you.'

'Suit yourself.'

'So. How much did they cost.'

'Eight pounds fifty,' I conceded.

'Don't believe you. What's Weston-super-Mare like?'

'Dreadful. *Upsetting*.'

'Oh dear. Why's that?'

'It's a long story. I'll tell you later.'

'Can't wait.'

'It's interesting, though, about music hall – '

'All right, all right. I don't want your autobiography.'

'OK. See you later.'

'See you later. Drive carefully.'

'I will.'

'You're a terrible driver.'

'I'm not.'

'Are.'

'Bye.'

'Bye.'

As I drove out of Weston, back past the supermarkets and out-of-town warehouses that could have been anywhere, I decided to head straight back up the M5. No more of this mawkish up-the-banks-of-the-Severn nonsense. Just motorway efficiency and with any luck a coffee and doughnut at the services.

It had been a funny old day, not least because in a minuscule way I felt that I was now part of comedy's expansive family, connected by the slenderest of threads to the Great Leybourne, the Great Vance and Dan Leno, but connected nonetheless. It's this sense of continuity and evolution which make Britain what it is, everything different but related. It's why we got music hall while the Europeans got cabaret. There were some similarities, but ultimately cabaret is more concerned with ideas and political satire. So in the end, we're still a nation that just wants to have a good time and get pissed while in France and Germany they tend to meet up and say clever, even revolutionary things about those that rule them and the systems by which they're governed. While we laugh at the silliness of the everyday world, they want to change it.

Well, it's a theory.

The Ross Noble CD had the unlikely premise of a Geordie comedian touring the world and then doing gigs in those countries. His material was based on the observations he'd made and the people he'd encountered during his stay. It relied to a large degree on Noble's relationship with the audience. He clearly has the ability to react to anyone in any place, and was immediately on easy, chummy terms with his crowds, even in Thailand and Hong Kong.

Maybe, I mused, this is what Dan Leno would have been doing today. 'Dan Leno Live in Sydney' would have been a certainty, but so would 'Den Leno in Cape Town' and probably 'Dan Leno in Delhi'. Continuity, you see. On the other hand, a few months ago on television, I'd seen Bernard Manning doing his act in India. He presented his familiar and mostly offensive set to audiences which comprised educated, middle-class Indians. Not surprisingly, he barely raised a laugh. Those that understood him at all were mildly offended, the degree of offence mollified by feelings of pity. So it isn't always about audience rapport; you have to have, er, appropriate material. Poor old Bernard. His humiliation almost made you feel sorry for him. Almost.

Though I was quite taken with this notion of continuity within the comedic community, as I drove away from Weston it also seemed as if something had been lost, or maybe discontinued. Weston-super-Mare was as much about endings as it was concerned with connections. In sombre but poetic ways, the empty pier, the neglected Winter Gardens, the brutalised architecture and the unused bandstand held a mirror to the passing of an epoch, to the gradual dimming of an earlier gaiety. Jimmy Casey and Eli Woods were echoes, living souvenirs, as much as they were still dynamic inheritors of a tradition.

Morrissey said something about this sense of death-in-life in his hymn to the melancholy of the English seaside, 'Every Day is like Sunday'. And so did Graham Greene, who observed that 'Seediness has a very deep appeal; it seems to satisfy, temporarily, the sense of nostalgia for something lost . . .' And Weston is nothing if not seedy.

Perhaps, though, it is John Betjeman's poem about wartime Britain, 'Margate 1940', which best captures the acute romanticism of a past recollected within an imperfect present:

And I think as the fairy-lit sites I recall
It is those we are fighting for, foremost of all.

But I didn't have much time to ponder these ghosts or muse how Weston represented a stage further back. Or even how the gentility and glamour of the past helps to frame the way we live today. I was going up north and I was bloody scared about it.

SEVEN

Grin Up North

To get to Manchester, the man at National Rail Enquiries advised I would first have to travel back to Oxford, where I could pick up a Virgin train, then proceed via Birmingham New Street, Wolverhampton, Stafford, Stoke and Macclesfield.

At our local station, we have three officials doling out tickets from behind the perspex. They operate a rota system of some kind. One official is a polite, efficient, matronly woman. Another is a resentful small-minded little shit whose main purposes in life seem to be selling tickets so slowly that passengers are soon in danger of missing their trains, being rude and never on any account giving out useful information about trains. And the third – the one who actually sells me my Manchester ticket – is a nice jovial man who looks as though he's worked in the office all his life and has developed an old-fashioned, even affectionate connection to the railways.

'Officially, our designated route is via Worcester Shrub Hill,' he observed, '*then* Birmingham New Street. But it *is* much quicker to go to Oxford. Less hanging around.' He sold me the ticket and handed it over with a look of conspiratorial roguishness. 'Don't say you bought this here,' he said, 'say you bought it on the Internet or something.' I grinned back, grateful though irritated that such mild chicanery should be required.

The train to Oxford was late. On arrival, I had only a minute or two to locate and catch the Manchester connection. One of the information monitors was out of action and the other was giving different intelligence to that being broadcast over the public address system. I lugged my bag over the footbridge, then heard the announcement, then sprinted back again, only to see the Virgin train pulling into the platform I had just left. As it arrived and I set off over the footbridge once more, another, second announcement apologised for the incorrect showing of the incoming train's platform on the single working monitor, then declared a different though still incorrect platform. All the other passengers who had, with me, been running from one side of the station to the other, finally learned the lesson and met the train using nothing more than common sense.

A few minutes later, my anger moderated by the gentle swaying of the carriage, a cup of tea and large choc-chip cookie, I recalled a similar scene in Jacques Tati's *Monsieur Hulot's Holiday*. Then, passengers had been confused by a virtually inaudible babble issuing from the station's rudimentary P.A. Like us, they had dashed from platform to platform, presumably with the same befuddled optimism and diminishing degree of trust. When the film originally came out, the leading French newspaper *Le Monde* ran an editorial about the return of 'holiday panic'. Following the Second World War, holidays had only recently become possible again for the French middle classes, and the paper remarked on the unending hassle and chaos of travel in a country that had barely begun to rebuild its roads and railways. Holidays, it concluded, were needed to allow travellers to get over their exhausting labours in getting there in the first place.

That was fifty years ago. The war itself has been over for sixty. You couldn't be blamed for asking what the fuck was going on even if it transpired our railway was involved in an obscurely complex homage to Tati.

I hadn't been to Manchester for a year or so, when I'd popped up to watch some cricket at Old Trafford with a writer and director called Jim Poyser who's produced a couple of my plays on Radio 4. After a bad start, I'm gradually being brought round to the idea of Manchester. My very first memory was coming up for a university interview. It was raining – no, there was a deluge of biblical proportions – and I remember being shown around the English department by an elderly man, probably an academic, who smelt of whisky and mothballs. Appalled by this man, the weather, the fusty department, the congested halls of residence, and quite likely all things Mancunian, I fled the scene without even attending the interview, skulking back to Birmingham barely an hour after first arriving.

Since then, Manchester has changed. It's been regenerated. It has two football stadiums so good they don't seem to belong in England. It has loft apartments and trams and plush shopping malls. It has become 'cosmopolitan'. A place even remote from the same city's Olympic bid more than fifteen years ago when an impressive range of hanging baskets represented the only impediment to Atlanta securing the committee's vote.

Nonetheless, as we pulled into New Manchester, I felt a

twinge of regret. Amid the construction, there were still a good number of dirty red-brick houses and a respectable contingent of ungentrified streets that would have passed muster in *Corrie*. I admit to liking this sort of thing. They strike a chord, probably for horrible, sentimental, arguably fogeyish reasons, but strike one all the same.

The buildings, of course, aren't the only thing to have changed. Humour, too, has moved on. There used to be a clear divide between comedy acts in the north and those in the south. Traditionally, the northern variety was slower, softer, less aggressive and with the humour tending to be directed against the self, not others. But that was ages ago. Even before Steve Coogan. Thirty years ago, J.B. Priestley detected a decline in the amount of genuine affection in humour ('the constant display of warm affection', he called it), locating the beginnings of the demise to the end of the First World War, though he reckoned it had taken another sixty years to die out completely.

On the other hand, I still felt uneasy about performing in Manchester, finding it hard to disown stereotypical images of gruff working-class men in flat caps roundly abusing my softly-spoken otherness. To put my mind at rest, I had arranged to meet the MC and gig-organiser of XSMalarkey, a comedy club on the Wilmslow Road. His name was Toby Hadoke and we thought a spot of lunch was needed to put me in the picture before I did my ten minutes later that evening. I'd only spoken to Toby on the phone and didn't know what to expect. In the event, he called me on the mobile and cancelled.

'Sorry, Steve,' he said, 'it's just that my father turned up unexpectedly this morning and I want to spend some time with him.'

'Do you not see each other very often?' I asked sympathetically.

'Haven't seen him for fifteen years.'

'Fifteen years?!'

'He went away on a course to Germany and never came back. Mum was furious.'

'I bet.'

'She paid for the course.'

'Oh well,' I sighed, 'Good luck. And see you tonight.'

'Yes . . . but hang on, I've sent a replacement.'

'For lunch?'

'Just after. Her name's Lavinia Murray. She's a comedienne. Among other things. Sometimes performs at XS. She's very interesting.'

We said our goodbyes and I walked to the hotel where Toby and I had arranged to meet and where Lavinia would now be arriving. I had about half an hour, so I ordered a burger, thinking I'd have just enough time to polish it off before she arrived. I had a hunch that Lavinia might be a vegetarian. Even if she wasn't, I'd recently developed a kind of irrational guilt about eating meat in public. And I didn't doubt that given twenty years or so, meat eaters would find themselves banished, along with smokers, to the back alleyways of office blocks, the two groups taking either furtive drags of their fags or discreet bites of their burgers.

Actually, Lavinia didn't eat anything. Over a pot of herbal tea she told me about her pets, however, which included a tame crow, so getting the burger out the way was probably a good move. Birdlike herself, perhaps a bit nervy, though also possessing a self-contained inner resolve, Lavinia had only been doing stand-up for a year or so. Though as Toby had indicated, she did indeed do a lot of other things besides. These things included robotics, clowning, physical humour, short-story writing, adaptations of novels and radio drama. Stand-up for her was part of a much broader process, what she called 'the joy of ideas' and her ambition to discover suitable ways of constructing then expressing them. She had, for example, just secured Arts Council funding for a show which investigates the development of vocal chords using evidence from archaeological digs.

'So how does stand-up fit into all this?' I asked.

'It's a kind of doorway,' Lavinia replied, 'just one of the ways I have of exploring thoughts.'

'What about laughs? Do you, er, play your material for laughs?' I suspected she didn't.

'Not really. Quite often people *don't* laugh,' laughed Lavinia.

'Don't they?'

'No. I don't think audiences always know how to take me. I once did a gig at a football club. I don't think they knew what to make of me. I suppose I'm on the lunatic fringe of comedy. I'm most interested in the evolution of ideas, in the difference between things rather than their sameness. People are often scared to encounter new ways of seeing things.'

'Yes,' I agreed, 'they probably are.'

'And being on stage, doing stand-up, allows me to let stuff go, release material, so that I can then go on and get more.'

'More stuff?'

'Exactly. Stand-up allows me to squeeze things out, then absorb life again and again. Better than accumulating ad infinitum. In that sense, I'm a leaky sponge.'

'I can see that.'

We turned to talking about the gig at XSMalarkey and my

wider enquiries into comedy, my comedic quest.

'Toby's very good. It's a very friendly club. Toby is very protective of us all. He even tells people off if they heckle.'

'I'm glad to hear it.'

'He understands how difficult it is just to get up there and do it.'

'It is.'

'Even if you're no good.'

'Absolutely.'

Lavinia was currently writing a piece for *Flux* magazine about secret societies. For the same publication, she had also written a short story called 'The Adventures of the Unborn Embryo' which had begun life as a performance piece. In another show, she represented England as a musical instrument, its railway lines being strings on a sort of giant fretboard. When the Germans tell the English not to make so much noise, we refuse and they hit Ireland with a broomstick.

As you can see, Lavinia isn't a conventional stand-up.

'A lot of mainstream comedians are like balm,' she continued, 'they're mostly there to soothe, whereas I want to challenge. Even if people don't laugh, it's what I want to do.'

Though she was whimsical, even surreal, Lavinia was also refreshingly childlike, perhaps gauche, something at any rate remote from the hard-nosed, cynical world of stand-up. I suspect she survived not despite this removal but because of it. She recalled how one crowd had been so bewildered by her Björk impersonation that it had been stunned into flabbergasted silence.

I thought I knew her well enough by this point to risk a cappuccino. Between slurps, I twittered on about my own shamefully plain routine.

When I'd finished, she said, 'I'm sorry, but I can't make it tonight, but what you're doing sounds *lovely*. No sense of performance. I like that. A bit Dadaist perhaps?'

'A bit dull,' I said.

After lunch, or at least my lunch, we swapped email addresses, Lavinia's involving the name 'Balthasar Starr' (real name, Marc Henry), one of the so-called 'Eleven Executioners' who founded Munich's first cabaret in 1901. The Executioners chose blood-curdling names for themselves; Starr's translated as 'corpse-rigid'. On Friday 13 April, the cabaret's opening night, Starr had stood on a high step overlooking the orchestra pit and welcomed the specially invited guests by name. He and the other ten Executioners, dressed in blood-red gowns with slit-eyed cowls and yielding executioners' hatchets, then danced on stage, joined hands, and sang a threatening song which effectively damned the bourgeoisie.

Starr was one of Lavinia's heroes. Undoubtedly, he accessed the psychotic with a vengeance. If she was interested in this stuff, I doubted she would appreciate the mundane banality of my own routine. And if she thought I sounded a bit Dadaist, that was fine by me. Best let sleeping dogs lie, I thought.

After meeting Lavinia, I felt a little better about things. After all, if she could bend the rules and wasn't overly concerned with an audience's greed for glee, laughter for laughter's sake and so on, there seemed a fair chance that I might be tolerantly received as a well-intentioned aberration. Possibly as a break from the main action, a kind of 'chill-out' room in the otherwise relentlessly mirthful hedonism of contemporary comedy.

Well, it was a nice idea.

We said our goodbyes and I heaved my bag into the centre

of Manchester and booked in at a Travel Inn. The only room available was the disabled one, the sort with a sliding bathroom door, red cord by the loo and Olympics-specified arrangement of bars and handrails. I'd stayed in one before and it had disconcerted me. Still did. But at around fifty quid, it was a bargain.

Toby had given me precise instructions about catching the Didsbury bus which, I found, went directly past the halls of residence I had been so snooty about all those years ago. The driver told me where to get off and quite soon there I was, an hour early, strolling round the car park at Sainsbury's, going over my lines, talking to myself, making faces, and frightening the early-evening shoppers.

That still left half an hour or so before I'd arranged to meet Toby so I thought a quick look at the performing space wouldn't hurt. Might actually be quite a good idea. I quickly found a largish pub, right on the main road, which sported the XSMalarkey poster in one of its windows. I assumed the comedy itself would be performed in a cramped, probably smoky room above the main drinking area. That seemed to be the way things were done. A door close to the toilets suggested as much. I tried it but it was locked, so I asked one of the barmaids whether Toby had arrived.

'Not yet,' she replied. 'Should be in soon, though.'

'May I go up and look at the space?' I inquired politely.

'What space would that be?'

'The XSMalarkey space. The space for the comedians. I'm, um, performing tonight,' I added with conspicuous humility.

'Malarkey's? You're standing in it. There is no other space. The comedy's down here.'

'But this is a pub,' I said rather obviously.

'The comedians use that stage at the side.' She gestured towards a slightly raised platform in what was a dark and distant corner. It seemed a very long way off.

'How many people, would you say, usually come to see the comedy?'

'It's usually pretty full. It's the end of the exams as well. The students will be in to unwind.'

'How many is full?'

'Two hundred. Maybe more.'

I nodded, turned, felt sick, walked directly out of the building, and trudged back to Sainsbury's. Then I did what I always do when I'm facing a crisis. I took out my mobile and called Pippa.

'It's HUGE,' I cried, 'the size of a football pitch. BIGGER. The size of a fucking aircraft hangar.'

'Don't exaggerate.'

'I feel dreadful.'

'Don't do it then.'

'What do you mean, "Don't do it"?'

'You don't have to.'

'I do. You don't understand. I do.'

'No you don't. Nobody will mind. Say you're ill.'

'I'm not.'

'You said you were feeling dreadful.'

'Not that kind of dreadful.'

'But dreadful all the same.'

'Yes . . .'

'Well, there you are then.'

I muttered something about self-respect and rising to the challenge, then Pippa mocked me and I felt better.

'Should I say goodnight to Otto?' I said.

I heard her asking whether he wanted to say night-night to Dad.

'He says no thank you he's watching CBeebies. It's the bedtime hour. "Blue Cow's" on.'

It was the 'thank you' which hurt the most.

I cut my losses and wondered whether Toby had turned up yet.

When I arrived back at the pub, it was being emptied of drinkers and restocked with comedy drinkers. Some were shuffling to the exit merely to have their wrists stamped before turning directly round and re-entering.

Toby was in the green room, actually a small space isolated from the rest of the pub by simply placing a large club-style sofa across its invented access. We introduced ourselves and I shook hands with a compact, politely pugnacious, lightly bearded man of around thirty. In another life he could have been a boxer at one of the lower weights. He was also wearing a T-shirt showing that he'd recently been in the Caribbean watching cricket. As it turned out, we'd been at the same game in Barbados. Ice broken.

Like many comedians, Toby had originally trained as an actor and almost by accident found himself on stage one night doing a routine. Then he discovered he could make money at it, something that didn't seem so straightforward with the acting, and his course was set. As a comedy venue, XSMalarkey had started life as a free gig but Toby soon introduced a cheap door charge, more to train the audience to be attentive than for any financial reasons.

Gradually, word spread that this was a tolerant venue – Toby insisted that acts were given due respect – and soon the bigger names were using it, also drawn by the fact that there wasn't much work on Tuesdays, the traditional Malarkey night.

The rest, as they say, is history. XSMalarkey won Best Comedy Club in the north for three consecutive years and has grown by word of mouth as much as anything else. Toby bemoans the lack of media coverage that independent clubs achieve in comparison with the established big hitters. He struck me as an idealist or at least someone with a nose for achievable ideals, driven by the desire to give comedy and comedians of all kinds a decent platform. Thus, he attracts newcomers and experimenters as much as Perrier Award-winners. And while acting as MC, he is able to hone his topical, satirical material which he then uses in more main-stream gigs. Ruefully, he also recalled a grim period at Caffe Uno, when things weren't going so well at the club. Still, he hoped he'd cooked his last overpriced spaghetti carbonara.

By this time, XS was about two-thirds full. Some of the other performers had arrived and made their way behind the sofa where Toby greeted them. It was a busy night for him. The acts, me, his father, and also his never-seen-before German stepmother somewhere in the room. He indicated the running order he'd devised, and everyone nodded in agree-ment. 'Thought I'd put you on second, Steve. I'll warm the audience up. Then Demitris. Then you. OK?'

I also nodded, though distracted by a bloke I took to be Demitris who was pacing around with a piece of paper, waving his hands, memorising gags. It was good of Toby to put me on at all. Though he was preoccupied, I especially wanted to ask him about regional humour. Tonight, there would be no good time to ask, so I plunged right in. Happily, it transpired he had a bit of a bee in his bonnet about it.

'Audiences can be very parochial,' he said. 'I've watched very good London-based comics doing great material and be barely acknowledged. Then a northerner will come on and make quite ordinary geographical references that strike a chord and be met with gales of hilarity. On the other hand, comics shouldn't moan about regional bias – they can't very well *blame* audiences for not laughing, can they?'

Toby's anti-BNP stuff had not gone down very well in Blackburn and Oldham, both BNP heartlands. The crowds there had become very uneasy when he did it and he kept it short. 'But at least I wasn't set on fire. And I had the courage of my convictions – that, to me, is often more important than getting a laugh on a knob gag.'

The poet Simon Armitage once told me that any artist who wants to make a living must know his constituency. Whether you're a poet or a comedian, you should sense the mood of the audience, feel the pressure it exerts on you, and then give it what it wants.

Actually, he also remembered trying to do his poems without a book in front of his face, and immediately feeling uncomfortable because, suddenly, he, rather than the poems, became centre stage. Stand-ups, of course, don't usually have props. They're on their own. That's why being responsive to an audience is so important. There's nowhere to hide. So, all things considered, Toby did the right thing by reining himself in.

Anyway, by this time, all the other acts had arrived, four or five of them, I think. We endured an awkward though friendly enough all-in-it-together round of introductions. Demitris had come all the way from Gloucestershire. That made two of us and I made an unremarkable joke about the area being a hotbed of comedy, 'unremarkable' in the sense that no one else actually acknowledged it as a joke. Ashley Frieze, a youngish, fattish, balding man who had come from Newcastle, told me he was in computers and was taking his act to Edinburgh later that year. 'I'm an analyst – some people call me an anal-ist,' he guffawed, illuminating the moment with a threatening ear-to-ear grin.

Another Newcastle comedian was hanging around. He looked sinister and undernourished, a bit like the novelist Ian McEwan. Though he wasn't actually performing that night, he seemed very suspicious of me. In fact, Toby apart, everyone seemed a little edgy. Perhaps it was a competitive thing. Sizing up the opposition. Then someone else shook my hand, a large ginger-haired bloke with a black T-shirt who looked like he might be running the student bar. He would be on after me. The only woman in our group was a petite blonde, sitting quietly by herself. She wasn't exactly being unfriendly, just uncommunicative, intense, self-possessed and sort of simmering. Later, I'd discover there were very good reasons for this.

I attempted to ingratiate myself with Ian McEwan by confessing I'd only done one proper gig and even then had faltered badly in the early stages.

'Zoned out, eh,' he chuckled, and walked off to the bar.

By this time, I was starting to worry. Not exactly nervous, as such, though nerves were of course part of the problem, but experiencing a terminal, dull ache of dread layered with dollops of foreboding. XSMalarkey was now full of students. Young folk. When they saw me, an old lag, lumbering into the spotlight, surely they'd be expecting a wise old bird's expert hand on the comedy tiller. They were anticipating a masterful, effortless draining of the comic juices. They had finished their exams and quite reasonably wanted a reward. Wouldn't it be an irritating, anti-climactic, anger-inducing disappointment to discover they'd have to show tolerant forbearance towards such an obvious novice?

Oh well. Too late for all that now.

Loud music played and built to a crescendo. Toby sprung on to the stage carrying in one hand a pint glass filled with water and in the other a trailing fag. He made a topical and funny joke which linked Jimmy Hill's chin to racism and then a self-deprecating one about his eczema: 'And a word of advice to any girl who wants to sleep with me tonight. Girls, bring a DustBuster along so you can hoover your vagina afterwards.'

Demitris did ten minutes or so, fading a bit in the middle section but picking up again towards the end, then Toby said a few nice things about his dad before giving the audience its first warning of the night, yellow-carding it. 'My dad's in tonight. So watch your language. Show some respect,' he said solemnly. With that, he introduced me: 'Ladies and gentlemen, he's come a long way, it's his first time at Malarkey's, so let's give him a right rousing welcome – Steve Jacobeee . . .'

I walked towards the stage, pushing as politely as I could past those who were standing in my way. More loud music greeted my arrival – it seemed familiar but I couldn't remember who or what it was. Though I felt a jolt of adrenalin, this time I resisted the temptation to break into a bound. I took my time. I tried to play the moment, though in playing it I felt I was actually walking in slow motion, maybe even backwards. I made it to the microphone, took it from the stand and held it tight to my chest. I smiled inanely at the audience and waited for the mild commotion to subside.

Other comedians I've seen have tended to use an audience's

energy, surf its vigour. Whereas I actually distrusted it. A few people, I could see, were beginning to wonder whether I would start at all, probably thinking that I'd 'zoned out big time'. Then I did start, carefully, perhaps a bit more slowly than before but with what I liked to think of as assertiveness.

Once people realised I was unlikely to change up from this trundling, lowish gear, they settled back and listened. Then they laughed, more or less in the right places too. Pleasantly surprised, I made the mistake of easing off and, for only a few seconds, casting an inquisitive eye over them.

I'm not quite sure why I did this. Logan would have berated me for escaping the moment, or at least as much of the moment I was ever likely to be in. Maybe I was so relieved things didn't seem to be going badly that I momentarily lost the intense kind of concentration that usually attends fear. Perhaps, on the verge of giving myself to an audience, bending myself to its collective will and becoming a properly dedicated comedian, I drew back, reluctant to commit in case things went wrong. Sort of protecting myself from possible calamity.

Whatever. I drifted away from my routine.

I couldn't speak for the lot at the back who were out of my range and probably more interested in drinking than listening, but the ones I could see were quiet and attentive. Not exactly hanging on my every word, not rapt, but definitely paying attention. It reminded me of being in the classroom and having a more or less captive audience. I was faintly appalled. Perhaps, I remember the thought striking me, I've stumbled into a new area of comedy which taps into memories of being back at school. In a Proustian quirk of fate, maybe I'd ignited some sort of nostalgia for childhood. Without knowing it, I'd possibly acquired a schoolmasterly bearing which now flicked some switch in those who were until very recently still at school, in a sense still were.

It took about a second to process these thoughts.

In that time, I forgot where the fuck I was.

'I'm terribly sorry,' I whined, 'I've lost my place.' A few people laughed. 'No. Really. I have.' A few more laughs. Perhaps they thought it was part of the act. I collected myself, rewound a few lines, and started up again. No one seemed to mind, so I just got on with it.

The rest seemed fine. I could hear Ashley Frieze laughing fiercely at my good bits (especially the SS stuff and the lederhosen sequence) and sometimes even at the bits that weren't so good. He had emerged from the green room and was standing at the bar only about ten yards from the stage. My only regret was the Mr Whippy joke at the end. Too visual, I thought. Or too intimate in that room. Or too obscure. Or maybe too visual, too intimate and too obscure. At any rate, I did it meekly, replaced the microphone and then slunk off stage apologetically.

There was some decent clapping. Perhaps someone cheered, though in a packed pub of post-exam students someone at some point is bound to cheer. Ashley thumped me on the back as I made my way past him. I didn't actually know where I was going. 'Well done. Some golden moments there,' I heard him say. The green room hove into view and I reasoned it was as good a place as any to go. Once there, the other comedians seemed more willing to be friendly. They'd seen me. They understood I was not a threat.

Meanwhile, Toby was up again and revealing to the audience exactly how much of a novice I was. He asked for another appreciative round of applause and, on my behalf, received it. Then he introduced Ashley, whose act incorporated a guitar and parodic songs, mostly laments at the expense of old girlfriends. All the time, he worked hard, never letting the audience go, maintaining a rapport with his audience. And I thought, I couldn't do that. Never could I put myself so absolutely and nakedly on the line. Be so urgent and so generously determined to make an impression. Give so much of myself.

When he'd finished, Jo Dakin took his place. She was top of the bill. The quiet woman I'd seen earlier sitting pensively by herself. As soon as she started her routine, I understood why she had set herself apart. The loud, elemental, energetic, manically gauche, nearly psychotic woman she exploded into on stage, had needed time to build up a head of steam. Suddenly it seemed, though of course it wasn't suddenly – it had been going on since she arrived – Jo transformed herself into a neurotic cartoon of man-hating, frustrated womanhood. For twenty minutes or so she wrung an exhausting performance out of her fragile body, afterwards slumping passively at the bar wearing a slightly dazed expression. Like most good comedians, she gave a 'performance' which had little to do with acting. Though it was too solitary for the interaction and cross-stresses of drama, it was nonetheless gruelling and concentrated.

'Jo's just given up her job to concentrate on the comedy,' said Toby to the audience. 'The marriage guidance office will really miss her.'

Soon afterwards, at the bar, I asked Toby about this. I was intrigued by the idea of people giving up jobs for comedy and at what point such decisions were made.

'It was a joke,' he said.

'About the marriage guidance? Well, obviously I know that, but giving up –'

'The whole thing was a joke. It's what I do. I'm a comedian.'

'Ah. Right.'

'And you did OK, Steve. Big laughs from the comedians in the room. Always a good sign.'

He turned to Jo again and I wandered outside to call Pippa.

'How did it go?' she asked.

'All right. I think I got away with it. Not actually *good* though . . .'

'I got Otto to brush his teeth,' she said.

A couple of blokes came out of XSMalarkey and heard bits of our conversation.

'You were good,' said one.

'Really?'

'Yes, really.'

'Quick, tell her,' I said, and handed him the mobile.

He took it.

'He was good,' the bloke said.

Pippa said something back and he laughed.

'What did she say?' I enquired.

'Nothing,' he lied, and handed back the phone.

'See, and he wasn't even drunk,' I assured her. 'Or gay. Better go – I've got autographs to sign, a public to meet – you know the kind of thing.'

I thanked the kind man. 'I meant it. You had a nice presence,' he observed eloquently.

'A nice presence.' It was something. It wasn't even too backhanded. Toby told me you couldn't hope to make everyone laugh. Even if beery men in Bury or a hen party in Chelmsford wouldn't appreciate me, someone would. You could do your head in wondering why some people laughed and others didn't. In fact, the more you think about humour, the more elusive and pointless the thinking becomes. Of course it does. Like the old adage which says that any analysis of comedy is like dissecting a frog. Nobody laughs and the frog dies.

Actually, I'm not sure it is an old adage, but it's an expression Barry Cryer once used to me. Barry doesn't have much time with theories about comedy. 'If something is funny it's, well, *funny*,' he said. Mind you, he also suggested I might be all right as the regional bias in comedy wasn't anywhere near as strong as it used to be. As an example, he cited Ross Noble, whose charm and soft Newcastle accent could, he claimed, relate to anybody, anywhere, any time.

I, on the other hand, now knew, or thought I knew, or had at least persuaded myself, that I could be passably funny or not consistently unfunny in reasonably rarefied circumstances, i.e. friendly clubs mostly full of quite educated and/or civilised people who knew how to behave themselves or were told how to behave themselves.

Not quite Ross Noble, but it was something.

And I hadn't yet been heckled. I felt ambiguous about this. I didn't particularly want to be heckled but at some point in the future I felt I ought to experience it. After all, I wanted to do the thing properly and doubted I would ever feel like a proper comedian until I'd faced a bit of well-aimed malice. My quest required the full comedic experience, even heckling, maybe especially heckling, and I was nothing if not thorough. I couldn't say that XSMalarkey had been enjoyable, but neither had it completely unnerved me. Though words like 'pleasure', 'zeal' and 'relish' remained distant and possibly unattainable objectives, in due course, maybe they would happen. Early days yet. Essentially, I was still quest-driven; a stiffly over-educated bloke used to passing tests and rigorously schooled to believe in seeing things through. Besides, I had invested too much to consider chucking it all in, and in truth I hadn't yet experienced real discomfort.

Not yet.

Briefly, I wondered how my resolve would handle severe reversal.

It was something to ponder, but for now all I wanted was to get back to my disabled room and sleep. All that nervous energy had left me feeling exhausted.

I caught the number 42 back to town and spent a restless night being kept awake by the boozed-up clubbers directly outside my window. I didn't fall asleep until three, partly because of the noise, though also because my mind was racing.

One of the things it raced about was Blackpool. Originally, I had planned to take an excursion there, though such a trip now seemed less appealing. My performance was over. I was pooped. It would mean another day on the hoof. And for the moment, I was tired of comedy – doing it, thinking about it, talking to people about it. Blackpool could wait.

I had been there once before, in the mid-1960s when I went with my father on a business trip. I used to travel with him quite often. For the Blackpool jaunt, I'd have only been eight or nine at the time. The routine was that he dropped me off for two or three hours and gave me a couple of quid. While he completed a round of appointments with high street jewellery shops, I liked to look at the sights and wander around empty football grounds. I liked going on these trips, especially if I could wangle a stay in an expensive hotel.

Blackpool was a double whammy. While Dad tried to flog

some of his jewellery, I found the football ground at Bloomfield Road then made my way up the Blackpool Tower. I remember taking the lift and literally bumping into Jimmy Clitheroe, at that time starring on early-evening Saturday telly in *The Clitheroe Kid*. Jimmy was an adult who looked like a child and played the part of a schoolboy always getting into scrapes. It was the first time I'd encountered anyone from the (for me) glamorous world of television, unless you counted the Christmas card we received every year from Barney Bamford, a TV presenter who sometimes introduced reports for the local arm of the BBC

In the flesh, Jimmy was both fantastic and frightening. So, overwhelmed was I by the experience, I fled the Tower as quickly as I could. Possibly it was this memory of him that had tempted me back. A ghost to exorcise. Unfinished business. A more likely factor was the 1995 film *Funny Bones* which had been set in Blackpool. On its release, this imperfect, ambitious, thoughtful movie had completely fascinated me.

Funny Bones is that rare thing in English cinema, a film of ideas. Specifically ideas about comedy. In it, a successful veteran comic (played by successful veteran comic Jerry Lewis) argues that there are two types of comedian: 'One is funny, the other tells funny.' The bummer for Lewis's son, Tommy – whom the film follows from Las Vegas, where he 'dies' on stage in front of his father and other luminaries, to Blackpool – is that he is neither type. He's just not funny. He hasn't got funny bones.

It's in Blackpool that Tommy hopes to buy material from the sort of comedians who inspired his father's early career. He views comedy as a commodity instead of something that springs from the lives and personalities of its performers. Jack (played by Lee Evans) is Tommy's half-brother, or Lewis's Blackpool laugh child. And Jack is as naturally, anarchically funny as Tommy is dour and defensive. Somehow, Evans is both hilarious and disturbing, and therefore at the heart of the movie's comedy and its argument. When a psychiatrist examines him about his deranged behaviour and asks him if he's lived in Blackpool all his life, Evans replies, 'Not yet.'

Blackpool was the right setting for the film, too. With its tacky beaches, sex, pubs, clubs, chip shops, kiss-me-quick hats and 'laffs', the place implies low comedy, the permissive populism of music-hall smut, survival laughter, what some people call the 'humour of necessity'. The kind of comedy that's required for those living on the edge.

It used to be a class thing, I suppose, using ugliness and vulgarity to help forge an identity, to fight back the smothering blankets of refinement, the pale levels of good taste. Blackpool was and probably still is a bubble of romantic tawdriness. The sort of place which permits the worst of us to come out for a holiday, the worst that Orwell identified as the 'lazy, cowardly, debt-bilking adulterer who is inside all of us'.

What sort of issues did *Funny Bones* raise? For a start, personal ones. Was I funny or did I tell funny? Easy answer. On the evidence thus far, I reckoned I told *quite* funny, though the telling was probably at the lower end of the telling scale. I certainly wasn't *funny*. Not many people are, mind you. But neither was I not funny, or not completely not funny. On the other hand, and on any given night, I could probably slide easily enough into being not funny. If I was a share issue, I would be a solid but unspectacular earner. Not blue chip. But not a huge gamble either. Over time you'd earn back your money on me, plus a little bit.

And what of places? If Blackpool was an appropriate setting for this enquiry into humour at the (literal) edge of things, what sort of comedy is conjured by other towns? Slough, Glasgow and Liverpool, for instance? And London, Bristol and Brighton? A recent newspaper article concluded that Lancashire is our national humour centre, asserting, 'A gentle breeze blows through the county, producing a whimsical people given to flights of fancy.'

Does the place make the comedy, or does comedy characterise the place?

A friend of mine, a comedy writer called Bernard McKenna, thinks humour is often more regional than national. For him, places and cultures make the comedy. Jewish humour, for instance, born out of adversity and traditional storytelling, and with a delivery that's to die for. The same for Scottish humour – though being a Scot himself, I suppose he would say that. Thus, he believes someone like, say, Jasper Carrott is more Brummie than English. And Peter Cook, with whom he worked a great deal, was 'very much an Englishman who could never do comedy without an accent – either he exaggerated his own and was a toff or, and more usually, he did northerners, cockneys, Germans and so on.'

Maybe Englishness is too diverse and complex a concept to properly embrace a unified idea of comedy. 'Even the Pythons,' Bernard observed, 'so often regarded as being zany and English, are only four parts English. They were also one part Welsh and one part American.'

Anyway, I probably wasn't going to Blackpool. So stuff it. But what of Manchester? Despite all the regeneration there's still a rawness about the place, and not only in the nightlife. On the one hand it exclaims loudly against gentrification while on the other it seems happy enough to embrace its comforts. I suspect many English cities are like this. XSMalarkey, I concluded, was precisely at this tense crossroads. Toby Hadoke was politically aware and saw his humour as a force for enlightenment. He was a stickler for respect and politeness, and said 'vagina' rather than 'cunt'. The club could host Lavinia Murray's cerebral comic experiments. It could also give someone like me ten minutes of stage time. But there was still an undercurrent. Toby worked hard to achieve a charged but controlled atmosphere. The club flirted with aspects of high and low culture.

That night, I recalled, he had admonished the audience for talking too loudly, not paying attention and even for clinking beer classes. A chap with a goatee had dared to exclaim aloud during one of the acts and thus became the origin of a Batemanesque caution from Toby: he became 'The man who shouted out in the middle of a comedy routine at XSMalarkey!' Mind you, someone once tried to punch Toby while he was on stage, so you could understand the readiness with which he quelled any sign of uprising. And I couldn't say that I was anything less than bloody grateful for his protective philosophy. I doubt I could have performed in the north twenty, even fifteen, ten, years ago. Not without being duffed up, anyway.

The clubbers on the street outside my room finally went home, or wherever. My mind stopped racing and I slipped into a deep but shortish sleep. I had about five hours of it before I woke up and decided to find an Internet café. The man behind the desk at the Travel Inn wasn't English and therefore knew just the place. He was a regular user, keeping in touch with his family in Mali. A sign of the times was that the machines were actually located inside an estate agent's which also sold coffee and pastries. I had two of each. I also flicked through the local paper which devoted a page to Madonna's forthcoming visit to Manchester and estimated the chances of bumping into her apparently biggest fan, Bernard Manning. 'I'm a big fan of her,' said the seventy-five-year-old comic. 'She's a lovely lady. We met at Marco Pierre White's restaurant, Mirabelle, and she said she liked my jokes and enjoyed my show.' Of course she did, Bernard. The paper also said that if macrobiotic Madge got peckish, she could pop into the Eighth Day shop and café on Oxford Road, 'which serves vegetarian and vegan cuisine'.

You see my point about Manchester having it both ways.

Before heading back to Gloucestershire, I'd arranged to pop in and see Jim Poyser at the BBC's Manchester headquarters, actually less than a hundred yards from the Internet café. We don't see that much of one another, Jim and I, but we stay in touch and have things in common. Cricket and comedy, for starters. He writes and directs comedy, sometimes for the Beeb, sometimes not. He can also be very quick. On our first collaboration, an afternoon play for Radio 4, I had one of the characters say, 'Dad was in such a good mood that he felt it was time to break open the marzipan.'

'Better be careful with that one,' said Jim.

'Why's that?' I asked.

'Could be construed as gay slang,' he explained dolefully.

You know your words are in safe hands when you hear things like that.

Jim was in the middle of recording a comedy series called *1835*, the daringly titled follow-up to the acclaimed *1834*. Broadly, it charts the progress of a hapless aristocrat called Belport and his sidekick Ned in their attempts to find things to occupy themselves with in 1830s London. Thus, they do things like joining the newly formed police force, going to the music hall and getting involved in industrial action on the new railways.

Though Jim has written the material himself, he is not shy of self-criticism and when something doesn't work, changes the lines accordingly. 'Sorry,' he tells the actors, 'spot of bad writing there. Give me a minute.' He is clearly most interested in the structure of jokes, of finding the best ways of getting to a laugh.

Though it does plenty else besides, Jim's script is also littered with double entendres. The crew in Studio 3 cracked up every time it was revealed that the object of Belport's affections, a bad music hall singer, had her knockers.

I wanted to draw Jim into my comedic quest, get his input, so to speak, and thought the best time to do this would be over lunch. In the canteen, we both had a roll and a fruit salad, though it turned out we both wanted something different. The fruit was just a new-man thing. 'I fucking hate fruit salad, don't you?' Jim said. Then he told me that he'd always had an obsessive thing about comedy. During his Mancunian youth he had memorised whole sections of British and American comedy programmes. He was sidetracked by serious literature at university and wrote what he calls 'a rather grim novel', only returning to comedy as a writer in his later twenties. 'Comedy is a serious business and no mistake,' he said. All the really good people he's worked with, including Griff Rhys Jones and June Whitfield, and me of course, are virtually teetotal, very focused and extremely intelligent. He longs for someone he admires to turn up late and pissed and not knowing their lines. But it just doesn't happen.

'On the other hand,' he suggested, 'I probably drink too

much strong Continental lager. It's not the best way forward.'

I thought back to the Herculean drinking of the Great Vance and George Leybourne. Also to that of Les Dawson, another local lad, whose career fumbled badly at one point, partly due to booze. I'd passed his plaque at the door of the Palace Theatre that same morning while walking to the Internet café. His sidekick in the famous gossipy women sketch 'Cissie and Ada' was Roy Barraclough, and he was playing the puritanical Uncle Danvers in *1835*. I'd been sitting barely ten yards from him for most of the morning.

'Very brave,' he'd said when I introduced myself to the actors and told them I was in Manchester doing stand-up.

'I used to do stand-up,' said another, '*very* competitive. They'll do anything to get laughs, most of them at any rate. I used to go on after a man who put a lighted firework up his arse at the end of his act.'

'Dysfunctional lot, stand-ups,' said a third, 'no offence meant. Mostly, they hate people. It's about bullying an audience, isn't it? That and getting something off your chest.'

The BBC has recently set up something called the Manchester Comedy Unit, in an attempt to bring more television production to the regions. London still has a stranglehold on commissioning and this initiative is seen as a way of either breaking the monopoly or casting the net wider. It depends how you look at it. Probably where you live. Jim, though, is sensitive to the notion of a large, state-run bureaucracy like the BBC effectively nationalising comedy. It is, he tells me, no coincidence that shows like *The Office* and *The Royle Family* were created and developed independently, long before the BBC got involved. That they found national audiences is a matter of taste rather than administration or packaging.

Comedy has long since burst its regional banks. I thought Toby Hadoke's moderated routines at noted BNP outposts didn't really demonstrate that parochial humour still flourished, rather that it existed but in a ghettoised form. The same with Blackpool's pickled sentiments. The north might still be a different country, but it also has Harvey Nicks, loft apartments and political correctness. Halifax is a plc. The electrified east coast line has turned Wakefield and Bradford into commuter towns. Four-by-fours and Jeeps prowl the Pennines seeking the best schools. The north is an old face wearing new glasses. Social and demographic developments have refined humour and made anachronistic curiosities of its more extreme symptoms.

I asked Jim my favourite question, at least the one I seemed to be asking everyone in Manchester, i.e. if he had any thoughts about regional humour. After all, he'd grown up in Manchester and had a soft spot for the gag-led humour of the sixties and seventies. He didn't have any thoughts, as it turned out. Not really. 'I'm afraid I don't have much to say – except to say I like writing for the Manchester accent as it lends itself to arguing and I think there's a lot of comedy to be had from good-humoured argument.'

I passed Les Dawson's plaque again on the way to the station. What would he have made of it all, the man who temporarily went out of fashion for making rude jokes about overbearing mothers-in-law? When he died of a heart attack in 1993, the *Sunday Times* observed that his passing was almost the end of the line for the English tradition of working-class, come-up-the-hard-way comedy. He was also, the paper said, nearly the last of the funnymen of the national service generation, one of 'the comics who are funny before they even open their mouths'. Funny, not tells funny.

In particular, Dawson was a funny man of the people, able to conjure up a lost world of northern austerity, rent arrears, ration books, old ladies carrying chipped mugs to the pub and (of course) affectionately ridiculed mothers-in-law. He was able to wring humour from any situation. The more unpromising the circumstance, the more likely Dawson was to be able to find a bolt of comedy in it. 'My wife's gone off with the man next door,' he once admitted. 'Ooh, I do miss him.'

Although his forte was often thought to be in the exaggeration of familiar music hall jokes, he gave new life to the clichés of northern comedy with his infectious wordplay and love of language. Those clichés no longer exist or have been pushed to the margins. It's the kind of thing he might have written about in one of his novels where he sometimes revealed pride in an England now vanished. Or at least in the vanished kind of place where northern mothers-in-law were a different breed from the genteel, middle-class ladies from the south, some of whom had mothered the young Oxbridge and university-educated comics of the eighties and nineties.

The plaque, I thought, is certainly a way of memorialising Dawson but also of politely putting him and his kind safely behind us. This is a cause neither for regret nor celebration. It just happens. We are intimately and at all times connected with our past – with past life and (indeed) with past humour. It's just a matter of seeing it. Only four hundred yards down the road, Roy Barraclough was still going through his lines in Jim Poyser's radio comedy. In 2003, the Manchester Comedy Festival inaugurated an annual Les Dawson Award for Services to Comedy. In the same year, Ted Robbins' tribute show, *Ted*

Sez Les, took on the subject of the mother-in-law joke. Performing these gags at the Comedy Store, he remarked that life had come full circle.

EIGHT

Cheeky Monkey

I'd had to do a bit of talking to worm myself into the Birmingham heat of Channel 4's *So You Think You're Funny?* competition. There were about twenty other heats scattered through the country. Lucky qualifiers would be heading up to Edinburgh for the semi-final in August. Dylan Moran was a previous winner so it was obviously a jolly good thing. Well worth the winning. Or well worth the winning if you wanted to win and wanted to become a comedian.

Which I didn't. Much

At first, and naively so, I thought the very idea of a competition for comedy wasn't especially apt. Aspiring comedians going head to head, trying to outdo one another, trying to be the funniest joker in the pack. Being a purist, I wanted to believe proper humour didn't work like that, couldn't be so nakedly adversarial. But, of course, when you think about it, it is. Quite a lot of comedy is about scoring points, putting one over on somebody, being the cleverest dick. So maybe a competition is comedy's natural milieu.

Not for me, obviously, but for others.

Other AmusedMoose alumni were already battle-scarred veterans. Their emails told depressing stories of being 'gonged' or 'belled' off the stage, or sometimes being heckled off by fiercely partisan audiences, or just being victimised by spiteful, foul-mouthed judges.

So when I called up Julia at Channel 4 to ask whether I could be fitted in somewhere, I was apprehensive. I also explained I didn't necessarily want to 'compete' in the literal sense of the word.

Actually, it sounded rather weedy.

'I don't expect to get through,' I said, 'but even if I did, I don't want to.'

'You don't want to go to Edinburgh?'

'Not really.'

'Why not?'

'I don't think I want to be a comedian. Well, not in the long run. I like watching – but watching from the inside.'

On reflection, this sounded rather pervy, so I told her about my comedic quest.

'I see,' Julia said, though I could tell she didn't see at all. 'I'm not sure you can be in the competition if you don't actually compete,' she continued.

'I promise I'll do the best I can,' I pleaded.

'How about if you're obviously good enough to go to Edinburgh?'

'. . . which I won't be . . .'

'. . . if you're obviously good enough, then you go to Edinburgh. But if it comes down to a choice between you and someone else . . .'

'. . . someone who wants to be comedian . . .' I added helpfully.

'. . . then on that basis, we wouldn't take you to Edinburgh.'

It sounded very reasonable and on that understanding we struck a deal.

I had asked specifically for the Birmingham heat, which would take place in the Cheeky Monkey comedy club at the Station pub in King's Heath. This is about three miles from the city centre. I knew the place well, had in fact grown up only four miles away. I was even able to conjure a picture of the pub, opposite the local library, close to the police station, and a short walk from the sports ground where I'd once played rugby for Moseley 3rd XV. It would be a kind of homecoming. This familiarity would also help me test my theory about the importance of 'place' in relation to comedy. Not really a theory. More a hunch. And maybe not a very original hunch, but still one worth thinking about.

In addition, I knew the whining Birmingham accent was the inspiration for the Australian insult, 'whinging Poms'. And before the war, 'Made in Birmingham' was the recognised trademark for shoddy, mass-produced goods. It follows, supposedly, that the list of distinguished institutions and people who have sprung from this satanic 'cemetery without walls', as it was once known, is not long: the Repertory Theatre, King Edward's Grammar School, Neville 'Peace for our Time' Chamberlain, and the comic geniuses Sid Field and Tony Hancock. When Kathleen Tynan recalled the first glimpse of her future husband, the dandyish theatre critic Kenneth Tynan, she said, 'Aesthetic, tall, appealing. I was riveted because you didn't see people like that in Birmingham.'

By common consent, England's 'Second City' is precisely that – second: second class, second-rate, second division. It's one of the anomalies of 'new millennium-style inclusive PC

Britain' how much of it *doesn't* include the Brummie accent, which still operates as a convenient trigger for mock revulsion and chronic merriment whenever it is heard on television or radio.

Which isn't very often.

Any number of Scousers, Geordies, cockneys or Scots can make their way in the national media by effectively having nothing more substantial to offer than a regional accent. But you'll never find a Brummagen accent reading the news or hosting a game show. To my knowledge, no one from the Second City has even appeared on *Big Brother*.

My thinking was that Brummies were a contrite, self-deprecating lot whose humour was based largely on the cheerful enough understanding that they were a bit crap. 'Crap', granted, but what the hell, you had to laugh, and thus, 'cheerful'. Genial and annoyingly enthusiastic, unless of course you also took a fatalistic attitude to being second-rate, in which case you become Eeyore, i.e. gloomily doom-laden, though still gloomily and *amusingly* doom-laden.

According to this theory, Brummies should be more than capable of having a laugh at their own expense. On the other hand, like Manchester and many other places besides, Birmingham had recently been regenerated, and I wondered whether this gentrification would countenance appropriate adjustments to the city's sensibilities, its civic ego and, therefore, its humour.

As I write, the newly rebuilt Bull Ring has just opened. The old one was completely and self-consciously flattened, thereby removing one of the principal causes of derision and starting the healing process. However, the city's true rejuvenation was begun a few years ago with the construction of Brindley Place.

This is a partly canalside, almost wholly pedestrian development near to the city centre whose cafés, restaurants, pub, bars and clubs are cannily positioned to exploit the never-ending stream of name-tagged trade provided by the NCC, the largest conference venue in Europe.

But Brindley Place is entirely fake. Much of it is a grim anthology of pastiche bistros and pseudo-brasseries and cosmetic down-to-earthness. Every undesirable high street chain has a branch down there. 'McDonald's for the waged,' as someone put it. All this was new or newish and entirely in line with what was happening elsewhere. So naturally I wondered whether the overweening influence of the briefcase-toters, the shufflers, the play-makers, the Rollieflex flickers and all the other faking stoats and weasels would have any bearing on my assumption that Birmingham used to be full of self-deprecating, relentlessly sunny losers.

Did Brummies, in fact, take much note of these changes? Had they created a stirring of municipal pride? Or did people just use the facilities to get pissed and treat themselves to an omelette and *frites* at Café Rouge?

I had more or less a whole day to kill before I needed to be at the Cheeky Monkey. And what's the first thing you do when you're back on your old stamping ground and hot on the trail of comedy?

The first thing I did was go back to my old school.

Actually, there's a good reason for this. An old school friend is working there, in senior management, so I pop in to see him when an opportunity presents itself. He's called Richard, or rather he is now. At school, he was just 'Rick'. I've never quite got to the bottom of the change, assuming that it was something to do with adulthood. It's quite possible he now hates 'Rick', maybe has always hated it, his 'Rick-ness'. Still, I can't manage 'Richard', never have done, so we end up having telephone conversations which start with him saying, 'It's me, Richard,' and me saying back, 'Oh, hello, Rick.' It's not ideal, but we manage.

Anyway, Rick and I were not merely in the same year group, but almost always in the same class and often in the same lessons. Count the hours. How much time must we have spent together since we were eleven? We both did English and history at A level, both read English at university, both became teachers, both taught in Singapore at the same school and at the same time, and both became heads of English departments at the same time. We also played a lot of cricket and rugby together. Just as important, we shared the same tongue-tied hopelessness at speaking foreign languages, were both crap at singing and both danced like Stephen Hawking. Apart from me, Rick is the only person I know who couldn't pogo. I suspect we've actually forgotten whether or not we actually like one another. It doesn't much matter. Our relationship is ineluctable, having survived all manner of disagreements, arguments and even a punch-up. Now, our lives seem so adjacent that when I was unemployed and the marriage to my practice wife broke down, he was immediately worried that his own life would soon be in similar turmoil.

And three years later, it sort of was.

At any rate, Rick's now back at our old school – which must be a bit weird. I parked up near the chapel and set off gamely towards his office knowing, of course, exactly where it was. At the end of one corridor there used to be a single step down, or there was twenty-five years ago, and my pre-programmed legs instinctively remembered what should happen and made the appropriate knee-jerk adjustment. Like many differently abled/unfriendly steps in England, however, the step has been ramped over, and I stumbled forward awkwardly, almost executing the perfect pratfall.

I commented on this to Rick when I saw him a few moments later, the semi-jocular point of the story being something to do with the unfathomably deep-rooted spell that school casts over us. 'Yes,' replied Rick, 'so just think what being here is doing to me. Every day. Every week. Every year.'

I wanted to talk to him about my stand-up and about comedy in general. He didn't necessarily know much about comedy clubs but he did know about me. So we walked out of school, past the multi-storey where I had once thrown snowballs at passing cars and been caned for my efforts by 'Ernie' Halstead. Past the petrol station where on Saturday nights I would put a gallon of petrol in dad's car and from the tendered one-pound note still have enough money left over for three pints. Past the sports shop where I bought my first jockstrap.

Happy days.

Rick and I found a café and ordered two 'Massimo' lattes, though for some reason we passed on the chocolate muffins. It was seasonally warm outside, so we found an empty table and sat down. It was at times like this I found myself wishing I smoked. Two blokes chatting over coffee in the sunshine, two blokes being intense and smoking fags. It could have been so Mediterranean. It might have looked sexy, even in Solihull. Even sitting opposite Boots and Next.

But Rick and I weren't sexy. Not very. We've had our moments, but they were few and far between and in the main occurred untold years ago. There have also been many embarrassing moments, and we knew about those as well.

Though we might not agree, this kind of familiarity made it very hard for either one of us to deceive the other. If he thought even for a moment there was a possibility of me being shit at stand-up, he'd be the one to tell me.

'Surely you're shit,' he said.

'You haven't even seen me.'

'Well, are you?'

'Pretty much. Not *absolute* shit. But pretty shit.'

'Thought so.'

We gossiped contentedly about the difference between comedy and humour, the sense of communal laughter being a delightfully public form of reassurance, and England beating New Zealand at cricket. Then there was much mutual head nodding about the thin line which separated tragedy from comedy, Rick citing Mercutio's dying speech in *Romeo and Juliet* as a good example of this. At least the dying speech in the video of Zeffirelli's *Romeo and Juliet*, a godsend to all English teachers as it takes up a whole week of classroom time, which has Mercutio announcing that he is a 'grave man', his friends laughing because they think it's a prank, then Mercutio dying, and finally his friends not laughing.

We also ordered another 'Massimo' each and chinwagged about national humour. I said I doubted that received wisdom about things like English irony and understatement were true. It was just too neat and uselessly generalised. Rick, though, thought there was something in it, arguing that irony was often a reflex of post-imperial culture, hinting at paradox and uncertainty, even doubt about its future direction. On the other hand, he said that newer cultures, cultures that looked forward, were less ironic, e.g. the United States, Australia and, er, Singapore.

'But Singapore doesn't have any comedians,' I countered.

He faltered, momentarily, then snapped back, 'My point exactly.'

And I remember thinking for a moment or two, he's right about this. As a country we've withdrawn from empire, and as the children of that lost empire, we're all children of diminishment. We're culturally aware of faded aspiration and so whenever we do hanker after anything, or even dream about it, we're embarrassed by it. Probably embarrassed to have aspirations at all. 'We've had our day in the sun,' we seem to be saying to ourselves, 'now get over it. Move on.' Individually, we're pocket imperialists regulating a colony of one, so of course we're abashed and disconcerted; hence irony.

So there we were, two middle-aged old school chums, sipping large milky coffees not four hundred yards from our Alma Mater, chatting about comedy. Naturally, Rick and I also share a similar self-deprecatingly doom-laden sensitivity for the frequently bizarre, managed restlessness of lives. The old school probably has some influence on this, too. Public schools, even major minor public schools, tend to be good at fostering an awareness of one's faults which can then be explained away as merely being part of a wider grotesque.

Rick had a meeting with the headmaster or maybe a lunch duty or possibly both, so we finished up and made ready to leave.

Then, at the last moment, he suddenly asked, 'Can I come and watch tonight?'

It was a mischievous request.

'Absolutely not,' I replied, with unbending stoutness.

'Go on.'

'No.'

'Please.'

'No.'

'Why not?'

'Because nobody can come and watch. Nobody I know, at any rate.'

'Because you're shit?'

'Because I'm shit *and* I'm embarrassed about being shit. I'd be embarrassed if I wasn't shit but I am shit and being shit makes it worse.'

He laughed. Well, laughed in a mocking sort of way.

'It's about identity, isn't it? All this interest in English comedy and humour.'

I recalled my original aims: getting to know myself through comedy, etc.

'I suppose so,' I admitted, 'Englishness and all that.'

'Not just *that*. Your identity. Who *you* are. Where you fit in.'

As I drove off afterwards, towards Birmingham itself, I weighed up what Rick had said. The interest in Englishness and English comedy was indeed an indirect though significant aspect of my self-enquiry. When you considered the facts, it was obvious. My great-grandfather was German, apparently losing considerable wealth when he was on the receiving end of a land war in the nineteenth century. He fled to England, where my paternal grandfather was born. By blood, he was half-German and my father, born in 1919, a quarter. Coincidentally, he then married a German woman, my mother, who was seeking employment in England after the war. This despite him being possibly the most un-German person imaginable. He couldn't even speak the language. All this makes me, theoretically at least, more German than English. It's a conundrum at the heart of my stand-up routine.

I suspect it's also something that exercised my grandfather. My mother certainly would not have been in any plans he'd made for his son. At the very moment when my father went away to do battle with the Boche – actually fighting against his future father-in-law, though of course not knowing this at the time – my grandfather presented him with a book. I have it on the table in front of me as I write. It's called *Life Worth Living* and it's the autobiography of C.B. Fry, a man many considered to be the quintessence of all-round Englishness. He was a great cricketer, a distinguished academic, a journalist and the commander of a navy training ship. The book was published in 1939 by Eyre & Spottiswoode. It cost 12s 6d. The full title is, *Life Worth Living – some phases of an Englishman*, and there's an inscription on the first page. It reads: 'Dear Howard, C.B. Fry has had a very full life – and is a great Englishman, having "Played the Game" not only on the cricket field, but in many other walks of life – which have been beneficial to this England. I confess to a tinge of pride, that you too, are now doing "Your Bit" for the Old Country; and wish you a speedy and safe return to the normal activities of life. Your affectionate father. Xmas 1939.'

Although my grandfather aligned himself strongly with 'the Old Country' he could, I suppose, just as easily have lined up with the Fatherland. He wasn't very good at cricket, my grandfather, nor did he properly understand it, but he made a dogged and determined effort to embrace the game. When he pitched up at Edgbaston cricket ground in his eighties, I sat next to him while he dozed, often for hours at at time, occasionally bringing him a cup of tea and a sausage roll.

The thing is, he was resolved to be English. His unflinching allegiance must have been sorely tested when my father brought home a German woman and then married her. Worse, *her* father was in the Waffen SS and for a time was even assigned to protect Hitler. While on duty, he had taken a photo of Adolf in civvies reading the newspaper. And I have that photo with me now as well, also on the table and next to C.B. Fry. It was originally in his SS issue photo album, which is suitably embossed with the dramatic and distinctive lightning-bolt insignia. That's upstairs somewhere. I don't often get it out. Though if I did, I'd soon be perusing a whole battalion of Ottos and Waldemars and Wilhelms.

The music hall was another of the ways in which my grandfather became a fully-fledged Englishman. He adored the Scottish music-hall entertainer Harry Lauder and would often sing his songs around the house. The connection went deeper than that as during one of his performances Lauder had singled out my grandmother for special attention. 'Harry and Nanna' became a sort of family joke. I can remember her being teased about it without even knowing at the time who Harry Lauder was. Lauder also provided the anthemic 'Keep Right On to the End of the Road' song which was adopted by Birmingham City and can still be heard ringing round the St Andrew's football ground.

Birmingham City was yet another of my grandfather's assimilation ruses. He may even have seen them play as 'Small Heath Alliance'. His relationship with football was much the same as it was for cricket; one of mostly uninformed enthusiasm. Ever willing, he once colluded in a letter my anxious grandmother wrote to my dad's school, asking if it was possible to use tennis balls when playing cricket. This disconnected dreaminess about sport was typical. He turned up, he gazed at the pitch and the players, he put in the hours. But he didn't know what the fuck was going on. Whenever we went to watch Blues play at St Andrew's and someone scored, he always stood up, looked about a bit and shouted, 'Who scored? Was it Summerill?' Summerill was for a time the only player's name he could remember. Before Summerill it was Vowden. And after Summerill it was Francis. He died before he could extend his repertoire any further, though on his hospital deathbed, determinedly English to the end, he did ask whether Francis had scored a goal, this time for England, I think in a game against Brazil.

Though my dad recalls him singing the odd tune around the house, he doesn't think my grandfather actually possessed much in the way of a sense of humour. Perhaps this was the unconsumed German in him, the Teuton's last hurrah. My father, on the other hand, does have a good, keenly developed sense of humour. Furthermore, it is classically, even parodically English; understated, ironic, restrained, apologetic, whimsical, somewhat absurdist. He grew up when music hall was in decline, his only trips being to old halls like the Hippodrome to see the big bands, briefly on tour to the provinces while their London venues were being refurbished.

My mother's comic sensibilities were equally stereotyped. As I indicated earlier, they were often sparked by a sharp sense of *schadenfreude*, being frequently coarse and sometimes crude. My own ungentle irony and tendency towards mockery and sarcasm are a neat alliance of both parents' styles.

I suppose it would be nice to say my comedy actually conceals an intriguing and fairly well defended inner melancholy, and that behind the laughter is the sad story of a complex man lacking in confidence who uses humour partly as a defence and partly as a way of gaining self-esteem. But it would mostly be bollocks. Though some of it might be true, probably is, it applies to most people, to a degree.

I did lead an odd childhood, odd for the most part because of my mother, but I don't recall being especially unhappy or hard done by. And the oddities only became apparent when I'd left home, when it was too late to do anything about it, so they can't have been very significant, or not decisively so.

Anyway, I was now on my way to Handsworth where my parents have lived since a ruinous bankruptcy in the mid-eighties. Much of the above was playing through my mind as I drove, taking the long way round because Dad had a chiropodist's appointment and didn't expect to be back until two at the earliest. Neither of them would be, as Mum would taxi him there, wait for an hour or so, then bring him back. He is now eighty-five years old and his various ailments don't permit him to drive. When Mum's looking the other way, he still asks me to get him another licence or smuggle him a set of car keys, or both. But it's all pie in the sky. His health means he won't ever get behind the wheel again. He can barely get into the car. Mum won't hear of it, of course, mostly for very good reasons, though I can never resist the feeling that for her one of the good reasons is simply withholding the keys, an act of malice which inevitably yields a warm glow of pleasure.

Handsworth is a poor, predominantly black and Asian suburb of Birmingham. Despite the council's attempts to improve the infrastructure, it remains down at heel and obviously shabby. Still, Mum and Dad have made the most of their lot. Over the years, she has badgered the council into providing a new roof, a new bathroom, a new stairlift, a new central heating system, and even a new downstairs ceiling. Despite all this, none of the house actually *seems* new. Such was the scale and scope of the bankruptcy, that the mortgage on the quite nice house in the suburbs (the one I grew up in) was only paid off about two years ago. This despite the bank seizing it twenty years ago. I don't imagine it's a good feeling to be paying good money for a house that you don't own and one in which you can't live.

I arrived at the Handsworth house and parked my car round the back. This is normal practice as anything on the road is regarded as fair game to opportunistic thieves. Years ago, I once had four tyres stolen from my Mini. Much later, when I invited him to the school where I was teaching to give a reading, I inadvertently discovered the thief was probably one of the country's leading dub poets.

Oh, how we laughed.

I walked up the drive, past the incongruously neat borders my mum still maintains. In among the plants and flowers were the Bambi figure and the plastic windmill she'd rescued from her father's house in Germany when he died more than twenty years ago. Mum answered my meaty thump on the door and immediately went into a story about one of the cats – one of the five or six cats, the numbers keep changing – which had been ill and sicked up all over the dinner service. The mess hadn't been effectively cleaned up, eggs were lain, and a few days later, when she opened a cupboard, around fifty fat bluebottles flew into the kitchen. She laughed while she told me this, then asked if I wanted a cup of tea.

'Er, all right,' I said, 'but not out of a cup that's had any of those eggs on it.'

'Right. Biscuit?'

'Just one then, thank you.'

I'd been suspicious of all food that came from Mum's

kitchen ever since she offered me a bar of chocolate which predated even the requirement to display a sell-by date.

We settled down in the front room, my dad already settled there because he didn't go many other places these days. He was watching one of the three television sets lined up in front of him and, because of his hearing or rather the lack of it, wearing a huge pair of Thunderbirds-style headphones.

'Is that a new car?' my mum asked suspiciously, looking furtively through the window. I thought I'd parked it far enough away not be noticed. Now there would be a probing interrogation about money and how I was spending it.

'Quite new,' I replied, 'though there's a nasty scratch. It was keyed along the side only two days after we bought it.'

I wasn't sure a seventy-five-year-old woman would know about 'keying', but reasoned that a) an explanation would soak up a bit of time, and/or b) it would anyway divert attention away from the newish car, and/or even c) she might feel a twinge of sympathy and therefore be less snooping about the money, but it would certainly d) allow her to complain at length about the delinquencies of modern society and maybe even to launch into her favourite argument for the return of hanging.

In fact, only a) occurred, even then not quite in the way I'd expected.

'I've done that,' she said.

'You've done what?'

'Keying.'

'You mean it's been done to you. You've been keyed?'

Actually, I doubted this, as anything of the sort would have been reported back in choleric, venomous language, probably with an appendix about the need for respect, in addition the need for someone like Hitler to instil it.

'No. I've done it.'

'What do you mean?'

'When I'm in the car park at Tesco's and see people who aren't disabled park in the disabled bays, I wait till they're inside – then I run my key along the side of the car.'

'You don't?!'

'I ruddy well do.' While she said this, she took out her car key, or at least some kind of key, and made a violent scything movement with her arm to demonstrate what she meant. Then she laughed. This, for her, was clearly a very funny thing to do. Mischief, damage and retribution, the Holy Trinity of my mother's comic world.

'How many times?' I asked.

'A few.'

'More than ten?'

She nodded.

I doubted whether my father had heard much of this, though he did stir, taking off his phones and asking me what brought me to Birmingham.

'Just to see a few people about something,' I replied obscurely.

I suppose it's shameful that I can't tell my parents about doing stand-up at the Cheeky Monkey, but it's just one of those things. Over the years, I've adopted the policy of never telling them anything which they might construe as disappointing. Or anything which might embarrass me. That doesn't leave much, but in the surviving though admittedly narrow connection which remains, we play out a relationship that more or less works. Part of me would like to be more chummy, part of me not. Whatever. At least my reluctance to share details of my comic journey spoiled the theory that I was only doing it because deep down I wanted to make my parents laugh.

Or maybe they did suspect something. On my last visit, I'd left early to talk with Ken Dodd, playing a date just down the road at Dudley Town Hall. Research, you see. I'd told them about that all right, though not its broader context. My dad guessed I was writing something, assuming it was a history of comedy or perhaps music hall. I didn't disillusion him.

When I'd arrived at Dudley, Doddy's assistant and long-term partner Anne Jones was preparing the stage. It was about forty minutes before the show began. She greeted me warmly and took me backstage where Ken Dodd was busy in front of a mirror, doing things with his hair, mostly tousling it, and applying make-up, making himself into *Ken Dodd*. He looks smaller, smaller and more rotund, than you'd imagine. And possibly older.

Though he was very accommodating, I couldn't help feeling that he was in charge. Completely in charge. Our chat consisted mainly of him talking in longish, relatively inflexible statements, and me sipping tea, asking the odd question and – well – listening. Anyway, everything on his terms. Maybe it was a habit derived from having to have command over large audiences.

I made a mental note: 'Establish supremacy at earliest opportunity.'

'Generally speaking,' he told me, 'I don't like acts where men get dressed as women . . . except for Barry Humphries when he's Dame Edna.'

'Why's that?'

'Because Dame Edna is a proper character. There's more to it than just getting easy laughs because you're a man dressed as a woman. Proper comedy isn't just using sex on stage. It goes deeper than that.'

Doddy, of course, doesn't resort to sex or bad language in his act. No easy laughs there. For the four or five hours he's on stage, he works very hard. Despite the surreal hilarity, a mildly puritanical ethic attends his performances.

'Beware the demon drink!' he warned me when I told him about my own stand-up plans.

'Oh, I'm not much of a drinker.'

'Not you. The audience. You'll have to battle with their alcohol intake.'

While we were talking, I looked round his dressing room. Dicky Mint – a sort of pint-sized alter ego that allows him to display his gift for ventriloquism, is neatly wrapped in a sheet of transparent polythene. The big bass drum he pounds is similarly sheathed, cues written on a scrap of paper and taped to its cylinder. A few tickling sticks lay underneath a chair.

When the great man flexed his mouth, the trademark teeth became obvious. Doddy chatted to me about his love for Shakespeare, his dislike of the cult of personality ('the modern disease'), his plans to establish a national archive of comedy to preserve the 'traditional' sense of humour and his determination to resist retirement.

Then it was time for him to go on stage.

'Sorry, Steve,' he announced, picking up a tickling stick and waving it round a bit. 'I have to go. Perhaps we could talk again . . . though only after you've been in front of a lively audience. Experienced The Fear.'

Those words came back to me as I left Handsworth. I knew a bit about 'The Fear' now and, momentarily, it made me feel oddly robust. I was, so to speak, one of the gang.

I reached the Station in King's Heath soon afterwards. It was still early, so I went for a walk down the high street and had half a pint of Stella and some pork scratchings at the Hare and Hounds. This used to be a folk-music venue, and in my wild days I remember seeing the Durham songster Jake Thackeray performing there, probably sometime towards the end of the seventies. Soon after that, the upstairs became a comedy club called the Four-X Cabaret, named after the sponsor, Castlemaine XXXX lager. I never knew whether it became 'comedy' at the expense of 'folk' or whether the two worked cheek by jowl, though each in their own ways were representative of the times which spawned them.

The Four-X Cabaret was not quite where Frank Skinner started out, but it was the venue which most helped to establish him as a stand-up of great potential. Every Thursday night for about two years he could be found there hosting other shows, finding his voice, building a reputation and, by all accounts, allegedly shagging lots of women.

I once saw him there and he performed very local, even parochial material that he knew would strike a chord with Brummies. A few years earlier, Jasper Carrott had done the same sort of thing, basing his early routines around funky mopeds, Reliant Robin drivers, the traumas of watching Birmingham City play football, and the dangers of the school-bus run through Moseley, barely half a mile down the road.

Before Carrott, there was Hancock, and before Hancock there was the genius of Sid Field, who like the others had learned to perform more generally accessible material, sometimes through recognisable 'types', keeping in check his Brummie origins, though at the same time reminding audiences whence he came. Apparently, there's something endearing about someone from the provinces being nationally appreciated but still being obviously provincial.

People are 'the same all over the place, in their own particular way,' Field once said, 'whether you find them in Balham or Birmingham. In London, I play Slasher [Slasher Green, a spiv and Field's most well-known characterisation] as a cockney, in Brum as if he was a local boy.' But even when he was being a cockney Slasher, he would remind an audience of his roots, enquiring politely to the members of the pit orchestra, 'And how are yooo to-day? R-r-r-reasonably well, I hoop?' Another way of doing much the same thing was to pronounce the name of the composer 'Shostakovich' in a broad Brummagen accent.

I had another packet of pork scratchings, finished my half, got up to leave the pub, and realised I felt slightly stewed. Woozy, at least. Pathetic, isn't it? On just half a pint of bloody Stella. But that's the way I'm made. Or maybe it's my metabolism. Sensing the peril, I tried to check through my lines – and couldn't. I'd decided to ditch the Mr Whippy joke and replace it with . . . well, what exactly? Couldn't remember that, either. Having eaten just a biscuit at my mum's and with a couple of 'Massimos' still swilling around inside me, I'd not had any proper food since last night. Desperately needing something to absorb the alcohol, I headed across the road to a small Indian restaurant, ordered a korma and rice, and then sat in solitary isolation waiting for the booze to work its way through and for my head to clear.

While it was clearing, I considered. Unlike comedians like Carrott, Skinner and Field, who made local reputations and then found ways of nationalising their product, I was doing things the other way round. I assumed the other competitors would be from Birmingham, or the West Midlands, playing before a Birmingham audience. I was a Brummie, too, though I didn't talk like one and hadn't lived there for over twenty years. I feared this would be a handicap. Probably a good excuse for some well-aimed abuse. 'Shuddup, yaow twat,' I could hear people shouting, with me wanting to reply, 'Look, I really am from Birmingham. I can't help it if I don't have an accent.' I'd recently read an article which said that one Birmingham suburb was the least gay area in the country. In my scrambled state, I half wondered whether I ought to alter my material and somehow accommodate this fragment of local knowledge, ingratiate myself, *connect*.

This anxiety, combined with my anyway nervous anxiety at what lay ahead, and further combined with the usual dull ache which was the familiar preamble to going on stage, now collaborated with the Stella and the korma, not to mention the pork scratchings, and in fact the free popadom and chutney, to form a debilitating knot of gastric dread in my stomach. My head was OK, just about and only OK, but the rest of me felt as if it was on the verge of a shuddering seizure.

I struggled to contain all this, more or less unsuccessfully, though several deep breaths were required and taken. Then I went through a routine of coughing and yawning, accompanied by some strange face twitching and a bit of gaping. The manager, acutely aware I was his only customer and obviously worried, came courteously forward and asked if everything was all right, which of course it wasn't, though I said it was and asked only for a glass of water.

I pulled myself together, paid the bill, and ambled the two hundred yards or so back to the Station. The comedy room, the Cheeky Monkey itself, was up a small flight of stairs and towards the back of the pub. To reach it, you went through a narrow corridor of no great length which was flanked by walls tiled with William Morris, or maybe William de Morgan, or at least some kind of nineteenth-century ceramic. Any hopes of Victorian grandeur these might have raised were quickly thwarted when I entered a low, squat, half-timbered, mock-Tudor room with Artexed walls.

Some of the other comedians were already there, huddled in a corner, with drink but not drinking, most looking anxiously at crumpled pieces of paper which they clutched tightly in their hands. They looked young, some very young, all anyway much younger than me. Except one, a woman of about my own age, who looked the most nervous of the lot.

'Hello,' I said, 'I'm Steve.'

'Hello,' she replied, and we shook hands. I forget the name she gave me.

'Done many gigs?' I asked. It wouldn't be many. I knew that. One of the competition's rules was that we should all be novices.

'None,' she said.

'A good time to start,' I said supportively.

'Not really. I'm only here to support him,' she said, and gestured towards an impossibly young boy to her left. 'I'm his mum.'

Soon enough, Julia from Channel 4 arrived with an assistant. In all, there were eleven competitors. Each of us would have eight minutes. After seven and a half, Julia (or her assistant) would flash a torch. We should not be on for much more or less than the stipulated time as it would harm our chances of making it through to the semis. Then we handed over photographs of ourselves, required for identification and discussion after the heat had finished. Finally, Julia wished us luck and announced a running order.

By eight fifteen, the Cheeky Monkey was more or less full. One hundred and thirty people, maybe a few more, maybe a few less; it was difficult to tell. The evening would be compered by Geoff, an established circuit comedian, and there would be two intervals. I was at number seven, the penultimate act before the second interval.

In the remaining few moments, I got talking to Annette, a lively black girl who lived in Handsworth, as it happened only a couple of streets away from my parents. She was distracted as her costume and props hadn't yet arrived. Then her boyfriend turned up bearing a cane, a wide-brimmed hat and a white trouser suit. As he handed them over, she told me he also lived in Handsworth, in fact right opposite Mum and Dad. I couldn't help noticing his car, a white Polo, which had a scratch down its near side, and I wondered if he had been one of my mum's car-park victims.

The audience had by necessity split itself into two distinct halves. Those towards the front had grabbed the seats and tables, seemed quite civilised in fact, while those at the back talked louder and, being closer to the bar, drank quicker. With dismay, I noted they were already rather boisterous.

Geoff began his warm-up routine, walking smartly out to the obligatory swirl of loud music. Straight away, he identified a nerdy-looking bloke in the front row as someone who might become the butt of his jokes. I think he was called Greg, and this Greg was wearing an England football shirt and sporting a pair of bookish specs. Geoff constantly referred to him as 'my friend', actually a phrase he repeated whoever he talked to, and an expression I immediately took against. In addition to disliking the phrase, I had the feeling that I also disliked or would come to dislike Geoff. I didn't know it then, but I was already preparing myself for this not being my night.

'And what's your name, my friend?'

'Greg.'

'And where are you from, Greg?'

'Sutton Coldfield.'

'And are you here by yourself, my friend?'

'Um, yes.'

'Any single ladies in tonight?'

Two women at the back said they were, one more loudly than the other, though both quite softly. Obviously they'd seen Greg and weren't too impressed.

'There you are, Greg – two lovely ladies for you, a bit on the quiet side, but it could be your lucky night. What do you say to that, my friend?'

'Very nice.'

'Come on, Greg. You can do better than that. One of the shy ones, are you?'

And so on and so forth.

I wasn't much enjoying any of this. They say the MC is important for working the audience, but what he says can also make a difference to the comedians. So already I felt out of place, not feeling for a moment as though I remotely belonged in the same room as Geoff or, indeed, any of his newly acquired friends.

Steady, I thought. Early days yet. Let's see how things go.

Craig was first up, a gay teacher who actually looked very like a gay teacher. His routine involved a long story in which he told his gran about being homosexual. Then Gary came on wearing a hat in the shape of a weight with the words '50lb weight' written on it. He immediately took this off and exclaimed, 'Well, that's a weight off my mind.'

Gary's act developed into a series of unlinked gags, most of them corny and involving convoluted puns. At other times, he fooled around with a number of props, including a stuffed cat and a *Clangers*-style flute, which he produced from under a billowing black cape. I didn't think he was particularly good, though he was certainly game. As what he did owed as much to variety as it did to stand-up, I immediately developed a tender, protective feeling for him. The audience, however, was distinctly restless. These days, as with ventriloquism, there wasn't much place for someone on stage working a puppet or using old-fashioned props. Not in the age of irony; not in the age of effects.

Annette was next up, and gave a loud, hysterically confident rant against mobile phones and dodgy children's television presenters, even overcoming a technical hitch when her music didn't work. I admired the relentless force of her performance, her panache and the colourful brow-beating of the audience, though the material, I thought, was a little stale. On the other hand, the crowd loved it. She'd even reached the beery lot at the back, who whooped and cheered throughout, and applauded wildly as she left the stage.

If I've overdone the details in the run-up to my act, it's only because I want you to understand the context of my evolving paranoia. Annette's act was the point at which I began to understand absolutely and with complete clarity that soon my own routine would sink without trace. From Annette on, I was merely contemplating the gallows.

Fighting against the message my senses had delivered, I tried to remain calm and think about the situation in a composed manner. Perhaps, I thought, my unease had something to do with the audience, which was entirely different from the well-wishers at the Enterprise or the celebrating students at XSMalarkey. This bunch had probably come directly from work. They were tired and bored. They wanted to be entertained and they wanted the comedian in front of them to put on a show, be easy on the eyes and ears, not make too many demands. Gay blokes with grannies, sassy women bellowing about mobile phones and television presenters. Recognisable types in discernible circumstances.

What they didn't want was effete knob babbling on about Plato and lederhosen. People like Jasper, Frank and Sid had developed ways of transforming their home-grown comedy into something that could be more broadly appreciated, making it BIGGER. I'm not sure comedians have to do this kind of thing any more, whether or not they can go straight on to telly and cut out the local clubs, experience of audience rapport and whatnot. Anyway, I realised I too had to find a way of doing it, of somehow cartoonising my restrained little soliloquy. And do it *right now*, for these people at this place in this town.

Yes. That was the way forward.

Though with alarm, I also realised I had no way of doing it. None at all. Obviously I didn't. No tools for the performance, you see. What I did was based on language, and though language could amuse and endear, had indeed amused and endeared in many places and at many times, it couldn't in King's Heath on a Tuesday evening. Mine was essentially a solo turn. Stephen Fry once pointed out that language could never come close to dance or song as a means of sharing an experience: '. . . in a culture like ours, language is exclusive, not inclusive. Those on terms with words are distrusted.'

I knew that as soon as I opened my mouth I would be perceived as being weird, a little outré, in old-fashioned terms, a bit of a wally.

So much for the homecoming. So much for the return of the prodigal son.

I was a dead man walking. I knew it in my blood and in my bones. And I'd reached the point where I was experiencing physical problems, nervously occasioned, bewildering jumps from constipation to the squitters, a churning apprehension, an anguished spasm of dismay. Also, I felt angry with myself for putting me in this position. For a moment, I was literally beside myself with anger. There was someone standing right beside myself who was in fact me, who kept shouting, 'Comedy! Comedy! How could you ever think you could do comedy?! You stupid, stupid bugger!' All the things I feared, or feared because I hated them, such as lawyers, bankers, sharks, jellyfish, lifestyle gurus, etc., rose up and were suddenly inside me, threatening to consume me, moving with irresistible purpose towards my vital organs. A snap of the liver here, a chomp of the heart there. Gobble, gobble, gobble. A guzzle at this, a gulp at that, until nothing was left. A comedic pig-out.

My end was nigh. Already, another act was on.

'Weirdo,' someone shouted from the back.

He was calling out to Dave, a smallish man dressed in a V-neck sweater and wearing a tie, a sort of poor man's Woody Allen, who delivered a routine based on his own sexual inadequacies and social incompetence. After an uncertain start, his recognisable, get-at-able type did well with the audience.

I retreated further into myself, a snail retracting into its shell.

The interval arrived and I trolled round the car park opposite the pub and adjacent to a furniture warehouse selling the kind of furniture I would probably pay to have removed from my house. I needed the air. I needed to pull myself together.

I can't say I feel calm at the best of times, calmness being an emotional and physical condition that's always eluded me. Nervous tension about what I did, my work, who I was, guilt for sins committed, dread about the fates and fortunes of those I care for, and I suppose dread about the fate and fortune of myself. This was my habitual, uneasy, cat-on-hot-bricks state. But curiously, at that moment, I could remember my routine, word for bloody word, with absolute clarity, better than ever before.

I went back across the road, inwardly churning, outwardly calm.

As before, I found my place at the back of the room. One woman, about thirty and wearing a red beret, had only just arrived and was busy talking too loudly to her friends. I'd forgotten how much I hated berets, adding it and her to my inventory of internal guzzlers.

Chris from Leamington was on, telling a story about how he taught his low-tech Chinese mother to operate a computer. Then came Matthew, a puny and obviously disabled bloke in his mid-twenties. And did he give us comedy which *didn't* rely on his disability? Did he fuck. Of course he didn't. 'I'm the only bloke I know who can go to the pub, get pissed and walk out in a *straight* line,' he jested, and the audience exploded with sympathetic applause. And laughter. Lots of it. The woman with the beret turned to her friend and said, 'So brave to talk about his handicap like that.'

Between every gag, each one making direct or indirect reference to his gammy legs, he hobbled forward to take a sip from a pint glass of beer or lager before hopping gingerly back and resuming his routine. The effect of this faltering manoeuvre was to give his performance some kind of rhythm (joke-shamble-drink-sip-shamble-joke) and also to render it as 'performance'. To see Matthew in action was to witness the living truth of Stephen Fry's words. By constantly reinforcing his impairment, he also drained the audience of its sympathy, exhausted its quota of compassion.

What hope for me, next on?

Matthew limped past me when he'd finished, and limped past to thunderous, raucous applause.

'Let's keep rolling right on,' said Geoff .

No warming of the audience, just me stepping straight into Matthew's space, Matthew's emotional vacuum.

I started my routine slowly, wary of an audience I already suspected was predisposed to dislike me. Though I gave probably the most faultless rendition of my material yet, it was delivered in a bloodless, almost defiant way. The audience, temporarily used up by Matthew, had nothing to grab hold of, no point of entry; no character, no warmth, nothing. Just words, hundreds of them, floating into the smoky mock-Tudor air, bubbling up and out the door, then along the tiled corridor, and out into King's Heath High Street for all I knew.

I wasn't a comedian, merely an awkward, distant, puzzling human being.

When I looked directly at them, which wasn't often, I saw they were contemplating me. I saw expectant, half-interested, half-baffled, half-baked faces. I suspect they were waiting for something to happen, another character 'type' to suddenly step forward and make it all right for them to laugh.

Naturally, none of this happened.

We remained staring at one another while the words continued to loop out of my mouth, a remote soundtrack to an unknown event.

In his 1974 novel about a washed-up cockney comedian who idolised Sid Field, the writer Brian Glanville has his main character say this: 'A great comedian's the most creative person you'll ever find. He's creating every moment that he's on his feet. He's sussing out the audience, gauging the temperature, changing his rhythm, cutting out some jokes, bringing in others, maybe ad-libbing. He never stops.'

Whereas I, of course, never started.

And still the words came out, in the right order, carefully sounded, but dejected, passive and, as far as the other people in the room were concerned, utterly incomprehensible. Bunkered down beneath layers of hardline irony, I didn't allow them to share the comedy. I *wouldn't* allow them to share the comedy.

Fuck them, I thought. Fuck him, they thought.

Some of them, I think, would have quite liked to laugh. Given a chance, they'd have warmed to me. Others, I'm sure, wanted to heckle. Given a chance, they'd have shouted very rude things indeed at me. In the event, I paralysed both camps.

The references to the SS and lederhosen drew quizzical expressions. The crack about the abortion clinic caused some to muster a sharp intake of breath. I bet myself that Beret Woman was one of them. Plato was ignored. The ironic criticism of my father was met only with stony-faced and no doubt disapproving silence. At one point, though I can't quite remember exactly which point, *I* laughed, but only because I felt it was polite and because someone ought to.

One hand clapping, as it were.

At the end, I did change the Mr Whippy joke to a verbal gag

which was like putting my finger in a dyke which had in any case burst. I grudgingly thanked the audience, reminded them of my name, and walked smartly off to the kind of applause most usually heard at the moment in old black-and-white movies when someone called something like Mrs Lotherington has just finished her talk to the WI about local flora and fauna.

I called Pippa.

'How did it go?'

'Not well.'

'Bombed in Birmingham, eh?'

'Not quite. More like stealth bombed. But, yes, still bombed, I suppose.'

'Heckled?'

'Nope.'

'Not all bad news then. Did people laugh?'

'Nope.'

'Not at all.'

'Not unless you count me.'

'I don't think we can do that, can we?'

'No. I don't think we can.'

I watched another couple of acts. One was a very young guy whose surname was Knobbs. He tried to make a number of politically correct though mostly mundane quips before, of course, falling back on a sequence of jokes connected with his name. Literal knob gags, I suppose. Inevitably, the audience also liked him. Then there was Christian, the second disabled comedian of the evening. I'd talked with him briefly during the interval, in the tiled corridor, and he seemed a thoroughly decent chap. Like Matthew, Christian also made fun of his handicap, starting with a joke which involved concealing his disabled badge whenever a traffic warden was lurking. Done in by Matthew, immobilised by me, warmed up again by Knobbs and drinking quickly as last orders approached, the audience was now back on best chortling and guffawing form.

MC Geoff was busy talking to effervescent Annette and nerdy Dave, telling them he could find gigs for them at local clubs, taking down their telephone numbers, their email addresses and no doubt calling each one 'my friend'. He caught my eye as I eased past him, not looking at me, not even nodding, making his point. You're about as funny as a rice pudding, I thought, so I don't care what you fucking think about me.

Before leaving, I asked Julia how long I'd been on stage. Previously, I'd timed my routine at around eight minutes; tonight, she informed me, I'd been on for seven minutes and nineteen seconds. Must have rushed it, I thought. While she was looking up my statistics on her clipboard, she carefully covered over the four or five lines of written commentary about my performance.

Terry Jones, the ex-Python, once told me that a comedian wasn't 'necessarily' a laugh machine. 'I'm not sure laughter and comedy need to be connected,' he said. 'People don't complain when they don't cry at tragedy, so why should they when they don't laugh at comedy?' For someone like me, this was a point very well made. Mind you, he'd also said that because laughter is essentially a self-conscious activity, perhaps even an unnatural one, it's important to create an atmosphere, a world, in which people feel at ease, where it's OK to laugh.

So I didn't score too many points on that one.

How did I feel as I left the Station? Older, fatter, balder, and shorter. I slipped anonymously into my newish (scratched) car and played Elgar at full volume all the way back to Gloucestershire.

For the next forty minutes, I gave myself to *The Dream of Gerontius*. It always works, though it could just as well have been Mahler's Fifth Symphony, Led Zeppelin or early Duke Ellington. Tonight it could even have been Status Fucking Quo.

It had been a bad night and I was in the mood to hate everything about it – Geoff, the cartoonised comedy of the other contestants, the mock-Tudor pub, the audience – everything. On the other hand, and by the time Evesham was only a mile or so away, I'd come round to thinking that people had made some sort of sacrifice to watch the show, given their money and their time, so they'd earned the right to disapprove of me or (more likely) be perplexed. I didn't care much for them and they didn't care much for me. Fair enough.

Being a comedian, I thought, is bloody hard work. Maybe impossible work for someone like me. I was quite good at being complicated and awkward, but crap at being a straightforward laugh, a bit of a hoot, a treat. Tonight I had brought gracelessness to the table, as Logan might say. I should have been a clown rather than being merely clownish.

But there you go. Frank Skinner once said that a comedy act is like a long street with the jokes as lamp-posts. The gist of his argument was the folly of not turning back or finding another street if the first lamp-post didn't work, but blundering on anxiously into the gloom, past each non-working lamp-post, hoping that you'll eventually come across one that works. You end up driving quickly and blind, without headlights, and all around is darkness.

It's an odd metaphor, but you know what he's getting at.

Also on my mind was Bob Monkhouse's observation that the British distrust smart alecs. They disapprove of people 'being too clever by half'. 'By the same token,' he said, 'the comedians we love uncritically are those who best disguise their depth of thinking and expose their humanity.'

Whereas I put up barriers.

Still, it was something to take on board. As was Skinner's other assertion that 'Comedy without laughs is just someone talking'.

Live and learn, as they say. Live and learn.

NINE

Ha!

I bet you don't know where I am now.

Go on.

Guess.

Give in?

I'll tell you. I'm in a Virgin Atlantic plane flying to New York.

For a while, I'd been dropping hints to Pippa that in order to gain an appropriate perspective on British comedy I really ought to try viewing it from a different angle, see how it stacked up against other kinds of humour. Like looking at the earth from the moon. Or like looking at English comedy from New York, I mused. Similar language. Lots of comedy clubs. That sort of thing. Though I'd been suggesting it as an ideal scenario, I didn't really think I'd get away with it. Another trip. That *and* the cruise – in the same year.

Not a chance.

Then, out of the blue, Pippa said, 'Did you know there's a British/Irish Comedy Festival on in New York at the moment?'

'No,' I lied, though actually of course I knew all about it. Dylan Moran was on, for a start. Plus Eddie Izzard. And some others I hadn't heard of.

'If you're planning to go to New York, now would be a good time. For your comedy thing . . .'

'Yes . . .'

'I mean, if you're going to go *at all*, if you're *serious* about it, you'd better go now.'

'What, right now?'

'Within the next few days. While there's a festival to look at.'

'Er, is it OK,' I asked sheepishly, 'I mean OK with you?'

'You already owe me a week at a health farm. So just put this one on the national debt. I'll think of something . . . maybe another week at a different health farm, or just a week at a really expensive one.'

So I Googled some comedy clubs in New York, found an open-mike spot at somewhere called Ha!, then found the cheapest flight/hotel package for three nights on last-minute.com. And before you could say 'Lenny Bruce', I was winging my way across the Atlantic.

Impressive or what?

In truth, I'd been a bit glum after Birmingham. It wasn't exactly a triumph. On the other hand, though I was down, I was far from out. Why was this? In some respects, now might have been the appropriate time to bring down the curtain on my stand-up career. After all, I'd done it, experienced a reversal, and come to realise my limitations. No need to flog a dead horse.

And yet.

It did make me wonder.

Just as I'd been detached from the audience while

performing, so I was also disengaged from the hurt I ought to have been feeling. The reasons behind my failure were also helping to ensure my emotional survival. As yet, I hadn't taken enough pain to seriously contemplate giving up. Certainly not enough to compromise my staying power – the will to see something through, not to give up and, perhaps more important, not to be seen to give up.

And there was the still unsatisfied ambition to actually enjoy it, affirmation I had become a proper comic performer. Other comedians had told me this was where the real motivation for being a successful stand-up came from, the feeling of boundless energy as you worked an audience. The thrill to be had from the chambers of your brain opening up so you were able to think and act on many levels at the same time. Your whole being lit up by a dazzling sense of invincibility as you tapped into hitherto impenetrable levels of your existence.

It all sounded rather nice.

Nor could I deny I had grown to quite like, on the occasions it occurred, laughter and applause, even if I'd never been able to enjoy them in thrillingly, limitless, uninhibited ways. Though temperamentally unsuited to euphoria, there was just enough hope, and not enough suffering, to keep me going. There was still more carrot than stick.

And New York was *New York*.

So it was all settled.

Virgin Atlantic has changed a bit in the twenty years or so since I first flew with them. I wouldn't like to give the impression I'm a frequent flyer or make a habit of just popping across to New York. But the dozen or so times I have made the journey, I've always tried to use Virgin. Though I did experience a Dan Air flight in the seventies when I bagged a student job in Denver, selling books about cowboys over the phone – 'student job' being a kind of shorthand for something which is horrible to do and pays shit money. In the end, someone called Fred sacked me. From cold calling I graduated to gardening (sacked again) dish washing (also sacked), and working in Wendy's Old Fashioned Hamburgers (not actually sacked, but eventually demoted from serving fries to picking up cigarette ends in the car park).

Anyway, Virgin has changed. In the early eighties, when Branson was seen as a maverick trying to make it with the big boys of air travel, the national carriers, it was all a bit of an adventure. The crew were jolly and there was a party atmosphere in the cabin. Though they are still pretty decent, you do feel the *brio* has gone. Virgin are efficient and capable, but now almost as humourless as their competitors. Just in case he started to enjoy himself too much, one frolicsome three-year-old was strapped in with brisk, businesslike pragmatism by someone called Janet.

In the good old days, I always used to ask for a second packet of peanuts: not now.

Still, the in-flight entertainment is, as you would expect, very good. All the usual stuff but more of it; two comedy channels, for instance. So I settled down to watch the new Woody Allen film, *Anything Else,* showing on the back of the seat in front of me and a few weeks before its official UK release.

The film tells the story of a pair of fledgling comedy writers, Jerry Falk and David Dobel. Falk is a rising star in his twenties whereas Dobel (played by Allen) is sixty and still holding down a job as a schoolteacher. Just as Allen himself has become an increasingly marginalised figure, especially in the States, so Dobel is an ageing, neurotic comic convinced that he's a member of an endangered species. So paranoid is he, that at one point he advises Falk to arm himself against the anti-Zionists who plan to wipe them out.

It's by no means vintage Woody Allen, though even mediocre Woody Allen is better than nothing and certainly better than most other films.

Sitting next to me is an Orthodox Jew whose real-life nervousness is a mirror of Allen's on-screen jitters. He's constantly on the move – up and down, checking his blanket, then his pillow, his earphones, his complimentary toothbrush and his luggage. At one point, he sends back his food (not hot enough) then disappears to the toilet, anxiously looking over his shoulder as he heads off down the aisle, perhaps afraid someone will take his seat while he is away.

When he eventually returns, the old meal has been replaced by a new one – or new*ish*, as he has been away for so long. He inspects this and, inevitably, sends it back for the same reason as the first one. I see from his passport, which he checks every five minutes or so, that he is actually a Swiss Jew, and from the brochure he is constantly annotating, I ascertain he is travelling to New York for an auction of Jewish memorabilia. He has his eye on a nineteenth-century candleholder (estimated price $1,375), which he emphatically circles with a thick black felt-tip pen.

I wondered why Allen's humour, his nervy-nerdy character, tends to play better in Europe than it does in his home country. Maybe it's his sheer edginess, his lovelorn apprehension of being in New York, which strikes a chord. In Europe, I suspect we rather like his ambiguity about being American, or rather being a Woody Allen who happens to be in America. In part, it reflects the way we also feel about being in America. In fact, most English people feel the same way about being anywhere that isn't England, but especially America, which intimidates us.

English humour is frequently presented as a consequence of this kind of awkwardness, the strange, tense sensation of assumed superiority cheek by jowl with the actual feeling of somehow, inevitably being inferior. Not being able to make sense of this conundrum is in part what drives our emotions underground, makes us vague, abstracted, ironic, apologetic. And these feelings are especially apparent when we travel to the US, an old colony that in so many ways seems to be getting on much better than the old country.

If our archetypal national sensibility was ever to crystallise in a single geographical location, that place would probably be New York. We're penitentially rueful the moment we set foot there. It magnifies our brooding suspicion of uselessness, our skulking sense of anachronism, our fear of being losers. Think about it. Could a film ever be called *British Beauty*, or a song 'British Pie', or a novel B*ritish Psycho*? And how about the film of the great American comedian Lenny Bruce, called simply *Lenny*? Even in England we know this is not about Lenny Henry. And could you imagine a movie called *Jasper* or *Frank* or (God forbid) *Brucie*? Or *Norman* or *Ben*? *Alexei* is a bit better, but what of *Dud*, or even *Pete* come to that?

As William Leith wrote in his short book *British Teeth*, Britain has become 'a place of indifference and envy, a place that had become ashamed of itself, a place where educated people hid their knowledge, where the middle classes grow up trying to imitate the voices of the poor. We had developed a taste for failure, in the same way that drunks develop an appetite for the self-loathing which drives them to drink even more. We had become known, and know ourselves, as a nation of losers.'

So this is one of the reasons why we, why I, connect with Woody Allen – his disenfranchised, peripheral also-rans denote a familiar, even cosy presence, a recognisable alter ego. And this was precisely the reason why I wanted to go. I was intrigued to know how my supposedly English humour would play in New York, and in addition how American humour might put it into some kind of context.

At Newark, though sprinting hard to overtake the first class, business class and club class passengers who had disembarked before me, I still queued for almost an hour to clear customs. Despite the melting-pot, land-of-opportunity, openness thing, America is devilishly difficult to get into at the point of access. You can drive from Belgium to France without even stopping at the border, but American immigration is tighter than a gnat's hoo-ha.

A beefy young man with forearms the size of Rutland asked me how long I would be staying in New York.

'Three days,' I replied confidently.

'Business or pleasure?'

'Business. No – pleasure. Wait a minute. A bit of both. Well, mainly business . . .'

'What is your business?'

'I'm a writer.'

He eyed me suspiciously.

'Sowaddyagonnabedoinhere?'

'Talking to people about comedy. Doing some stand-up. You see, I'm interested in . . .'

His eyes had already glazed and were in the process of hardening.

'Get outta here!' he smirked. 'Oh . . .'

'Yes?'

'. . . and have a nice day.'

'Thank you. You too,' I chirped.

On Manhattan Island, my hotel was on the East Side, in the mid-sixties, though so far east it was virtually in the river, and adjacent to a vast, rusting bridge which ceaselessly carried traffic into the centre of town. It might have been the bridge on which Sherman McCoy took a disastrous wrong turning in Tom Wolfe's novel *Bonfire of the Vanities*. Then again, it might not have been, but I liked the idea, and for the moment it stuck.

'We've upgraded you!' beamed the bloke at reception.

'What does that mean?' I asked, perhaps ungraciously. I didn't really want to be upgraded. Being English, it had the suggestion of bringing into play complex issues of debt and gratitude.

'Bigger room. Much bigger!'

'Not more expensive though, I hope?'

'No, sir. Just bigger.' Then he handed me the key card.

He wasn't kidding. The room was huge. The furniture, even the king-size double bed, was dwarfed by it. A shabby armchair was marooned somewhere near the centre, its leg supports fully extended to fill up a bit more space. On closer inspection, I saw it actually had several cigarette burns on it. The air-conditioning unit thrummed noisily beneath the windows, windows which anyway rattled and whose blinds were closed because of the nearby bridge. Though they weren't actually nailed shut, the apparatus which operated them was so complex as to make being shut a more or less permanent state of affairs.

I felt as if I'd strayed into a Bill Brandt photo, one of the interior nudes.

Though, as Kingsley Amis once said, bigger doesn't necessarily mean better.

I intended to spend my first full day, a Monday, getting my bearings, contacting Ha! to cement my open-mike position, and maybe watching Woody Allen play clarinet at Michael's Pub, apparently something he did every Monday night. I also planned to catch a train to somewhere called Morristown to visit an Anglo-American comedienne called Alison Larkin. A month or so earlier, I had seen Alison perform at the Soho Theatre as part of the London Comedy Festival, and she struck me as being someone who would understand a great deal about English comedy. We had spoken briefly after her show, exchanged email addresses, and made the usual noises about meeting up and chatting if I ever happened to be in New York.

Well, here I was.

The flyer for Alison's show explains why she is able to provide such a unique perspective on transatlantic comedy: 'Alison Larkin thought she was an English rose . . . only to discover that she was actually an American redneck! Adopted at birth and raised in England, she discovered her roots in Bald Mountain, Tennessee.'

Her one-woman performance delivers the true story of a very English upbringing, which involves the Home Counties and boarding school, then the quest to find her birth mother and the subsequent trip to the States. It begins with Alison sitting at a breakfast table reading aloud from a letter to her mother, her adoptive mother. When she speaks, it's with a perfect Middle England, mid-century English accent. She sounds like Margaret Rutherford or Joyce Grenfell. But on her head she wears the reversed baseball cap of dress-down American classlessness, and says, 'My name is Alison Larkin and I come from Bald Mountain, Tennessee. I'm a redneck.'

It's like listening to Margaret Thatcher suddenly revealing she's an Eskimo.

In America, it brings the house down. Even in England, people laugh loudly.

To get to Morristown, you have to catch the New Jersey Transit from Penn Station. As you'd expect, American trains are bigger and shinier than ours. Everyone gets a seat, even in the rush hour. And it's exactly on time. Extraordinary. On the other hand, nobody eases a trolley through the throng of passengers and offers you a cup of tea and a KitKat, but you can't have everything. The journey time was about an hour. By and large, it was not a pretty journey, though it's always interesting to gawp at unfamiliar landscapes through a train window. As we pulled away from Manhattan and the dense industrial zone which surrounds it, small towns made familiar by TV and the movies arrived at regular intervals. Whitewashed wooden houses with decks. Cute white churches with working clock towers. Minor-league baseball parks. You know the sort of thing.

Alison met me off the train and said we should chat over a typical American meal at a typical American restaurant, by which I assumed she meant a hamburger eaten somewhere earthy. We drove around for a bit, during which she told me about her husband, Jim, an expert on English comedy. They and their two children had been in Morristown for twelve years.

'Comedy is so much about context,' Alison said, 'and Jim shared many of my own reference points. Simply had to marry him.'

'But does he know who Shep is?' I chuckled.

'He does now,' Alison laughed.

She said Jim sent his apologies but his computer was on the blink and tonight was crucial, or crucial enough, for it needing urgent and immediate repairs.

After some more driving, we settled on Arthur's, which from the outside was all neon and inside all gingham. Though she enjoyed living in Morristown, Alison was tentative about its restaurants, but from what she'd heard, Arthur's was fine. We drove about a bit more trying to find a place to park. When we did, Alison reversed rather too quickly and cracked into a wall. 'Not to worry,' she giggled, 'everything is absolutely fine.' She sounded even more like Joyce Grenfell when she said this. Twelve years in Morristown had altered her accent not one jot. When I commented on this, she replied in what I can only call 'broad redneck', saying something graphic I would hesitate to include even in these august pages.

We walked into Arthur's, ordered a couple of burgers, and set about discussing comedy. I was still resistant to notions of a national comedy, of humour that could be defined by geographical or even cultural accident. Alison, however, begged to differ.

'It's the English class system which gives English comedy its distinctiveness,' she said, by which she meant its frequently unspoken sense of hierarchy, things not said, or not quite said, and rarely said openly. Everything was in a kind of code; ironic, I suppose. 'The US is far more democratic and open,' she continued. 'There's less baggage. Everything is more direct. And *that* shows in the comedy.'

I was still sceptical. The idea of an entire nation's funny bones being designed by essentially non-comic factors was somehow irksome to the comic purist. There's some old black-

and-white TV footage of Ronnie Corbett, Ronnie Barker and John Cleese each representing the lower, middle and upper classes. The smallest in height and stature is the lowliest. He looks up to the middling man, who in turn looks up to the upper-class chap. The sketch was written, performed and filmed in the 1960s. Forty years ago. It might have been true then, but surely not now? Not in Blair's classless meritocracy, not in a Britain which has considered abolishing the Lords, fox-hunting and the Order of the British Empire?

I said something like this to Alison, but there was no shifting her. She maintained that successful comedy relied on making a connection with the audience – which includes but also goes beyond appropriate cultural references – and this is why it is more complicated to find affinity with an English audience: there's so much 'else' going on and the comedian therefore has to be less direct.

'But Americans can be ironic too,' I countered, 'even more ironic than the English. What about *Six Feet Under* and *Curb Your Enthusiasm*?'

At the time, I hadn't actually seen *Curb Your Enthusiasm*, but I'd read about it and knew it was ironic, sneering, sarcastic, whatever. Even the title had a defensively Larkinesque lilt to it. And now I have seen it, I know it was the right thing to say. Its writer, Larry David, was the writer and co-creator of *Seinfeld*. In this new programme, David actually plays the main protagonist called, er, Larry David. He comes across as an unwittingly obnoxious schmuck, calls himself a 'bald turd', and generally puts himself through humiliating, wringing torment in the name of comic effect. It's a bit like watching a Mike Leigh character, or maybe John Cleese (as Basil Fawlty), and it's intensely absurd and ironic. Anyway, I immediately liked the idea of David when I heard how flummoxed audiences were when he used to do stand-up. 'On many, many nights,' said an old friend, 'the audience would just stare at him like carp looking up from a pond.' Larry and me, you see. Misunderstood comic geniuses.

At any rate, Alison nodded when I mentioned *Curb Your Enthusiasm*.

'Of course Americans can be ironic, but it's never dependent on class and an awareness of social hierarchy. It's rarely about undercutting someone's status. English humour is more cynical.'

I didn't necessarily want to swallow this either, though much of what she said struck a chord. Think of all the best English sitcoms, for example: *Dad's Army*, *Steptoe and Son*, *Till Death Us Do Part* . . . all of which depend to a large extent on an awareness of social mobility. Even *The Office*, of course about the futile comedy of work, is also about aspirational delusion, a bedrock of class awareness.

We are, I suppose, a fairly distrusting, unbelieving, scornful, insecure lot. Uncomfortable with ourselves, uncomfortable with being English. Maybe that's why we're most at ease with our swollen catalogue of plucky losers, like . . . well, like everyone who plays sport, for example Tiger Tim, Eddie the Eagle, Frank Bruno, et al. On the other hand, we laugh at people who do try to better themselves, and love it when those who have succeeded fall flat on their faces. We sneer at anyone who owns a flash car or dares to build a swimming pool in their back garden. Perhaps Alison had a point. We are cynical.

By this time, we had reached the coffee part of our meal. I had my eye on a large slice of cheesecake. Plus ice cream. Maybe plus syrup too, though I wouldn't have pushed it.

Alison, though, needed to get back to her children. And I still wanted to find Woody Allen.

My coffee was cold, but when the waitress asked how everything was I just looked at her and said, 'Fine, thank you.' Which was typical, i.e. weak and evasively apologetic. But then we're so precious about ourselves that by social osmosis we make the same assumptions about others. We call it 'good manners' though I suspect Alison might call it something else, like 'dishonesty' or 'being disingenuous'. And it's more or less what Alison talked about now. Perhaps she had noticed the beady look in my eye as I said 'Fine' and clearly meant something else, meant the opposite, in fact.

'What occurs to me every time I see a British comedy – old or new – is how much it relies on the central character not wanting to be rude, or at least caring so much about what other people think. If Hyacinth Bucket's neighbours were American, they'd move, or say NO when she invited them to tea. It seems to me that the British inability to say no is cultural. Americans don't give a damn what people think, generally speaking, which is a much more honest way to live, and possibly one of the reasons I live here. It's the "I'm fine" syndrome when the whole world is crashing around you. So much British comedy is based on that.'

I listened to Alison and stared at my cold, actually disgusting coffee. Our waitress wandered past again and this time I nearly did say something, if only to prove Alison wrong. Nearly. But not quite. Because if I'd said anything, I knew it would have come out badly, sounded somehow personal, been not just about the coffee but about the waitress, her job, her silly gingham dress, her lowly status, what having to work at Arthur's implied about her parents, her grandparents, her uncles and aunts and nephews and nieces, where she lived, the kind of car she drove, or didn't drive – all sorts of things, but not just about the coffee. I'd have sounded rude, not because I wanted to be rude, but because the burden of not being rude weighed so heavily that rudeness would inevitably feature. Our waitress caught my eye while much of this was spinning round my head.

So I smiled at her and drank the coffee.

Despite all this, I wanted to debate the point with Alison, but merely nodded in her direction, giving the impression that I agreed with her, or at least didn't disagree with her, and anyway feeling that no matter how I responded I would lay myself open to accusations of being disingenuous or not wanting to be rude – something – all of it to do with being too English. So I kept quiet and asked instead what kind of British comedy did well in America.

'Benny Hill, obviously.'

'Obviously.'

'And that old sitcom, set in a department store . . .'

'Not *Are You Being Served?*!?'

'That's the one.'

'Why on earth do people like that?'

Actually, Alison didn't much care for it, so maybe that was the Brit in her coming out, but she said something about the show being a good barometer of Englishness. Presumably this had to do with the rigid social hierarchies on the shop floor, John Inman's campness and the suppressed vulgarity of phrases like 'Mrs Slocombe's pussy'. All as delightful and whimsical as afternoon tea. Or to put it another way: the programme provides Americans with an archetype of Englishness – quaint, fussy, snobbish, sexually repressed, socially maladjusted, essentially harmless. Not so far from Basil Fawlty and all the others, in fact – and they seize on this as proof of archetypal behaviour in the same way I suppose we embrace convenient models of American behaviour. Neither Alison nor I could put a finger on exactly why this might be so, though the unaffecting portrayal of old colonial masters as bumbling buffoons must, we thought, be part of it.

Actually, come to think of it, America, and indeed the rest of the world, like Benny Hill for quite specific reasons, most of them to do with pornography. When it first aired in New York, one reviewer complained of its 'pornographic grubbiness', though a year later he had revised his opinion, saying that it was this 'pornographic grubbiness that makes him so special, so subversively sane. He's a music hall lech . . . [who] remembers that life's a nasty treacherous comedy and sex a glorious joke.' Benny was also compared to fish and chips and room-temperature beer. It was the apparently irresistible combination of smut and Britishness which came to so captivate the planet.

I pondered all this on the return journey to Penn Station and had to admit that my natural scepticism to national styles of humour had absorbed a few telling blows. In addition, Alison had also cautioned me about US conservatism and to be careful with my routine. 'I'm not sure the references to the SS will go down terribly well,' she said, 'you might think about tweaking your material.'

So that was something else to think about.

In the film *Pulp Fiction*, the famous hamburger dialogue between John Travolta and Samuel L. Jackson concludes with the assertion that it's the small things which make the difference in questions of national identity. French fries and mayonnaise in Belgium, for example. As my train rattled back towards New York, I looked out at the overgrown triffid-like vegetation which bordered the track, vegetation that could have been almost anywhere, almost in England, perhaps – almost, but not quite – and appreciated the sentiment. Sometimes it's difficult to explain why things are different; they just are. And perhaps comedy is a bit like this. You hear an English joke, even a non-culturally specific English joke, and you just know it's English without quite knowing why.

It's in your blood and in your bones.

For example: our irony is different from their irony even though the word fundamentally 'means' the same thing.

By this time, I was tired and jet-lagged and maybe even a bit muddled. Maybe that accounted for the weird version of relativity that was forming in my mind. The kind of relativism which suggested the need for American irony to help appreciate English irony. Which suggested that, after all, there was no universal or absolute law of comedy.

As I drifted into a light sleep, my old English teacher, Ken Ellison, came to me in a moment of Proustian recall. He was a small, dapper man with heavily pomaded ginger hair who had been at Oxford with Kenneth Tynan and pronounced 'piano' as 'pea-ar-know'. He had been the first one to alert me to the difference between irony and sarcasm, telling us how sarcasm was derived from a Greek word meaning 'the tearing of flesh' and that irony was its gentler relation. In times of stress, he said, the one 'shaded' into the other. I always liked that word, 'shaded'. Once, he sent me out of the room for impersonating his habit of slapping one hand with the other when making a point.

The fantasia of Ken then shifted to one of Woody Allen, a

man of similar stature. There was panic in this dreamworld. Woody-panic. What the fuck was I going to learn by watching him play the clarinet? Would I see something in his reed work that would somehow illuminate an entire comic world? In my improvised dream, I imagined hanging around the pub door after he'd finished playing and, like something from a fairy tale, being granted a single question. What would that question be? 'Mr Allen – what if any in your opinion are the differences between comedy and tragedy?' Famously, Allen has said he's not much interested in comedy, and that life is 'a monstrous, monstrous thing'. Maybe he'd read Horace Walpole, who said that, 'The world is a comedy to those that think: a tragedy to those that feel.' Surely, I thought, you can do both, think and feel? But maybe Woody had done enough thinking for one lifetime.

The train jolted to a halt and as I woke up I realised my face had become stuck on the brown leatherette seat. I quite wanted to stay there, all night if necessary, but eventually peeled myself free and set off on the subway, the address for Michael's Pub jotted down on the back of a dollar bill.

An hour or so later, and after a bit of walking, I found the address, though not the pub. The bartender at what would have been the pub next door told me that Michael's had closed down. I was dead on my feet so didn't push for any more information, for the moment just thankful that I could head back to my hangar and get some rest. It was probably a good thing. There are so many ways of making a tit of yourself without being arrested for pestering Woody Allen about comedy. In my hotel room, I jotted down ideas for a brand new routine at Ha!, and fell into a deep, more or less untroubled sleep.

Rather than tinker with the material I had, I decided to try something completely different. I also decided this was the moment to come clean about my comedic quest, make buddying-up jokes about President Bush, and then launch into an essentially light-hearted, teasing attack on the US. This would consist of a list of ten points which outline the ways in which America was imposing itself on the rest of the world, thereby altering its cultural landscape and ensuring comic homogeneity.

In other words, it wouldn't be long before we were all laughing at the same things.

I sketched out my new routine in a lined writing 'tablet' I'd bought at Penn Station for under a dollar. I'd also bought some chewing gum and a Hershey bar. Oh, and an ice cream.

At one o'clock in the morning, drowsy, jaded, dazed and confused, it seemed like a really good idea.

I woke up about an hour later, and like the John Self character in Martin Amis's *Money*, was immediately convinced I'd slept through a whole night. I felt energised and restless, ready for the challenges of a new day, even though that was actually around five or six hours away. I switched on the television, which didn't work, then tried to read Ted Heller's novel about two American comedians, *Funnymen*. Gradually, and without moving much beyond the first couple of pages, I dropped into sleep again. This time until around 6 a.m. when the traffic outside my window woke me up.

The one good thing about my hotel was bagels and coffee in the cafeteria on the twenty-first floor.

I nabbed a seat by one of the full-length plate-glass windows and watched New Yorkers arriving for work in Manhattan. They came by car across the bridge outside my room, by helicopter, by ferry and, a long, long way below, on foot. There was even a plane, though only one, and even then some distance away. For a time after the World Trade Center attack the phrase 'that's so 9/10' had entered the vernacular as a way of describing a particularly enjoyable period of time.

All this was going through my mind because Michael Moore's new film *Fahrenheit 9/11* was playing at the cinema only a couple of blocks away, and I wanted to see it. There were a couple of mid-morning shows and I planned to catch one of those. All other performances were sold out.

Watching it was a strange experience. The audience filled about half the auditorium and consisted mainly of students and pensioners. I wondered if they would be laughing at the same things as me and in the same way – and, perhaps surprisingly, they pretty well did. A knowingly outraged but still relatively restrained ripple of amusement. Still, this was New York, not necessarily typical of America, and the audience was educated and/or chock-full of age-giving wisdom. It was also, I think, a mostly Democrat gathering. Three people left within half an hour, actually at the bit where Bush is informed of the attacks and just stares balefully at a children's reading book for seven full minutes, and I assumed they were either angry Republicans or old-timers with a toilet problem.

The film itself was a moving and powerful indictment of Bush's presidency, though I didn't necessarily think it was very good. The obvious appeals to emotions over the carefully crafted argument, and the appeal to the personal rather than the abstract suggested the roller-coaster ways in which Americans absorb information these days. As one critic wrote, 'It's autobiography and pop culture that move American consumers, not sense and sensibility.'

Mind you, it's much the same in England these days, film and television having narrowed the differences between our national susceptibilities. You suspect, for example, people would be more interested in Jordan's opinion on terrorism than a tightly researched, investigative, ninety minute documentary which refused to grant precedence to one meaningless viewpoint over another. And if you want to make a film which changes minds, then Moore's way is probably as good as any.

Afterwards, I chatted to a few members of the audience and three young Democrats who were handing out leaflets inviting people to a concert for John Kerry at the Radio City Music Hall. Kerry would be supported by Jon Bon Jovi, Wyclef Jean and Whoopi Goldberg. It's not quite the same as the Tories calling on Jim Davidson or the Lib Dems wheeling out John Cleese, but the intention is much the same.

Incidentally, Eric Morecambe was once asked why so many comedians were Tories and he replied it was the money, by which I assume he meant (simply) that it was easier to keep the stuff under the Conservatives, rather than giving it away through taxes. And when Doddy was being put through the wringer by the Inland Revenue, he made the point that money was the only tangible sign a comedian could have of success. The stuff assumes a weird significance and is never just 'money'.

That aside, all the people I speak to recognised the film's hysterical methods while still believing it was probably the most effective way of dealing with Bush. 'It does persuade people,' smiled an impossibly tall young man who at the same time presented a mouthful of ongoing and no doubt expensive dentistry, '*and* it sways the waverers.'

Rather than catching the subway, I decided to walk to Ha!

which was on West 46th Street, just off Times Square. I'd glanced at my muddled notes from the previous night and decided not to write a more concrete version and then learn it by rote.

As far as I could, as far as I dared, I'd be winging it, maybe even living in the moment.

Being so far away from home somehow made this easier. Or at least made it easier to think about doing it. No chance of seeing anyone I knew, the sense of isolation puncturing the familiarity of context, actually easing the knot of habitual self-consciousness. So when I arrived at the club and put down my name on a list for open-mike spots, I was relatively relaxed, even calm, about the whole thing. There were seven other names on the list by the time I arrived, though the Italian-looking bloke who seemed to be organising it said others were bound to follow. He was playing a game on his computer and seemed put out at having to deal with me, especially when I asked him some questions.

'I will get on?' I asked.

'Yeah, yeah. You'll get on OK.'

'It's just that I've come a long way.'

'Yeah. Really.'

'So I don't want to be disappointed.'

'You won't be. And it's five dollars. That OK with you?'

'It's all right. I don't want money. Give it to charity if you like.'

I even wondered whether I ought to tell him about my comedic quest, that I was a man with a mission.

'No. You pay us,' he said without glancing up from his computer. 'Five dollars buys you six minutes of stage time.'

Apparently, the open-mike night was a platform for

comedians to try out new material in front of any other comedians who wanted to try out new material, plus whoever wandered in off the street, stumped up three dollars and bought a drink. Not quite what I'd imagined, but different, and definitely worth a go. I paid up and the Italian bloke gestured to a flight of steps which disappeared into an inauspicious gloom.

Ha! actually has two stages. The main one is on the ground floor and is considered tougher because the audience is further away and therefore more comfortable shouting out or creating their own private parties. It is also more formal, laid out like a café, while the upstairs lounge is more intimate, with high bar-stool tables lining two of the walls and stumpy tables surrounding a minuscule stage. Ha! has a reputation as a home for starting comics. It's the kind of place in which you would want to begin but not finish a career.

Ten minutes before showtime around fifteen comedians have paid their money and around ten others have come in off the street. An audience of twenty-five or so would make the upstairs lounge feel very cosy. A thin, pale man, probably in his mid-twenties, introduced himself to us.

'Hi, I'm Dave,' he said, 'your MC for the evening. Has everyone paid their five bucks?'

We all nodded, apart from one woman, who must have been in her seventies. She identified herself as Sandy Kane and was wearing a canary-yellow cowgirl outfit topped off by a large Stetson. She fumbled and blustered for a few moments before finally producing the money. Apart from her bosoms, which exploded out of a revealingly tight shirt, and a bright orange wig, she looked like an outsize banana.

Dave explained how things worked, giving each of us a

number, and indicating a red light opposite the stage. When a comic had one minute left, he would flash this. 'But don't worry about me,' he drawled, 'just do your thing.'

I just had time to ask Dave about the main shows at Ha! which happened later in the evening, usually over ninety minutes. Dave was one of the club's regular performers and MCs, often using the open-mike session to hone his act. 'This is a good club for a new comedian,' he told me, 'up to a third of the time in the shows proper might be given to barkers.'

'Barkers?'

'Sure. The guys you see out on Times Square handing out discount flyers for the club. You write your name on the back of each flyer you distribute – that way, you get credit for it.'

'What kind of credit?'

'Stage time. But you can also get credit for bringing in an audience – usually people you know. You're not a barker then. You're a bringer.'

Dave also told me that barkers didn't get paid for their sets but after the first five credited customers they could claim two dollars a head. That way, Ha! fills more than two hundred slots with novices. It has to, as there are often four shows a night. Turnover of comics and audience is high, even for New York.

'The amateurs also do a lot of grunt work.'

'Grunt work?' I was beginning to sound like an echo.

'Yeah – cleaning, mopping, sorting empty bottles in the basement. And walking Anthony's dog.'

'Anthony?'

'The owner. Anthony di Napoli.'

Apparently, when Anthony bought the Ha! premises the idea was to convert it into a piano bar called 'Sweet Caroline's, named after a favourite Neil Diamond song. A gay comic – or maybe he's a comic who happens to be gay, you'll have to ask him – called Exiene Lofgren asked if he could book comedy shows during the club's downtime, and by October 2002 the comedy had more or less taken over and the club became Ha!

Dave excused himself in order to make some trial lighting checks before the open-mike session started, and I settled into a corner of the upstairs lounge, nabbing one of the high bar stools, waiting for the off.

I fished out my writing tablet and got ready to take some notes.

Within a couple of minutes, Dave had bounded on to the stage and was apologising about the state of the toilets – the smells, the appearance, the squalor; the grunters obviously weren't taking their grunt work seriously enough – though this merely acted as a preamble to a series of new jokes he was trying out about haemorrhoids. Each haemorrhoid story he told trumped the previous one for grotesque detail, and whenever one pushed the boundaries of humour too far and didn't actually come across as a joke, he chatted warmly with the audience and admitted his mistake with happy-go-lucky nonchalance. 'OK, OK. I must remember not to do that one. Anyway, moving on quickly, how do you like *this* one . . .?'

Such sangfroid, I thought. I wondered if an English comedian would be able to be so easily, so authentically indifferent to not raising a laugh. 'Authentically indifferent' that is, as opposed to pretending to be indifferent or (more likely) being ironically sensitive and thus feigning indifference, which isn't the same thing at all. Or maybe I was still thinking too much about what Alison had said about class, about the way English people are always thinking about who they are, what kind of society they belong to, and where they themselves belong in it. All of which would make authentic indifference, Dave's authentic indifference, very difficult to achieve.

After Dave had completed his warm-up, he introduced the first comedian, Tom, equally as confident and at ease with the audience, and equally unflappable when a joke didn't work. He made a good Michael Moore joke – I can't recall the context, but he said that someone in one of his stories 'moved faster than Michael Moore going for a box of Twinkies'. I guessed that Twinkies weren't a kind of salad.

We laughed at that, all twenty-five or so of us, and Tom took the opportunity to add, 'OK, he might have made a good film and be on the side of the angels – but he's still FAT. Right? RIGHT!'

More explosive, unbridled laughter, though not quite so much from me. I had come from a place where we're still very polite about the fat, the skinny, the otherly abled and the differently formed. And I thought America was the home of political correctness.

After Tom came a shaven-headed man wearing an expensive tan suit. He'd obviously just come from work and I saw his routine beautifully typed out on a couple of sheets of thick, creamy paper. He delivered a competent though unremarkable joke-led set before someone called Catherine took the stage. She immediately launched into a series of impersonations, though not impersonations or impressions of well-known politicians and celebrities. No, she presented cruel caricatures of her 'most hated homeless', people she saw begging on the subway or panhandling on the pavement. Twisting her body and face into all manner of unsympathetic, demented grotesquerie, she got big laughs, especially from a couple in the shadows just to the left of the stage, a couple of bearded men in their early thirties who were, I thought, even in this company, laughing too hard and too readily.

Though I also laughed, it was laughter without conviction, its hollowness once again a hangover of, what precisely – manners, guilt, restraint, oversensitivity? I was beginning to think that in America there was far more scope for mocking the afflicted than is generally presumed.

Next, a woman in her thirties (I think called Erté) told how her father used to hit on her school friends, more than once asking her to remind whichever friend was sleeping over that 'old pops still likes to lick out the old salt block, so if you can fix it for me, I'd be grateful'. Then Sandy Kane, the banana cowgirl, delivered a stream of vicious jokes about black people. 'Remember when this country used to be WHITE?' she started. 'So it's good to see so many of you white folks here tonight.' Chris, another comic in a suit, took up the theme, though for good measure he trashed blacks *and* beggars, inviting them to get jobs, even if they didn't possess arms or legs: 'Get a job!' he shrieked. 'Get a job, GET-A-FUCKING-JOB. You can't be that happy doin' what you're doin' . . .'

Admittedly there weren't so many laughs by the time we'd reached Chris, though I was still a little numb from what I'd heard. Then, before I was quite ready, Dave introduced me and invited me on to the stage. A sprinkling of applause and a couple of whoops as Dave 'bigged it up' for me. Hurriedly, I took a final glance at the few points I'd jotted down the previous night, strode to the microphone and delivered my routine. (For those of you interested in such things, you can find an outline of it at the back of this book; Appendix 2.)

There was some polite laughter and the usual bewildered/slightly amused stares, but it didn't seem to be going too badly.

Then, quite suddenly, as I was working my way through the supposedly joshing catalogue of the ways in which Americans imposed themselves on a vulnerable world, something took over. I don't know whether it was the rhythm of the list itself, or an involuntary response to what the previous comics had dished out, or the liberating sense of being so far away from home. Maybe I was, finally, 'living in the moment', or at least living a bit closer to the moment. Logan would have proud of me. Anyway, what happened was that I became increasingly aggressive and hysterical. What started out as a light-hearted tease soon became a cold and rather sinister rant.

'Number eight!' I snarled. 'The Concept of Choice. What's that all about? You lot spend so much time worrying about what combination of dressings best suits your fucking salads or what fillings you'd like in your sodding burgers that you don't have time to worry about THE THINGS THAT REALLY MATTER. That's not choice. That's filling your head with meaningless nonsense, with bollocks. It's just a way to stop you thinking about the important stuff, making choices about those that some people call "having opinions". War in Iraq or pickle and mayo on my burger? Urrrr. That's a tricky one . . .'

Everyone apart from Catherine (the beggar hater) and one of the paying audience was looking at me with a sort of hurt disbelief, perhaps edging into annoyance.

I stumbled through number nine on my list, a joke against the kind of political correctness already demolished by the other comedians, and surged forward to number ten, 'The Mangling of the English Language'.

Now Dave was out of his seat and pointing at the red light, which was flashing impatiently. Fuck it, I thought. I've paid my five dollars. Actually, when you think about it, I've paid a lot more than that. They can bloody well hear the rest of it. I've got ten points and I'm going to finish them. So I carried on, with Dave up and down out of his seat, the red light twinkling away, the rest of the room mostly quiet, and me saying things like, 'Better out than in? What the fuck does that mean? And it's not true. Believe me. It ISN'T. Better in than out, I say. BETTER IN THAN OUT . . .'

'Apart from now, eh?' someone chortled, out of the gloom.

'Who wants to know what everyone else is thinking or feeling? Not me . . .'

'Nor me,' the same voice said.

'. . . and "Love you". Why do you say that? Even at the end of a telephone call. You've got us doing it in England now. There was a reason we didn't say it before, because it was important, not to be bandied around willy-nilly –'

That was the moment Dave reached the stage. 'Thank you, Steve. Let's give it up for –'

'– you can't have everyone going round telling everyone else they love them. It's indiscriminate. Cheap. But we're doing it in England. We're doing it in bloody England. So you've won. Well bloody done –'

'Thank you, Steve. Really great –'

'– before all that we found it hard enough to admit we didn't loathe one another. We never told people we loved them even when we did love them, which probably wasn't that often. But it was a kind of rule. You weren't allowed to say it. It was private, see. Not a word to be shouted down the phone while you're in the supermarket –'

'Well done, Steve,' said Dave, now on fully on the stage and this time taking the microphone from me. I stomped back to my seat, a smattering of applause trailing behind me. 'Well,

Steve, the reason why we eat so quickly in America, the reason why we have fast food,' Dave said, recalling number five or maybe number six on my list, 'or why we cut to the chase and tell people we love them, is because we don't have time to waste, we're too busy saving the Free World and defending your ass.' And here he looked directly at me and smiled.

I sat down, flicked open my writing tablet with breezy nonchalance, or more likely feigned breezy nonchalance, and watched the next act, in fact a double act. The two young men with clipped beards were next up, and they began a disjointed though otherwise fiercely offensive rant about blacks, gays and beggars. One particularly distasteful moment featured a discussion between them, actually more a reminiscence, about the size of a gay man's penis. Even if they'd been a couple of affable blokes the material would have been monstrous. As it was, they came across as the kind of men who lived alone in a trailer in the middle of nowhere, played rock music too loudly, drank beer from a bottle, kept a stash of porn and preyed on pre-pubescent girls.

The small audience became twitchy. Even Dave was quite shaken.

'Er, thank you,' he mumbled, when they'd finally finished. 'Well, Steve, what number was your point about political correctness? Number eight, was it? I think that one's been pretty much trashed.'

From this point, the evening descended into farce. A woman called Linda spent much of her time on stage giggling or shrieking hysterically – it was difficult to tell them apart – and describing the kind of elemental yawn she undertook when getting out of bed in the morning.

The open-mike session was ended by someone called 'G', a

man in his fifties, wearing shorts and a T-shirt, who should have been on before me but had temporarily disappeared when his turn came, apparently to get stoned.

As he floundered on to the stage, virtually incoherent and very wobbly on his legs, G hurled a FedEx package against the back wall and then threw a baseball glove to the floor. His unintelligibility neither started nor travelled anywhere in particular, though somewhere towards what would have been the middle I thought I detected a series of threats being made against me for my attack on his country – though it was difficult to be certain.

He ended his act by screwing up bits of paper, attempting to do the splits and then sort of collapsing.

'Let's give it up for G,' said Dave without much enthusiasm, 'though I wouldn't blame you if you didn't. Thank you and goodnight. That concludes this part of the evening's entertainment.'

We shuffled out of the lounge, back down the stairs and into the still quite bright light outside. The remains of the day. The air was soft but somehow alert. Most of the audience had already disappeared by the time I exited through the club's small, slightly grubby door. New York's nightlife was just staring up. The restaurants and bars along West 46th were beginning to fill, and I saw one, which advertised a Judy Garland impersonator, was particularly busy.

I chatted with Dave, a very pleasant, sociable bloke, who said if I wanted to watch any of the shows that night, to just mention his name at the door. Then we sat down, perched really, on the steps leading up to some apartments directly above Ha! To break the ice, I made a comment about G and the bearded duo from the swamp.

'Both acts are here fairly often,' Dave said, 'he's usually stoned – or worse – and they're always offensive. Sometimes they come on stage and try to sell their motorbike. Still, it's a free country.'

'And I thought Americans were so politically correct,' I mumbled inanely.

'Officially we are. Kind of. I don't think we'd ever let the double act near a stage for the main part of the show. Even if they were to somehow make it funny. G once got on the big show of the evening. I don't know how. Maybe we weren't paying good attention. Just as he got on stage, Nicole Kidman and Sean Penn walked in. They didn't stay long.'

By this time, other people had joined us on the steps. One of the paying audience, who introduced himself as Matt, Catherine and Exiene Lofgren, the gay comedian who'd been at 'Ha!' since the beginning.

Matt thought we were all proper comedians warming up for telly appearances. He was there because he was bored with his job and was looking for ways into the comedy business. None of us was able to help him much, though Dave made the right noises about working hard and not being daunted by failure. Catherine said she'd majored in drama at college and had originally come to New York to put on a play she'd written about Thomas Crapper, the inventor of the flush toilet. Things hadn't gone as she'd planned and the play was still waiting to be produced. Meanwhile, she's reinventing herself as a comedienne and her husband is a chef in a swanky Manhattan hotel. She told me how much she loved English comedy.

'What sort of comedy?' I asked.

'*Are You Being Served*?' she said.

'Oh. Anything else?'

'Python. Eddie Izzard. And I loved that show about Wise and Morecambe which played here.'

'*The Play What I Wrote*?'

'Awesome.'

'How could you like that?' I asked. 'It's so English. You have to know all about Eric and Ern, for a start.'

'They changed it a bit, I think. So the English references didn't go over our heads. But I loved the physical humour, the vaudeville.'

'But it's the language of English humour we like,' added Exiene. Now I looked at him properly, I saw Exiene had the kind of pale, deathly pallor which suggested he hardly ventured out of Ha! Like an overworked miner. I think he sees himself as a kind of stage mother, someone who looks after some of the budding comedians, his protégés. I guessed he could also undermine performers he didn't like. He had a flat, shiny face and a camp, slightly whining Scandinavian/Broadway accent. As far as one can be certain of these things, Exiene is obviously and unequivocally gay.

'When Ha! first started, I was told I ought to let the audience know I was gay the moment I stepped on stage. I mean, how obvious do you have to be? I think it's pretty fucking obvious. What do they want me to do – blow a hamster out of my ass?'

Mind you, I thought he'd probably have done it in the right circumstances. James Thurber once wrote, 'The line is thinly drawn between American comedy and American insanity.' At one point in the 1960s, US 'sicknicks' had a reputation for pushing the bounds of decency and taste. Their area of discourse was relatively easy to define: the unspeakable. They gagged about insanity and malnutrition, amphetamine and drug addiction, H-bomb fallout and nervous breakdown, perversion and disease, violence and horror. They derided the wholesome virtues of the square world – faith, hope and charity. And from what I'd seen, the strain still flourished in a semi-underground sort of way.

A few months before my New York visit, Frank Skinner was taken to task by the television presenter and actor Matthew Kelly for jokes Skinner had made about accusations of paedophilia. In his autobiography, the audacious Black Country gagster says there are no 'no-go areas' in comedy, and his only criterion for making a joke is its being funny. I suspect Roy 'Chubby' Brown thought much the same when he cracked a joke to an audience in Middlesbrough about a paedophile ring which had just been uncovered in the area. I'm only guessing, but I suspect the difference between them and the American 'sicknicks' is that the Americans don't care quite so much if they're *not* funny. Or to put it another way, Americans can be effortlessly more extreme and uninhibited about such things. They have an agenda beyond the gag which is, actually, what makes it funny and all right to laugh. They are also, I think, more involved with nationhood, perhaps with being patriotic. Things matter. Which is perhaps why their humour is often broader, more direct, more implicated, more dangerous than ours. Our edginess in no more than a calculated smirk; theirs is a full-blooded convulsion.

After I'd finished at Ha!, I went into a small club in the Village which promised 'uncensored comedy'. The comics who performed here were legging it between different venues, probably doing two or three turns a night. Again, there was the same unabashed ribbing of gays, blacks and, in this instance, a couple from France, who copped a lot of flak from all three of the comics I saw. Though picking on members of the audience is standard fare in all comedy clubs, and even though it was practised here with remorseless intensity, I never felt it was unpleasant or even mildly fearful. Whereas in England, whenever I have seen it happen, no matter how lightly or sparingly, I invariably believe that every word is laced with xenophobic bile. Maybe it's back to our old friend irony, never saying quite what we mean, and therefore meaning something much, much worse than anything we might say.

Even though the club I went into was a pretty liberal place and all the comics made jokes about President Bush – one, a Jewish woman whose boyfriend stood at the back of the room, menacing in Stetson and pointy boots, pointed out that while Bush was Governor of Texas, guns were an acceptable part of the culture whereas dildos were illegal; how could she vote for a man with those values? – they still performed in front of a large Stars and Stripes. They love their country, the Americans. We love our country, too, of course, though in a different way. In a generally diffident, apologetic way that occasionally flares into quasi-imperialist swaggering whenever there's a major football tournament. Rory Bremner would never perform in front of a Union Jack. And to take another comic whose act often had a political slant, Ben Elton never did. The only one who might is the Pub Landlord, Al Murray, and then only in a semi-ironic, I'm-not-really-being-serious sort of way.

I'd come to the Village because Dylan Moran was performing there as part of the British/Irish Comedy Festival. I'd missed the first hour or so because of the session at Ha!, and the people in the box office had refused to let me in at a reduced rate. So I thought 'bugger them' and went to watch the uncensored comedy instead, then sneaked in anyway once they'd closed the box office. I watched the last thirty minutes through a half-open door. The small theatre was barely half full despite the good reviews. I may have been wrong, but I also felt it wasn't going too well. Not badly, but hardly a triumph. The laughs were polite and attentive, and I felt that Dylan was struggling a bit; definitely not in the moment. When he finished, there was never any danger of him coming back for an encore, appreciative though the crowd was. I'd seen him once before, in fact, a few years ago at Lewisham Town Hall, where the audience was much bigger and far more receptive.

As Dylan left the stage, I nipped in and asked four people in the front row whether they'd mind talking to me about the show. Just for a few minutes.

'OK,' said one, a woman of around twenty. 'We're not going anywhere, are we?' she asked her boyfriend, a looming presence with an athlete's body and a strange, slightly small head. Not quite a pinhead, but close.

'I guess not,' he said, and prepared to be questioned.

They'd all come to see Moran because the publicity had compared him to Eddie Izzard, who it seems is greatly liked in America.

I asked them what they liked about Moran.

'The way he goes off at a tangent,' said one.

'Yeah,' said the guy with the small head, 'like it doesn't seem to going anywhere. She likes him more than me.' And he indicated his girlfriend.

'This is the second time I've been,' she said.

'It's different from most American comedians,' interrupted someone in the row behind us, a speccy man with a mustard-coloured shirt. 'More inconsequential.'

His companion joined in, a woman with enormous thighs

and a bumbag. 'Sometimes you feel that American humour is like a maths equation. You know, $x+y$ = punchline. It's a bit impatient. This is a good antidote to that.'

'I prefer it,' said the first woman.

'Yeah,' said her boyfriend, 'that's obvious.'

'You like it too.'

'Not as much as you.'

'You *said* you did.'

'I do. But not as much as you. Sometimes I wait so long to laugh I forget what it is I'm meant to be laughing about.'

And then he laughed.

The general gist was that the British/Irish humour they liked was the kind which was zany and a bit surreal. Its difference from American comedy was what attracted them. And the charm. Izzard especially was perceived as adorable, being funny at no one else's expense. 'You want to take him home and have a drink with him,' someone said.

A couple of my captives mentioned 'whimsy' and thought Americans weren't so good at being eccentric or quaint or, well, whimsical. New York does have a reputation as a place that likes a bit of a moan. 'The secret of survival in the city is to complain entertainingly,' Don DeLillo wrote in his novel *White Noise*. So maybe British comedians were seen as subtle, softer, more deft.

This cultural voyeurism for Brit whimsy showed up in the choices that had been made for the other slots in the festival. The Hollow Men, a Cambridge-educated comedy foursome, little known in Britain, did very well with their literate, absurd, even Pythonesque brand of humour. Lou Viola, the veteran New York talent scout who uncovered them, said, 'Being British makes the Hollow Men seem funnier than they are.

Because, like it or not, in America the English accent speaks of higher intelligence and education.' Hmm. And then there's Iranian Brit. Omid Djalili, who does a routine that's focused on the Taliban, Bush and political machinations. He was slightly shocked by the reception he received, at the depth of the laughter. And when Izzard performs, he claims there is no concession to a transatlantic audience. He is as rambling and eclectic as ever.

If stuff like whimsy and irony and abstract absurdity are received so warmly, it follows there must be demand for it and (ergo!) it must also be a part of the US's comic consciousness. And, of course, it is. You don't have to cast your net too far to find it. For instance. *Six Feet Under* is an excursion into darkness, anxiety and death, leavened by sharp humour. The eccentric comedian Andy Kaufman, who died in 1984 from an inoperable brain tumour, swore that he would reappear exactly twenty years later. Accordingly, in May 2004, a venue was booked in Los Angeles for *The Andy Kaufman: Dead or Alive?* show. And what of the teasing ridicule behind the title of the film *American Splendor*, a portrait of the comic-book writer Harvey Pekar as a shambling, grouchy American Everyman? Or the appointment of arch ironist Englishman Anthony Lane as film critic for *The New Yorker*?

Instinctively, I felt Americans could be every bit as weird as Britons – even whimsically, ironically weird – but I couldn't ask my four volunteers to hang around any longer debating the point. In the end, I let it pass, said my thank-yous and took the subway back to my cavernous room. I had a shower which was followed, despite being dead on my feet, by a night of almost no sleep at all. My body clock was still locked in combat with actual fatigue, one insisting I should have been wide awake, the other telling me not to be so stupid. So I woke every hour, on the hour. I eventually fell deeply asleep at about six thirty, by which time the traffic was building up nicely outside my window and the air con was thrumming along at maximum rattle. The deep sleep lasted about forty minutes before the noise made it impossible to continue.

I cut my losses, had another shower, then went upstairs and had a cream-cheese bagel, a blueberry bagel and three large cups of strong coffee. Awake and bloated, I headed across the street to a payphone. Public phones in America are very different from ours: they're smaller, they're not enclosed or weather proof, they're not very private, and they are often dirtier. Oh, and they work.

'Back today,' I said cheerfully when Pippa answered.

'He was up at five thirty this morning,' she said.

'Otto?'

'Who do you think? Tom Jones?'

Pippa has a thing about Tom Jones, so I sniggered feebly into the receiver.

'Would he like to speak to me?'

'Hang on. I'll ask . . . no. He doesn't want to talk. But he says he'd like a present.'

'What sort of present?'

'Something with a battery. Use your imagination – he's very keen on Spiderman.'

'Right. Any news?'

'You left a bottle of dandelion and burdock in the freezer. It exploded.'

'Sorry about that. I could look for that bra you wanted.'

'Oh please . . .'

'Rightio.'

'How did the gig go?'

'Not bad. Not good, either. I'll tell you about it tomorrow. I get into Heathrow at about eleven.'

'See you later, then.'

'Right. Love you.'

'Missing you already.'

'Bye.'

'Bye.'

Pippa had lived in Los Angeles for several years so she knew the lingo. The nice thing about 'missing you already' is it's already souped with irony. English people can use it with impunity.

I spent the rest of the day buying a submarine (with batteries) and a Kinks CD, watching a couple of movies, then taking a cab out to JFK for the evening flight.

An hour or so later, I took my place at the end of a long check-in queue which inched forward more slowly than any other queue I'd ever been in. Directly in front of me was an Indian family, flying back to Delhi via London and struggling with a mountain of luggage and two small children. The youngest one, an impish boy of about three, kept running away. Well, you would, wouldn't you? It's the only sane thing to do in a crowded airport. But this kept either Mum or Dad occupied, leaving the other poor bugger to somehow keep the bags moving forward, keep an eye on the older and only marginally less untrustworthy daughter, and fend off questions from airport security who clearly thought they constituted some sort of risk. They were, after all, Indian, awkward and nervous. Just asking for it.

Our slow-moving anaconda eventually snaked on board, an hour or so late, by which time my body clock, in any case fucked, was now in pieces. I had simply forgotten how to go to sleep. The in-flight entertainment offered the last two episodes of *The Office*, which I watched back to back with a glass of warm beer and three packets of bacon crunchies. I recalled how much capital the English press had made of the fact that the programme had received a cool response from US viewers. It was generally assumed this was because Americans don't have a sense of humour – whereas, of course, they absolutely do. This, despite the fact that *The Office* had won two Golden Globes, US TV's highest award, and their critics knew it would be destroyed by attempts to remake it. 'See *The Office* now, before NBC ruins it!' predicted one.

There is something unpleasantly smug about the English insistence on possessing a superior sense of humour to Americans – to most other people, in fact. It's a myth. It's like all those people from Liverpool who insist on telling you all the time how friendly or funny they are rather than just *being* friendly or funny. Or the myth of English eccentricity, our smiling tolerance of which is supposedly proof of the diverse nature of Englishness, whereas in reality – just like the assumed ascendancy of our humour – it merely allows us to indulge in complacency over our own lack of imagination. It's all right, we tell ourselves, that the country is going to the dogs and we're incapable of thinking beyond the need to decorate our houses or primp our gardens, because we've still got Our Famous Sense of Humour. We're still Laughing England, a bit mad, a bit bonkers; nothing boring about us, nothing Swedish or German about us. We're unique. No one like us in the world.

Except, of course, that's bollocks.

TEN

Oi! Oi!

I was still sceptical about the existence of a national, pervasively all-embracing kind of humour. New York hadn't changed that. Individuals develop their own systems of comedy. Humour is universal; irony is universal.

Still, coming back to England did *feel* like coming back to England. When we touched down and the Virgin pilot announced, 'Welcome to London, ladies and gentlemen. The temperature on the ground this morning is a sultry thirteen degrees . . .' you knew something was different. When they heard this, the English passengers smiled quietly to themselves. The others looked anxiously out of the windows, wondering how it could possibly be so cool and yet so sultry.

So I was still equivocal. Or being English, relatively equivocal.

George Orwell observed it was 'not easy to discover the connecting thread that runs through English life', though he also said 'but all English people . . . feel that it exists'. That 'feel' does a lot of work. And so it is with the awareness of a shared sense humour – slippery, elusive, shifty, maybe even inconsistent, but somehow sensuously *there*.

I have an American friend, Rick, another Rick, who is a well-educated, liberal, intelligent, creative man. What's more, he quite often laughs at my jokes. However, there remains the strong suspicion that we do not share the same criteria for comedy.

Sometimes it can be quite tricky.

Once, while we were teaching at the same school in Cambridge, Rick persuaded me to to stand in for him at the last minute in a balloon debate. You know; one of those things in which each debater argues the case for a particular (usually famous) person being allowed to stay in an imaginary balloon which supposedly needs to shed some ballast in order to prevent it crashing to the ground.

When I say that Rick asked me at the last minute, I mean that the debate had actually started when he suddenly remembered another, apparently more urgent appointment.

'Steve – listen, I know it's asking a lot,' he whispered as Mr Harding was putting the case for Winston Churchill, 'but I'd be grateful if you could fill in for me right now.'

'Er, OK.'

'Thanks. Good luck.'

'Rick?'

'Yes.'

'Who are you meant to be?'

'Pardon me?'

'In the balloon. Who are you?'

'Baryshnikov.'

'Who?'

'The famous ballet dancer.'

'Never heard of him.'

'*Never heard of him*?'

'Afraid not.'

'I've brought along a cloak and a pair of ballet shoes.'

'Have you? Why?'

'You could wear them, get into role, do a few jumps.'

'Fuck off, Rick.'

'You mustn't let him down. He's a great man.'

'Couldn't I be someone else?'

'Who?'

'I don't know. Philip Larkin.'

'Aaaagh! Not that gloomy, boring English poet who talks about dull train journeys.'

'That's the one.'

'No. It has to be Baryshnikov.'

'Rick – I don't know anything about ballet.'

And so it went on. In a way, though very much in its own way, I thought it was actually a very funny situation, one in which I might have even been prepared to have a go, if only for its incongruous absurdity. In fact, only for its incongruous absurdity. I could have had a bit of a laugh, sent the the thing up a bit. But Rick couldn't see the funny side of it. He was worried I would disgrace the great ballet dancer.

Also, of course, he wanted to win.

On the other hand, I was English and therefore particularly good at disguising my inadequacies through humour. Dunkirk again, you see. Not to mention the Blitz, Eddie the Eagle, wobbly bridges, and so on and so forth. My fall-back position. As Orwell would have said, an example of myth setting up a type or a persona, being embraced and becoming fact. I was prepared to make light of my shortcomings but Rick, despite having a keen sense of humour most of the time, didn't do 'shortcomings'. They were outside his comedic range. If anything, they were viewed as opportunities or challenges, not something to be glossed over with a display of ironic, self-deprecating brio.

It's probably why he went on to be a headmaster and I didn't.

It also illustrated a point once made by the great cartoonist David Low when he observed that the English have a sense of humour but no sense of wit, the suggestion being that English people are so mindful of humour that they carry a sense of it with them at all times, able to see comedy in almost anything rather than in a situation which invites it more specifically.

Anyway, I was back in England and aware of a certain fatigue seeping into my comedic quest. So far as comedy itself was concerned, I felt that any kind of defining revelation was almost as far away as it had been when I started out. As with the creative use of statistics, I thought I could prove (or disprove) anything I wanted. It depended which combination of comedians and audiences you believed.

More to the point, I was wearying. Wearying, that is, of doing something for which I was totally unsuited. Thus far, I had sort of got away with things without ever being able to properly convince either an audience or myself that I was a stand-up comedian.

I was also coming to the conclusion that many comedians weren't actually very funny people. Hardly a revelation, perhaps, though talking to them at gigs always left me feeling, well, frustrated. Not because they weren't being funny but because they lacked a fully functioning sense of humour, as if comedy was best saved for performance. For much of the time, the time when most of us do our living, it was therefore kept under wraps.

Kingsley Amis it was who pointed out that there were generally two main types of professional funny man: the chap who is such a scream at parties that his friends persuade him to go public, as opposed to the performer with a probable theatrical background who has started his career in the business. Very few, he said, are the same person on and off the stage, and many are as 'about as funny as armpits'.

One comedian told me he found himself sitting next to a woman at a dinner party who was fascinated at him being a stand-up.

'You don't *seem* very funny,' she said, after they'd been chatting for a while.

'What do you do?' asked the comic.

'I'm a doctor.'

'Well, you haven't examined me once tonight.'

Fair enough. It had crossed my mind on several occasions that people became comedians for many reasons, not many of them to do with actually being funny folk. Getting laughs, the evidence of funniness, is merely a symptom of something else they want.

Somebody else (not a comedian, though involved in spotting talent and commissioning comedy programmes for television) remarked how attractive a career in comedy must be. I asked why.

'You get to go out most nights, often to a pub or a club, and lots of people express their liking for you by laughing.'

At the time, I nodded politely. A few months earlier, I might have thought a bit the same, though only a bit, and now every bone in my body dissented. Don't get me wrong. Even though I can't hold my drink and am not in any case much of a drinker, I don't mind pubs. But not for four or five nights a week. And I think I'd be in psychological trouble if I relied to any extent on gaining some kind of emotional dependence from the uplifting kicks of a successful gig. Though I'm not great, I'd survived well enough so far to think I wasn't too bad. I'd had my moments. And don't get me wrong about this either – when they happen, it's a nice enough feeling, as far as it goes, but ephemeral and ultimately pretty shallow.

I'd had a conversation with a comedian about this in Birmingham, trying to say something about being older than the others, having therefore been round the block a few times and seeing adulation or love or whatever as, I don't know, *suspect*, let's say. The gist of it was I was more comfortable with caution and discretion. Experience had made me watchful of flattery.

I didn't explain it very well. Clearly he thought I was a tosser. But he gave me a hearing, tried not to look as though he'd been patronised, described the rush he got on stage, especially when 'riding' an audience, and said, 'You must be very grounded not to feel the same.'

'Not really,' I chirped, 'just differently dysfunctional.'

Anyway, for whatever reason, actually several reasons, I was beginning to feel the energy draining out of my quest. Perhaps if I'd persisted for (let's say) another four or five years, really committed myself to the idea of becoming a solo comic performer, things might have been different. I'd have poured my soul into it, gradually found my voice, discovered ways to communicate with an audience, maybe made a modest name for myself on the circuit, become reliable, acquired bookings, done Edinburgh, written material, cultivated a performance, perhaps been noticed by someone at the Beeb or been nominated for an award, maybe done a bit of telly or radio, become a comedic personality, then decided that I wanted to 'develop' and become a serious artist, use my reputation, having paid my dues, to publish a novel and/or find my way into films and/or television drama. Finally, after a few years of this, I would tell the world how much I was missing comedy, my first and truest love, and was planning a one-off stand-up tour called something like, oh, I don't know, 'Steve Jacobi: the Quick Comeback Tour'.

But I wouldn't be having any of that. Instead, I decided on a different kind of tour, a much shorter one which would take me to East Anglia, the south coast and London. The areas not yet covered by my comedic quest. I'd do my original material, really give it my best shot, pin down thoughts about regional comedy while keeping an eye on the wider picture. It would, I supposed, also be a last-gasp try for a window on my soul, though I was pretty sure I now knew where I stood in the epiphany department: a calcified non-performer who was emotionally incapable of taking to the stage and being simultaneously thick- and thin-skinned, the horrible balancing act that becoming a comedian seemed to require.

So not quite doing it gonzo, but semi-gonzo; gonzo-lite.

Still, I'd give it a go. A final go. It would be my 'Definitely No Comeback' tour.

I immediately ran into problems on the East Anglian leg.

Well, you would, wouldn't you?

Admittedly it's one of the more sparsely populated areas in England, though you'd have thought some kind of comedy would have been happening there in July. I Googled for hours on end, but could only come up with a few clubs, even those (in places like St Neots) only operating on an occasional basis, and never on an occasion convenient to me. More likely places such as Cambridge had clubs all right, though none which were actually open or not being renovated. Otherwise, it was an open-mike night in Chelmsford or a trip to Scunthorpe, neither strictly speaking in East Anglia, and both in any case unappetising.

So much for giving it a go.

Perhaps there just wasn't much call for humour in East Anglia. It wasn't that sort of place. You know, the Norfolk Broads, agriculture, fenland, Hereward the Wake, Constable, lots of history, but nothing to actually tickle the funny bone. Nothing to be ashamed of, mind. Some people and places are just like that. Comedy-free zones. East Anglia. My mum. Margaret Thatcher. The Third Reich. Parts of Wales.

On the other hand, I did know of one comedian from the area. Born and bred in Great Yarmouth, he found no jobs to cater for his lively mind but did his national service and met an enigmatic stand-up comedian from Lancashire. They formed a partnership and became national celebrities, many millions tuning into their television show. Even after fashion had turned against them, they remained an indelible part of English showbiz history.

So what was this comedian's name, the unlikely one from Great Yarmouth?

He was called Ted King.

And who was the one from up north?

His name was Arthur Upward.

King was always the straight man, Ernie Wise to Upward's Eric Morecambe. Kenneth Tynan, no less, praised them for their 'surreal whimsy' and the affectionate tension that characterised their relationship. Like most comedians from Great Yarmouth, you guess Ted King had to head for the city to make a go of it. Not much call for provocative, lively humour in a part of the world which is so orderly, conservative and generally unobtrusive.

But here comes the twist. Ted and Arthur don't exist. They're fictional characters from a novel called *The Comedy Man* by D.J. Taylor, and Ted is based at least in part on his grandfather. Though Taylor is most well known for his incisive literary criticism and heavyweight biographies, I wondered whether he might be the nearest thing to the centre of East Anglia's comedic vortex. He'd also written an article, I recalled, in the *TLS*, broadly concerned with the so-called 'golden age' of British television comedy in the 1970s, and in particular Ronnie Barker, *Dad's Army*, and Morecambe and Wise.

I fished out the relevant piece and discovered some welcome nuggets. Here's one: 'It would be impossible to imagine any classic English comedy show taking place in a society that had achieved genuine social equality.' Thinking about it, the word 'genuine' is crucial, especially in today's Blairite, supposedly less class-ridden but actually faux meritocratic society. Or as Taylor put it, 'In an age where class, status and position are as fluid as the audience that still, mysteriously, relishes their exposure, comedy's room for manoeuvre becomes ever more limited.'

So rather than heading off to perform in Great Yarmouth or King's Lynn, or even St Neots, I did the next best thing, probably the only best thing in fact, and arranged to see D.J. Taylor at his home in Norwich.

I know this could be construed as copping out. It didn't feel like that, which doesn't necessarily mean it wasn't true. I wanted to go to East Anglia. I wanted to speak to D.J. Taylor. If a club had been available, I'd have performed.

Still. One down, two to arrange.

I tried to get a gig at a gay club in Brighton, which wasn't having any, though I received back a nice enough message from the booker saying that she knew of another *quite* gay club which might serve my purposes. Eventually, I found a club in Eastbourne. Things were tricky, not just because Edinburgh hopefuls were busy honing their material around the country, but because comedy clubs are viable businesses these days, the premises frequently operated by a larger organisation in the way that pubs are beholden to the breweries. They didn't want to take risks with people like me, an unknown quantity, who might smirch their product.

I'd also decided to finish off at Up the Creek in Greenwich, where my quest had sort of begun. Though this is a big and prestigious club, and I didn't have high hopes of being allowed in, Jane Hardee, who was organising things, listened politely to the story of my adventure, the sense of symmetry that ending in her club would allow, the closure if you like, and she was very welcoming.

'Why not?' she said. 'Though I can't be responsible for the audience, how they treat you and so on.'

'I'll take my chances,' I replied with trouperlike resilience. Part of my thinking was that a bit of heckling might be useful.

It seemed a good idea at the time.

With the last pieces of my comedic jigsaw in place, I set off for Norwich.

Now, those of you who know anything about travelling in the UK will know that travelling horizontally across the country, in either direction, is about as easy to arrange as getting to grips with quantum mechanics. In addition, Pippa and Otto had already taken the car on holiday, so I hired an old Toyota Corolla, which smelt of cheap perfume mixed with mosquito repellent and had wind-down windows, and headed east.

Before she left, Pippa had left me with a final good-luck card, which showed nothing more than a chopping block and an axe. I think she was hoping things would go horribly wrong this time. She felt I'd been lucky thus far. Final and complete humiliation was needed as evidence of there being any justice in the world, really of there being any point to life at all.

I propped up her card on the dashboard. It fell down on the outskirts of Coventry. Then the lock on the glove department broke and the radio stopped working. There was a button which said 'CD' and I'd brought along a bit of Benjamin Britten, *Round the Horne* and an old Little Feat album, though in the end I was buggered if I could find how it worked or where the disc was supposed to go.

I'd got as far as Cambridge when I hit the first of two massive traffic jams which stretched, it seemed, all the way to Norwich and perhaps beyond. I consoled myself for the first thirty minutes or so of humid standstill with the thought that in a way, though only in a way, things like this merely emphasised the remoteness of East Anglia. It belonged to a different era, when travel wasn't so convenient, when the difficulty of making a journey protected small towns and villages from tourism and casual trippers. It was a bit of Merrie Englande which hadn't developed at the same rate as the rest of the country. No motorways. Slow, charming, detached and different. A price had to be paid for this nostalgia, and if sitting in an old and smelly Toyota was the tariff, then so be it.

After two hours, I wasn't quite so sure.

As a kid, we used to pass the time in our car by singing interminable tunes. Sometimes we'd count the other Minis on the road, or the other blue Minis, or the blue Mini Coopers. Dad had a special, limited-edition Radford Mini which had a statuette of a golfer on the bonnet. It also had electric windows, something of a luxury in the mid-1960s, and something more than the Toyota I was travelling in.

Or, at this moment, not travelling in.

None of this would have helped me today as the only cars I could see were the one behind and the one in front. No traffic at all was coming the other way. Instead, I passed the time by thinking of writers other than D.J. Taylor who are known through their initials rather than a name. J.G. Ballard, G.K. Chesterton, A.N. Wilson, J.B. Priestley, F.R. Leavis and V.S. Pritchett, for a start. And of course J.D. Salinger, though he's American and doesn't really count. Why did they choose initials over names in the first place? To lend themselves a certain gravitas, to suggest mystery, or just because they had embarrassing Christian names?

This game didn't last very long. About five minutes. So I started to think of other novels, besides *The Comedy Man*, which were specifically about comedians. Actually, *The Comedy Man* is like most other novels on the subject, being about much more than comedy, especially about what Taylor called 'the social topsoil in which humour takes root and prospers'.

At one level, his novel is a nostalgic celebration of a form of comedy, grounded in live performance, which is going out of fashion. The skill needed to milk an audience for laughs, be sensitive to its sense of community, is anatomised with great sensitivity. It also implies a pre-Thatcherite world, after which humour was lumbered with a social conscience.

Brian Glanville's 1974 novel *The Comic* shares a similar perspective. It's about a comedian who idolises the old music-hall comic Sid Field and endures the same kind of progress as Taylor's protagonist: the hard slog in provincial clubs, climbing the greasy showbiz ladder, becoming top of the bill at the Palladium, through the trauma and inevitable compromises of radio and (especially) TV. Then, downhill into drunkenness, fear and a spectacular crack-up at the Sunderland Empire which, you assume, is not the best place in the world in which to have a breakdown. Both novels suggest a style of humour which has become extinct in a technologically and politically correct, speeded-up world – meditations on the 'Condition of England' in fact, viewed through its humour, though there are in addition the usual subtexts about comedians existing only to make people laugh and the error they make in mistaking laughter for being loved.

There are some interesting variations on this theme. William Trevor's *Children of Dynmouth* for instance, where a scarred and intensely inquisitive individual called Timothy Gedge terrorises and blackmails an otherwise peaceful seaside community until he gets his wish to do a macabre comic turn in the local talent competition.

And then there's John O'Farrell's novel, *This Is Your Life*, in which Jimmy Conway, someone who always wanted to be famous, finally gets his chance when a top comedian dies and Jimmy 'inherits' his material, passes it off as his own, and uses it to become an award-winning stand-up. However, all is not as it seems, and O'Farrell suggests that becoming a comedian has not a little to do with self-loathing, creating another version of yourself, and coming to terms with the gap between who you are and what you want to be. Not so much getting a life as getting a different life. As if becoming a stand-up would in some way compensate for all that awful degradation of youthful optimism.

As if.

Sad, isn't it? Though I guess it's the twin allure of celebrity and laughter, something of a double-whammy in society these days: power and trustworthy likeability. It's what Tony Blair does. (Coincidentally, I saw a letter in the *Independent* around this time which said: 'Sir, What do you do if you've helped to pack hospitals with cluster-bombed babies and children? An obscene stand-up comic routine in the House of Commons.')

If Tony B. was a comedian, who would he be? There's a bit of Monkhouse about him, maybe a hint of Bygraves. And what of the others? Maybe Prescott as Tommy Cooper, Mandelson as Julian Clary, Brown as Paul Merton, Robin Cook as Paul Daniels.

Before he was a novelist, O'Farrell used to be one of Blair's speech writers. And before that, he was a stand-up comedian. Occasionally, you still see him, popping up on television to brighten up otherwise turgid political discussions, though I saw him recently with Ken Clarke (Roy 'Chubby' Brown), and Clarke was much funnier.

There are also some comedians who write novels. Ben Elton is the most obvious example of this sub-genre, though his musicals tend to be funnier than his books. Then there's Rob Newman and David Baddiel, of course. And recently, Jo Brand. These days, it's almost de rigueur to write a novel if you're a comedian, or famous, or even just a bit well known.

Not for many of the old brigade though, the old-style

comedians who made their names just as comedians without being part of the media and publicity circus. Still, Eric Morecambe wrote one. It's called *Mr Lonely* and was published in 1981. It's an odd book, though it has great curiosity value. *Mr Lonely* is cast in the form of a biography of comedian Sid Lewis written by . . . Eric Morecambe. Sid, we're told, is a superb comic performer and a real family man who takes on stage a character called Mr Lonely who is the key to his meteoric rise. Through all the successful television series, Christmas spectaculars and performances in Las Vegas, Sid remains the same, lovable warm-hearted bloke he was at the start – someone who just likes making people laugh.

Les Dawson wrote not one but several novels. The titles are promising (including *A Card for the Clubs*, *Well-fared My Lovely*, *Hitler Was My Mother-in-law* and *A Time Before Genesis*), and the work itself is idiosyncratic. They also show off Dawson's characteristic love of words while being more than merely playful; one is an ambitious, apocalyptic, state-of-the-nation work, for example.

What Dawson's and Morecambe's novels share is a wistful sense of a disappearing past, not quite nostalgic perhaps, but certainly a little maudlin. They are vignettes of social history, harking back to the time and set of circumstances which spawned their humour. To a certain extent, they were of a piece with their comedy. This is rather different from today's college-educated comedians, most of whom are quite able to write books that look suspiciously like a novel, and fancy their chances at being all-rounders. 'Look!' they seem to be saying, 'I want you to laugh. But I also want to make you cry and think. How clever is that?' Maybe it's because, as Taylor says, in an age where comedy's room for manoeuvre has been diminished, people are finding different ways of being funny, or channelling what would once have been the starting point for funny material into other media.

As I inched towards Thetford, one further novel came to mind. This was Gordon Burn's *The North of England Home Service* which tells the story of Ray Cruddas, comedian, TV presenter and eventually, under Thatcher, a sort of Downing Street court jester. Dropped from the Prime Minister's guest list, he accepts that the good old days are over and returns to Tyneside. Here, he dreams up Bobby's, an authentic club, complete with industrial mangles and such like, where the decor feeds the apparently bottomless appetite for a heavy industrial past. Illusions, the novel suggests, are essential; in all sorts of ways, grim reality is necessarily buttressed by the imagined and the imaginatively recalled.

It's not a controversial suggestion, even in a comedy club. The heritage industry has long been used to plant the thought that we really do care about the past, aren't moving forwards with complete disregard for old values. And the same with comedy. Brucie, Bob, Ken, Tommy, Frankie, Eric and Ern et al., have all been welcomed back into the business, lending it a familiar, unaffected lustre far removed from the ostentatious, ambition-fuelled, celebrity-driven game it has actually become.

Perhaps *The North of England Home Service* is a little too sentimental for the past, and too open in its disdain for modern life, describing its 'round-the-clock, leisure-and-pleasure hedonism . . . and fleeting entertainment experiences, [where] work was . . . fun; work was . . . recreation'. For Burn, and for his protagonist, you sense this represents a betrayal of 'true' comedy where humour and in particular regional humour were used to show deep affection and understanding of the people and places a comedian had been immersed in all his life. This in contrast to the matey, ephemeral chirpiness of many of today's circuit comedians – today in Leicester, tomorrow in Chelmsford – with their 'Anybody here like football?' blokeishness. Presumably, the former category represented the sort of comedians that people like John O'Farrell (or me) could never have been, and who Les Dawson and Eric Morecambe once were. The point is that humour was never simply about being funny, but about developing relationships, defining communities, asserting identity. Whereas now the implication is that it's all part of having a laugh, having a good time, in the same bracket as getting pissed, watching football, playing video games, shagging, shoplifting . . .

Wait a bit. The queue's moving. Funny what you think of when you're stuck in a jam for a couple of hours. Luckily, I'd allowed plenty of time for the journey, even hoping I might manage a trip into Norwich itself, maybe to look round the castle. Now, there was only time to get off the A11, grab a petrol-station sandwich – oh all right, and a Mars milk drink – and find D.J. Taylor's house.

The last bit was easy. His directions were, as you can imagine, crisp and precise. As I turned into the drive and parked in front of a large Victorian house, a small boy, presumably his son, or one of his sons, opened the front door. For a moment, I wondered whether to ask if 'D.J.' was in, but I needn't have worried, as almost immediately David appeared, ushered me through the house and into the back garden, where we plonked ourselves down under some shade-giving trees and prepared to banter about comedy.

One of the first things you notice about David is that he is very clever indeed. Very nice, but also very clever. Quite often they don't go together very well. Though he must be about the same age as me, he looks much younger, energetic, almost gamin. Slumped next to him, I felt like some ancient rotting hulk, a medieval sea wreck, a vast shell of slothful, unrealised uselessness. Still, it was nice sitting there talking about comedy, actually not talking about comedy at all to begin with, but talking about cricket. David said he used to watch test matches at Trent Bridge when he were a lad, and could remember going to his first England match, in the 1970s against New Zealand, when Tony Greig and Dennis Amiss scored centuries. England's win had been delayed by the Kiwi captain Bev Congdon scoring a big hundred. The sad thing is, I can also remember it. He scored 176. I watched it on television. Afterwards I went out and pretended to be Dennis Amiss, throwing a tennis ball against the wall in our back garden, then hitting it back with my size six Green Stripe Slazenger bat I had been bought the year before at Ray Hitchcock's Sports Shop for £12.95. We ate hot dogs for tea. We had to. It was Tuesday.

Anyway, David had just written an article for the *Tablet* about a Sikh comedian from Walsall who he thought was very interesting though still a little uneasy with his self-mocking material.

Well, we've all been there.

I sympathised, like the generous old pro I was.

We chatted a bit about this Sikh chap and the idea that jokes are nothing unless they're dangerous, on the edge of things. And this brought me to his *TLS* article and the observation that there were now fewer things to make jokes about. It was very hard, he said, to make jokes that were morally repugnant even if they were technically brilliant. David remembered one such gag from his teenage years: a black man goes into a pub with a parrot perched on his shoulder. 'Where did you get that, then?' wonders the barman. 'Oh,' squawks the parrot, 'there's fucking hundreds of them in the jungle out in Africa.'

Even though this was Bernard Manning territory, I couldn't help laughing, though laughing or at least trying to laugh in a way which suggested ample moral scruple in addition to comic appreciation. A sort of throaty gurgle, implying I was trying to resist anything so vulgar as an unimpeded, politically incorrect guffaw.

It's happened to us all, this kind of thing, I'm sure. The one I recall from my youth was Stevie Wonder being asked what it was like to be blind. 'Could be worse,' he answered, 'I could be black.' There were loads of them then, and not just about black people; homosexuals, fatties, starving Biafrans were all, at the time, fair game for a well-crafted joke. They were beautifully designed things, the insensitivity of content in some way counterbalanced by a flawless technique.

Well, moving on.

In addition to writing a biography on Orwell, David also has one on William Makepeace Thackeray under his belt. Thackeray was a famous Victorian novelist whose masterpieces are *Vanity Fair* and *The Memoirs of Barry Lyndon Esq.* Part of David's research led him to Thackeray's great-great-great-great-grandson, none other than the comedian Al Murray, the self-styled 'Pub Landlord'.

'It's an odd link,' David said, 'but when you see him in profile, with that pugilist's nose and forehead, you can see exactly where he's come from.'

Apparently, some of Murray's audiences don't appreciate the irony behind his xenophobic little Englandism. They come dressed in England football shirts and wave flags with the cross of St George and so on. So much for English irony, though David wouldn't be drawn on the notions of national humour, playing a pretty straight bat about, for instance, American wisecracking and the mild sarcasm of the English.

'Class is still a significant part of our humour, though,' I ventured, 'even though we're meant to be less class-conscious these days.'

'Perhaps more interested in status,' David replied. '*Dad's Army*, for instance, was obsessed with status just as much as class – it's full of people trying to impose their personalities on colleagues and subordinates. Even Private Godfrey, though he does it by default.'

'And Fraser,' I said, '"We're all doomed!"' though, obviously, without even attempting the Scottish accent.

'Yes.'

Actually, though I didn't say so, I thought 'class' and 'status' amounted to much the same thing in twenty-first-century England (though not in America where status is determined solely by money). Thus, the south is predominantly middle-class, a class which is still rising and defines much of England's character. Years and years ago, E.M. Forster said much the same thing, observing that 'the heart of England is in the middle classes'. He went on to describe them as being, among other things, cautious, efficient, unimaginative, hypocritical and with 'an undeveloped heart, [though] not a cold one'.

And now? Private schools flourish as never before. People who have money want their children to acquire the appropriate social trappings, and such things often begin with the right kind of education. These days, Nike trainers, a knowledge of rap music, assumed working-class speech patterns, the use of

American colloquialisms are as much a sign of being middle-class as a side parting, saying 'good heavens', listening to Elgar, having a working knowledge of Latin, and knowing that Bev Congdon once scored 176.

Anyway, this sort of thing passed through my mind as David strode off across the garden to disentangle his two sons, the youngest of whom was trading relatively good-natured blows with his older brother.

'Where were we?' he asked once he got back.

'Class,' I said, though we weren't really. It was more where I was.

'Ah, yes . . . status,' he said. 'Humour is very important as a means of defining yourself. Having fun at the expense of those around you helps to determine who you are.'

'How about in Norfolk?'

'There's always been teasing of the simple folk from Suffolk – and vice versa.'

'Maybe the more crowded and sophisticated a place is, the more it has to rub up against, and therefore the more material it has – it needs – for this kind of characterising humour . . .?'

'Very possibly. It used to be that a person from one part of the country couldn't be understood by someone who came from a different part. Accent and dialect was significant in that respect. Not so much now, of course. In the nineteenth century, *Punch* made a lot of jokes about the monarchy, though actually those who made the jokes understood that the royals were as bourgeois as them, actually one of the gang, so to speak. The humour here was a way of establishing a workable sense of difference. And they did much the same to the working classes.'

'A bit like creating a sense of familiarity through teasing?'

'More or less.'

I left not long after this, bracing myself for more hold-ups along the A11. Just before leaving, David had touched on the memory of his grandfather, in part the inspiration for Ted King. He was a concert party comedian, a quiet, reserved man who came alive on stage. He was a man transformed – funny as though being in front of an audience really meant something.

'The same for you, I assume,' David said.

'Er, no,' I replied, though sparing him the details.

It made me chuckle, did that, on the way home, and I thought again how relieved I was to be nearing the end of my comedic quest. The more I experienced life on stage, and the more I heard about other people being transported by the occasion, the more I knew how hopeless it was for me. For all kinds of reasons, some of them no doubt unpleasant and disobliging about my deep-rooted lack of public generosity, my die-hard determination not to give anything away, and my sheer bloody-minded, reserved, fuck-you, anti-social grumpiness. I just didn't belong. I was a stranger to its miraculous alchemy.

Or maybe I just wasn't very good.

I got the old Toyota back to the car-rental place, Blu-Tacking the broken ashtray so it didn't look broken, and headed home to collect myself before the Eastbourne gig. There were three phone messages waiting for me. One was from Jim Grant, the accommodating bloke who ran things at Eastbourne Oi! Oi!, to say he thought I'd asked for a September date, had indeed booked me for September, but now gathered it was *this* Sunday I wanted, i.e. not September at all, but could still squeeze me in, looked forward to seeing me, and would be starting the comedy evening at eight or thereabouts. Another message was from Max, my other and eldest son, actually older than Otto by almost twenty years, who was doing astrophysics at university and was wanting a special pair of chromatic spectacles for his birthday, spectacles which would apparently help in his struggle against dyslexia. They would cost three hundred quid. Give or take. Rather sourly, I wondered who *didn't* have dyslexia these days. The last was from Pippa, who was in France with Otto, who was fine, being very funny, at least funnier than me, and was looking forward to seeing me at the conclusion of my comedic quest, and had already fixed up a gig at the local village hall in Normandy.

This was a dig at my piss-poor ability to speak French, which was ridiculed every time I opened my mouth. Even attempting the comparatively straightforward '*bonjour*' in the local *boulangerie* immediately established me as a tongue-tied, flat-accented '*rosbif*'. Eddie Izzard, apparently, got to grips with French so he could do his material in, er, France. He has plans to learn German, Spanish and even Arabic, and then perform in those languages, too. Brave man, I thought; it showed a touching faith in the universality of humour.

Incidentally, Izzard is also dyslexic, as is Ross Noble, and I can't help thinking that their characteristic brands of humour, the free-form riffing which resists the claustrophobic format of television, is somehow tied to this.

Maybe that's the reason I *can't* do it.

And maybe, of course, not.

I took the train to Eastbourne, rather looking forward to the trip, perhaps as a knackered marathon runner anticipates the stadium at the end of his race, not really caring where he's placed, just glad to be there at all, still running. There were other reasons, too, though: the Towner Art Gallery in Eastbourne had a good collection of paintings by Eric Ravilious, one of my favourite artists, and it was always nice to be by the seaside.

I have a lovely guidebook of the area, *About Britain No. 3*, published in 1951 in conjunction with the Festival of Britain. It informed me that Eastbourne is one of the few 'planned' resorts on the English coast, the Duke of Devonshire having laid out wide streets and squares, with trees and gardens, between the old town and the lower slopes of Beachy Head. In addition, it's part of a pretty iconic stretch of coastline, though much of the imagery it evokes is now somewhat tarnished. Hastings is about twenty miles away, run-down and tatty, though there's talk of updating the rail links and an injection of European money to refurbish the place. There's a strongish gay community there ('Gay-stings'), too, always good for house prices and a sign that things are probably on the up. About a year ago, we were staying with friends there and on a whim almost went to see Max Bygraves give his last ever UK performance before, I think, emigrating to Australia.

Almost.

Actually, it was a missed chance. One of the few survivors of the music hall/variety era strutting his stuff for the last time at a well-known resort theatre. Awesome. The last of Max at the last of England. Instead, we'd stayed in, eaten some shepherd's pie and watched a *Thunderbirds* video with Otto.

Eric Ravilious liked this part of England for several reasons, one of which was the chalky downs which represented for him, and others, all that was enduring and good about England – ancient, civilised, resilient. Vera Lynn thought so, too, though she expressed it rather differently.

After all this, Eastbourne itself is inevitably a rather down-at-heel disappointment. I walked from the station through a hideously plain shopping mall, packed with foreign-language students and a number of old or old-looking blokes slumped in doorways clutching bottles, mostly of cider I guessed. One of them asked me for money, in fact asked me very politely, so I handed over a quid. It's like the Alan Bennett line about Waterloo Bridge – best to treat it as a toll bridge and you won't feel affronted.

'Just off the train?' the man asked.

'Yes.'

'What have you come here for?'

'I'm doing some comedy at a club.'

'Good place for comedy,' he wheezed, then returned to his doorway with a cheery wave.

A few minutes later, I booked into a seafront hotel, thirty quid a night, thirty-six with full English breakfast. Though it was clear the place was full of pensioners on coach holidays, I didn't much mind. I'm at the sad stage of my life where there's certain kick to be had from being addressed as 'young man' and merely walking up a flight of stairs puts you in the running for a crack at the Olympics.

The room was, as anticipated, dreadful, though it did make me feel momentarily at one with those fabled old comedians who did the circuit, staying in unappetising digs with grasping landladies, developing a sort of gallows humour about their existence, sacrificing comfort for their art. That sort of thing.

I went out for a walk on the pier, gorged myself on fish and chips (and mushy peas) at the Chippy on the Pier and strolled to its furthest point. More blokes slumped around, though also a couple having a snog and a young lad fishing.

The sagging figures reminded me of a minor character called Gorgeous George in Angela Carter's novel *Wise Children*. He was an old-time vaudevillian upon whose torso a map of the world had been tattooed, with the empire all in pink. This illustrated man is 'not a comic at all but an enormous statement'. In his Union Jack 'gee-gee string' ('I would have kept a horse decent') he is the pasteboard, knees-up, end-of-the-pier incarnation of hope-and-glory Britain, and he ends, rather like the thing he embodies, as 'an old cove in rags, begging'.

It was still early, but after a bit more walking I found the café-bar which 'became' Eastbourne Oi! Oi! every Sunday night. It was on a sort of high street, surrounded by other bars and clubs, all colonised by young and very young people. Eastbourne seemed to be a place either of geriatric antiquity or pubescent unreadiness. Nothing in between. Nobody like me, in other words. I began to worry about my audience.

A girl who couldn't have been more than fourteen, maybe thirteen (maybe *twelve*), walked past the comedy club, then paused. She was drinking from a bottle and wearing something like but wasn't quite a bikini, the bottom half of which was partially covered by a colourful yellow bandage which she had wrapped around her waist. It suddenly felt as if I'd not only strayed into the wrong place but was marooned in the wrong century. And I feared for my comedy. Would she go in? Would she and her mates constitute the core of my audience? A CBeebies crowd?

Luckily, she walked on and disappeared into the building next door, two meaty bouncers asking her age ('eighteen and a half') before waving her in.

Expecting the worst, I entered Eastbourne Oi! Oi! and

introduced myself to the barman, a doughy-faced man with a quizzical, vaguely amused, lived-in look about him. Like most barmen, I suppose.

'Um, is Jim here?' I asked.

'Not yet. He's late. Actually, he's usually late.'

'Are you a comedian?' asked a a youngish but by no means impossibly young woman sitting at the bar.

'In a manner of speaking.'

'Hello – I'm Jim's girlfriend. Have a seat and a drink while you wait.'

So we sat and chatted for a few minutes, waiting for Jim, which I gather she did quite a lot of, and talking about Jim's comedy.

'He's usually ever so quiet off the stage, almost shy. But when he's up there, he's like a man possessed. Something just gets into him.'

'He's transformed.'

'Absolutely.'

Actually, I was getting tired of hearing about all these magically charged alchemists – they were making me feel odd, inadequate, as if not being somehow electrified was a black mark – so I changed the subject and asked a mundane question about the layout of the club. For example, the whereabouts of the stage. There didn't seem to be one. There was a gallery to the rear of the room, suspended above chairs and tables, which at the moment hosted computers. This, apparently, was also an Internet café, though the area became a sort of green room once the comedy got under way. As for the stage, comedians walked down the metal flight of stairs and performed on a small, square of steel about two or three steps from the bottom, actually on the staircase itself.

It was an odd set-up. Still, I felt strangely calm about the whole thing. I didn't feel the need to find a car park and roam around it reciting my material. I just knew the words were up there, somewhere, floating around, waiting for their release.

Jim eventually showed up, a small, perky, efficient man probably in his mid-twenties. He said hello to his girlfriend, then rushed around getting things organised, setting up the mike on the stairs, identifying which comedians had shown up, then ushering us up to the gallery. One anorak was still logged on, from what I could see attempting to track down a new wing mirror for his 1979 Capri.

We were introduced to one another and a running order established. Unusually, the headline act, Pat Monahan, would be opening, in fact doing two sets, also bringing the entertainment to a close. There was a burly bloke from London who worked at NatWest, and a northern comedian with long, gingery hair and a been-there-done-that, Deputy Dawg sort of expression.

Pat Monahan himself was perfecting his Edinburgh routine: he'd already had a crack at it in Guildford earlier the same day, and had literally just driven down. On the bill, he was advertised as 'Mad Pat Monahan'.

'Why's he called that?' I asked someone with a beard who was hanging around, helping Jim, and chatting to us all in a friendly way.

'Because he's fucking mad,' came the reply.

Be that as it may, Pat seemed very likeable and charming, possessed of a suppressed, dangerously roaming energy. Though he's a Geordie, and does sound a little like Ross Noble, he is also of Irish and Iranian descent. Imagine Noble crossed with the boxer Naseem Hamed and the footballer Roy Keane and you probably get someone quite close to Monahan.

A Londoner, a northerner, an Irish-Iranian Geordie, and me, Posh Kraut, all on the same bill in Eastbourne. Clearly there was no such thing as regional humour any more. The old boundaries of difference, of geography and distance, had been obliterated by technology and travel. Comedy clubs were where comics from other places searched for things they might have in common with a disparate audience. These days, comedians were mercenaries, parachuted in to give people a good time, to find laughter's equivalent of the Common Denominator.

Nothing wrong with that, of course. In medieval times, there were all manner of professional fools around, especially at the court. The fact that he was an 'outsider' was even an important part of his status. He was literally a 'nobody', someone who could observe and comment upon, but never participate in, the aristocratic courtier's competition for power. The absurdity of the jester's dress both symbolised and helped create this distance. And the privilege of this detached foolishness was liberty of utterance: the ability to say things to the King through humour which would otherwise have cost a courtier his head. Simple, innate foolishness, it was believed, acted as a shield against worldly corruption and the Devil's wiles.

So there you go. In some small way we were part of an honourable tradition.

Soon there was a bit of the obligatory loud music, then Jim was up, doing a nice warm-up, jollying the lively crowd along, exorting them to shout 'Oi! Oi!' whenever occasion demanded, though I can't now recall what the occasion was, and generally setting the scene for Pat's opening set.

His Edinburgh theme was children's games, and after some banter with the audience, actually a lot of banter, Pat being famous for going off at a tangent, he invited volunteers to come up and do cat's cradle with him. There was much mirth when it became clear how crap men were at this, though it wasn't really rib-tickling stuff, just gentle and agreeable. At one point, he discovered a woman from South Africa in the front row and told the old joke about having a washing machine from her country ('It doesn't let you do a mixed wash'). This was followed immediately by an abject and fulsome apology for resorting to such material.

Very different from New York, I mused, with beady-eyed, old-trouper savvy.

It struck me while all this was going on, even over such a short time, how used I'd become to the atmosphere in comedy clubs. The loud introductory music, the genial MC, the friendly backchat from the audience, and so on. I could even hazard a guess at the other comedians' material – the bloke from NatWest would most likely make self-deprecating comments about his size and lack of success with women, while Northern Man would be comically sour and sarcastic. So when Jim introduced me, after the interval and sandwiched in between these two, I was sort of ready, or as ready as I could have been, and as a consequence, fairly relaxed.

I ambled down the steps, took up my position on the metal plate, fiddled with the microphone, and began the routine. I was immediately aware of someone on my left making the odd comment. I didn't respond, though I do remember glancing in the direction from which the disembodied noise was coming, maybe even managing a withering glance, and just getting on with it.

The laughs came, more or less on cue, and I found myself gaining in confidence, consciously slowing down the material, reinforcing the odd line, letting the audience know when it was their turn, secure with my material, establishing, I suppose, a bit of a relationship, even a rapport. Somewhere deep, deep inside me a performance was stirring. Never showy, probably not in the least convincing or compelling, but a performance of sorts, and the sensation not necessarily of enjoying things, never that, but of not *not* enjoying them either, of doing something more than merely enduring. Not 'in the moment', but then not absolutely out of it, either.

When I'd finished, even being playful with the concluding joke, I received warm, no, *admiring* applause. I turned and headed back up the stairs, recalling how I always rushed off stage and aware that here I was doing it again, back to the gallery where the other comedians were friendly and appreciative of what I'd done.

'Fantastic material,' said Mad Pat Monahan, meaning I supposed that I had delivered reasonable material slightly less expertly than a retarded baboon. But it was nice of him to say it.

'Never seen hecklers dealt with like that,' said another.

Hecklers? I thought. What hecklers?

'You just ignored them and carried on. Couldn't give a toss whether they got you or not.'

'You delivered on your own terms, man,' said the bloke with the beard.

All this was news to me. I hadn't heard anything. Just as well. Still, any praise was gratefully received.

'Er, thanks,' I said.

Someone else chipped in with a comment about thoughtful

material and my 'odd manner', which, he claimed 'forced' the audience to listen.

Of course, I had very little idea any of this was going on, but thinking about it afterwards, I reckoned the intimate venue, a pleasant crowd, the chemistry of the other, very different comedians and my casual manner all helped. 'Dying from trying' is an old adage. This was its opposite: 'charming by calming'.

NatWest man, Sean I think his name was, said how high he was after every gig. Did I feel the same? How did I feel now?

It was an invitation from one performer to another to justify what we did; to shoot the breeze, collude, natter, reminisce, give one another a funny handshake, to remind ourselves of the buzz to be got from making people laugh, to confirm to one another how important This Thing was, how much it affected us.

But I couldn't in all honesty say so.

Things had gone reasonably well in Eastbourne. I was pleased, sure enough, though still more relieved than euphoric. In any case, I wouldn't have known what to do with euphoria. Before he had gone on, I noticed Sean exercising himself, taking deep breaths, pumping his arms, flexing his shoulders, that kind of thing. It seemed very odd. How disengaged I was from all that, and ultimately from caring too much about the audience. And yet a few weeks ago, I had been literally shitting myself. Whatever change had occurred was shielding me from becoming too intoxicated or jubilant, though it also prevented me from sinking into a depression if things didn't go well. It protected me all right, this indifference, but it also reinforced the understanding that I could never be a proper comedian, one who exists only to make people laugh: 'They laugh, therefore I exist,' as Johnny Lucas says in Brian Glanville's novel. *Rident ergo sum.*

The scale of my disconnection was made more apparent by Mad Pat's closing set. He is a noted performer, is Pat. He loves doing it. As soon as he's on stage, he's sets off towards the audience like an excited puppy. He is as determinedly inclusive as I am stand-offishly private. Even though his material is uneven and he has to improvise wildly and sometimes chaotically to keep his audience, you can't help warming to him, wanting to like him. 'I'd love to take him home with me,' I overheard one girl say to her friend afterwards, and I don't think she meant it in a sexual way.

Pat's act ended with a lengthy montage of classic TV and film music during which he whirled Postman Pat's cat Jess around, somehow embodying the essence of each programme and movie. As required and on cue, Jess climbed, span, fucked, cuddled, whirled, ran, slept and talked. It was a vibrant, exhausting tour de force. He came off after fifteen minutes or so of this glistening with sweat and puffing heavily. You couldn't not admire the sheer unabashed energy of it.

After the show, I stayed around and chatted, not that keen to hurry back to my hotel room. Jim said I'd be welcome back at any time, and Pat gave me his card ('Patrick Monahan – COMEDIAN – Big on the Irish/Iranian/Geordie circuit'). Then I talked with someone young enough to be my son who had chucked in his job and was writing material for a mate of his who was doing the performing end of things. He wanted to make a living out of comedy and naturally enough wanted a few tips. I told him I wasn't the bloke to whom he should be talking, but it didn't do much good, so I babbled on a bit about being true to yourself, finding your own comedy, writing material that meant something to you, that sort of stuff.

God, I sounded a prat.

Then I walked back to the hotel. Even though it wasn't so late, the place was locked and I had to disturb the night porter.

'Sorry about the noise,' I said, referring to the loudish bell that had to be rung.

'Don't worry, mate,' the porter replied, 'everyone here is well tucked up, hearing aids turned off. Not a problem.'

Next morning, in the eight o'clock breakfast queue, two women behind me were talking about their night's sleep. At a pinch, both were well into their eighties.

'Did you sleep well last night?' asked one.

'Not really. At home, of course, I have one of those things that makes your bed go up and down. How was your night?'

'Oh, all right. Though I've only got a shower in my room, which can be a bit tricky come the morning ablutions.'

'I've got a shower. And a bath.'

'All right for some.'

'It's not like home, though. At home I've got one of those things that lowers you in and out.'

'That's nice.'

'And one of those orthopaedic chairs.'

'My son's getting me a chairlift for Christmas.'

'They're very useful – I don't know that I'd do without mine. It's got two speed settings. Top of the range, apparently.'

'It gets more difficult every year, doesn't it?'

'This coming-on-holiday business?'

'Yes.'

'It does.'

'Such a problem getting my tights on. I do miss Ronnie.'

All this seemed much funnier than anything I could ever say on stage.

And I still didn't absolutely understand why people felt such a need for comedy clubs. But there you go – maybe I'm just a miserable old fucker who's out of step with the rest of the world.

Anyway, only one more gig to go. Up the Creek in five days' time. Then I could hang up my teeth, or whatever it is that comedians hang up, but at any rate hang it up for ever.

ELEVEN

Up the Creek again

Even before I arrived in south-east London for the Up the Creek gig, I had a feeling that something wasn't right. The journey on the Docklands Light Railway, for instance, which took me through strange, futuristic, post-industrial developments before dumping me at Greenwich, was unsettlingly false. This would be my last gig, and already I felt relieved, disjointed, becalmed, a spent force.

Though the achievements of Eastbourne were still pretty fresh in my mind, I knew there would be no more gigging after Up the Creek. No matter what happened. I'd made a plan and seen it through. That was what I was good at. And I'd sort of got what I wanted from the whole experience. To go on would have meant conceding there might have been some sort of future for me in stand-up, or that I was obsessively striving for one.

I had come to understand the limits of my comedic ambitions and was comfortable with them. Though I felt quite satisfied with the events at Eastbourne, I was also aware that they represented some kind of ceiling. I could have responded in one of two ways: either be enormously encouraged by my apparent progress, or mildly disappointed at the pleasing but ultimately moderate level of achievement.

Obviously I opted for the second.

There's no way of fooling yourself. I knew, just *knew*, that stand-up was not for me. Eastbourne was like trying on a very expensive suit and seeing that you looked OK. But only OK. In the end, it made you appreciate that dressing up just wasn't worth all the bother. Not your bag. So when I say that I was a spent force, you have to understand the context.

So, although I approached Up the Creek with anxiety, it was an anxiety fortified by a sense of already having done a job, and done it reasonably well. I'd proved something to myself and had nothing to be ashamed of. Now I could let go of the whole performing thing with my pride more or less intact. To get on stage at all, I'd put myself through the mincer, become a stranger to myself, taken a ghastly holiday from my habitual character. I had nothing to lose.

Even so, this last gig felt wrong. Somehow, well, rotten.

Earlier in the day, I'd met Tony Allen, who founded Alternative Comedy more than twenty years ago with people like Alexei Sayle and Keith Allen (no relation). When he asked how the stand-up was going and I said I was sort of getting away with it, he replied, 'Getting away with it isn't enough really, is it?'

Tony believes that stand-up is about transcending the cheap laugh to reveal the truth beyond, which obviously wasn't quite my thing, but I knew what he meant. He is serious about being a comic performer, arguing for the kind of heartfelt ideas and spontaneous sincerity which can only come from the nakedness you feel on stage. Now he's moved his act to Speakers' Corner in Hyde Park where he's known as 'Lofty Tone'.

The point being, I always sensed that my relative indifference to stand-up would eventually be exposed. There were many ways to be committed, and I wasn't bound to any of them.

Without meaning to, Tony reminded me of the void at the centre of my act.

It didn't make me feel any better.

I also wondered whether anyone I knew might be in the audience, and the thought further unhinged me. Tony Binns, the old friend I hadn't seen for a year or so, had moved to Greenwich, knowing him probably into a loft apartment with fake wooden floors, a fancy kitchen, and at least one power shower. One of my ex-wife's friends, a tall angular woman, the sort who Takes Sides when relationships break down, also lived in the area.

They probably wouldn't be at Up the Creek of course, but just supposing they might, the mere thought of them being there, didn't help.

Thus far, I'd got away without telling many people about the stand-up. Pippa was banned. A few others who had uncovered my guilty secret had now given up attempting to prise dates and venues from me. However, in the last week, news had somehow leaked out to my sister and then to my parents. Even though they would never make the journey to London, just knowing that they knew made me feel uncomfortable, vulnerable, exposed.

Families. They're such bad ideas. Why can they have this crippling effect on you? Over the years, I've met people who are able to call their parents by their Christian names, relate to them as human beings, can even spend an entire Christmas period with them, and both sets of their new partners, *and* all their sons, daughters, stepsons, stepdaughters and, in one case, the half stepson acquired during a one-night fling. These people are always jolly and friendly with one another, the relationship merely a happy accident that allows them to meet and spend time with like-minded folk who in the normal run of things they would have anyway got on with like a house on fire. This, I suppose, is better than being hamstrung and emotionally disabled by the unavoidable fact of just having a mother and a father, who though they don't mean to 'fuck you up', unfortunately have. Actually, I do think they mean to, but that's another story.

Still, if you want to be a comedian and your parents haven't fucked you up then maybe they've *really* fucked you up.

Well, it's a theory.

In our house at Christmas, even pulling a cracker and donning a paper hat were potentially crippling moments of self-conscious awkwardness.

Anyway, they *knew*. Even though they had nothing to do with it and nobody said much – my sister said, rather blankly, 'Good for you, Stevie'; I think it was the 'Stevie' which did it for me – they still knew. And I knew that they knew, and they knew that I knew that they knew.

And all this was no doubt playing on my unconscious as I arrived in Greenwich.

It was also a sultry, pre-storm, end-of-the-week, Friday night. As soon as I emerged from the Underground station, I could sense the expectancy, the explosion waiting to happen. Not a good omen if you're looking for patience or a thoughtful engagement with understated humour.

The club wasn't quite as I remembered. The bar was actually a separate space to the side of the stage area and the food (exclusively Chinese, I think) was served upstairs. Mere details, however. It was still the same place; felt the same.

There were three other acts on that night, the proper acts, and the MC, Nick Wilty, apparently a Falklands War veteran. We all introduced ourselves in the tiny dressing room, up another flight of stairs from the Chinese-food outlet, and Nick said he'd like to begin with Rhod Gilbert, whom he knew would get the evening off to a good start, then go to an interval, after which there'd be me and a Canadian called André Vincent, eventually finishing, after one more interval, with another Canadian, this one called Craig Campbell.

(Actually, André Vincent may not be 'André Vincent'. He was billed as André Vincent and on the night I called him 'André', though I've since discovered there's another comedian called 'André Vincent', who often wears a beret and looks a bit like Phill Jupitus. So maybe my André isn't André after all, even though I'll continue to call him André.)

I would effectively be the penultimate act as Nick wanted to split the two Canadians, though for unspecified reasons, maybe something to do with the accent, possibly the feeling that there would be too many consecutive jokes about moose, but anyway disentangling them.

This meant I would be up near the top end of the bill. Up to this point, my strategy had been to get on early, sort of get away with things, before the audience were properly warmed up, and then get off quick. I didn't want a warmed-up audience; I wanted cold, numbed ones that were too sluggish to respond.

I went down to have a look at the punters. They were a noisy lot. They also seemed to know each other. I commented on this to Jane Hardee who confirmed that the club had a regular core who knew their comedy.

'Are they, er, very demanding?' I asked sheepishly.

'Can be,' she smiled.

'So this is their patch?'

'Mmmm.'

Then I went for a pee and pissed down my trousers. André Vincent was also in there, actually in a cubicle, though the door was open and he was looking very tense. He'd just been sick.

I gathered he was fresh over from Canada, was trying to develop a name in England, and this was one of his first gigs. I'd already heard him chatting to Craig, wondering how his material would go, that kind of thing. Craig said all the ordinary points of reference were different, from parking your car to buying a beer. It was the small things which often made a difference with comedy – you had to be aware of them as they were often the keys to a joke or line of thought. While I eavesdropped on their conversation, I noticed that someone, presumably another comic, had at some time drawn a cartoon on the dressing-room wall. It depicted a man with a contrived, nervy smile, with a speech bubble saying something like, 'I'd much rather be doing something else.' Probably many comedians felt like this before going on stage. But after – ah, well, that was different.

Unless you were me, of course.

As Nick took the stage to get things going, I thought again about the anachronistic absurdity of regional humour: Friday night, and a group of south Londoners were being entertained by two Canadians and a Welshman. No cheeky-chappy cockneys, no local knowledge, just four blokes wondering whether they could strike the appropriate chord.

Actually, that's not strictly true. Nick said he lived in Herne Hill, about twenty minutes or so by car from Greenwich – or an hour by bus, with three changes. So he was relatively local. I know Herne Hill. It has a serviceable though decaying velodrome, once used (I believe) for the London Olympics. It abuts Dulwich on one side and Brixton on the other, so is a mix of the reasonably impressive and the not-quite-so-grand. Nick, however, apologised for living there and described it is a place where people carried around books of poetry with them, not necessarily something I recognised, though it got a laugh.

'They deserve a good kicking,' he continued, 'it's the least they fucking deserve'.

The audience sniggered its approval. Nick had found their level and delivered what they wanted to hear. It was called being professional.

And it was about this time that I realised with certainty that tonight, Steve, you would be shite.

Nick is a blokey, likeable guy who gives the impression he's seen a bit of life. In the modern manner, he's simultaneously cocky and self-deprecating, puts people at ease and obviously finds it easy to relate to an audience. He also has a weapons system which he occasionally displays – a sharp comment here, an admonishing word there – just in case there's a smart alec in the audience who fancies his chances. My routine, of course, doesn't have this built-in resilience, and from the raucous nature of the audience, I knew I could be a target tonight. They would try me out, see what I had to offer in the weapons department.

Not much, I mused.

If I'd got it right, Nick had his Falklands experience to stiffen the sinews. He was no softie. My only related ordeal occurred in my gap year, working on one of the cruise liners that later did service as a hospital ship during the conflict.

Maybe Nick had been on the same ship, wounded in battle, gritting his teeth while a bloody tourniquet was loosened. The closest I had come to an 'engagement' was when someone, to wind me up, had sent me a bottle of hair conditioner, supposedly from Malcolm, the ship's gay hairdresser. I spent the rest of my time on board hiding from Malcolm, terrified he would get his homo hands on me.

Watching Nick, watching the audience, I thought how different I was from them. My accent, my clothes, my age; just the way I was. I still looked a bit like 'Man at C&A', a hint of the kind of chap who buys his pants from M&S. Of the others, Nick was wearing an old patterned shirt underneath a crumpled, creamy, lightweight suit. Rhod was, well, just young. And the two Canadians looked vaguely grungy, André with long fair hair and a shambling, slightly truculent gait, Craig wearing some kind of large sock on his head, so with his bulging eyes, big ears and grim-set lantern jaw, he seemed a little like Marty Feldman, though Marty Feldman without the looks. In addition, each one had an interesting non-English accent, whereas I not only sounded aloof, but looked a bit like a bank manager on holiday.

I suppose these sorts of differences had existed before, at other clubs, but only now did they seem to matter, to have a bearing. And all of them would have been defensible, if only I had a defence. But I didn't.

Rhod was next on, and he delivered a very accomplished set, drawing on his Welsh background, which included good jokes about playing football with his grandmother's pancreas (long story), and a few minutes on old toys like Kerplunk and Mousetrap! And this, which I liked a lot: 'When I was in prison I played football for the stalkers. We weren't bad players but when one of us went for the ball, we'd all go. There was no one looking for space.'

A little bit surreal, a little on the sick side, was Rhod, but it all seemed to work for him, the audience not taking against his Welshness as they had done a few years earlier when Rob Brydon had been sent packing, his accent a cue for prolonged sheep noises.

I should also say that Rhod was in addition quite charming and vulnerable. Not good as far as I was concerned. Charm and vulnerability could have offered me a kind of default position, and now they were all used up.

During the interval, Jane obviously picked up my foreboding and said, 'Quite boisterous tonight. That bloke on the fruit machine has been calling things out and inciting his mates. There's a small group of them. I'll be keeping an eye on him.'

She gestured to a shortish, thickish-set man with a shaven head, trousers that stopped just short of the ankle, and a pair of white trainers. He was giving the fruit machine a frantic bashing, then gazing at it with intense enmity. When he turned away, I saw he had a dent imprinted in the back of his head, a depression slightly larger than a two-pound coin. There was something Dickensian about him, a touch of the Magwitches, perhaps.

'Where's he sitting?' I asked.

'Near the back,' Jane smiled, 'well, at the moment he is.'

The second portion of the evening began. Nick did some more material, then André came on stage, all nerves and taciturnity beforehand, though now confident and adept. He did ten minutes or so, again going well with the audience. By this time, I felt completely though abnormally calm, even nerveless, which was perhaps a very bad thing. When Nick introduced me, I sort of glided up through the audience, impassive and unemotional, though also enervated, unfocused, and flaccid.

I took a moment to get going, shielding my eyes from the spotlight and foolishly looking right into it. The audience at this point was very quiet, 'too quiet' as they say in the movies.

Usually, there's a laugh or two at one or other of the opening lines, or at least a splutter, but now there was nothing. The inside-out line which reveals the exact nature of my grandfather's war experiences ('1935 . . . joined the SS) was met by an uncomprehending shelf of silence. I looked down at the first two rows, half wondering if anyone was there, and saw a group of girls nudging one another, much as they might have done at a school assembly when an especially dull guest speaker had been invited, brought in to address them about something like ornithology or careers in the Post Office.

Slowly, at first intermittently, then with growing awareness and connivance, one or two began to giggle, the kind of pitying snigger most usually reserved for incontinent grannies or farting dogs.

I ploughed on, not quite bungling the material, but suddenly distrusting it and occasionally garbling, alert to the small eddy of titters spreading through to the other rows. Someone had started up on my right and there was a definite stir of disapproval rippling through the ranks, even a few communal groans of dissatisfaction.

By this time, any laughing I could hear was wildly out of sync with anything in the material which could have been construed as 'comic', the effect like watching a badly dubbed film, actually no, the effect a realisation they were laughing *at* me.

I rambled through the lederhosen story feeling that the

confessional nature of the material, usually an important ingredient in winning over an audience, merely confirmed to this one that I was a prat, that lederhosen-wearing was precisely the kind of thing I would do.

At least no one was booing.

Well, not yet.

At the point where I admit to deficiency, it may have been about language or parenthood, I can't remember which and it doesn't really much matter, at the moment where I say, 'And I'm also unsuited to . . .', someone shouted out, 'to . . . COMEDY! You're unsuited to comedy. Get off . . .'

And this seemed to kick open some kind of door for the rest of the audience who now knew it was more than all right to have a go at me.

It's a strange experience being heckled, at least being heckled with some intensity and such focus, being the sole object of derision in a room of three hundred other people. I could have simply walked off, but I was determined to finish. It was, after all, the only achievable thing left to me, not being bullied off stage, so on I went, tripping over lines, repeating others, barely holding it together, missing out chunks then going back and inserting them at nonsensical moments, in any case rearranging stuff so it didn't make much sense and punctuating what I did say with things like, 'I'm not going, you know. You're going to hear the end of this whether you like it or not.'

'We don't!' someone chortled.

'I'd rather be at home watching paint dry,' another chimed.

I smiled, well, sort of smiled, and said, actually, I would prefer he was at home watching paint dry, too, and that watching paint dry was probably at the upper end of his intellectual capacity, no, beyond it, but if that's what he wanted to do it was fine by me so why didn't he just fuck off and do it, have the courage to do what he was threatening . . .

Though of course that isn't what happened at all. Maybe I did smile, but after he'd shouted out – it's usually a 'he'; the women just titter, which is just as hurtful, probably more if you can bear to think about it – I thought how little experience I had of this kind of thing. I guess people respond in different ways, though all of them must stem from a sense of being wounded and wanting, somehow, to fight back. Remember, for example, Bob Monkhouse's unconscious punching of a heckler? Jo Brand has a five-point plan: take a good look at yourself, assess your heckler, grade your put-downs, pretend you don't care and swear. Some comedians heckle the audience, getting their retaliation in first. Thus, Pat Condel used to ask if there were any secretaries in the audience. On getting the required 'yes', he would say, 'Nip out and make us a cup of tea, love.' Some comedians thrive on being heckled, getting a sort of adversarial kick from it. Gerry Sadowitz opened a show in Montreal with 'Hello, moosefuckers', only to have one of the moosefuckers jump up on stage and beat the shit out of him. And Sean Hughes recalls being booed and having to duck plastic glasses, carrying on anyway, though not being able to leave his bed for the next three days.

Any half-decent comic should be able to deal with hecklers. Not me, though.

Rather than confronting it, I simply retreated into myself, going on with what was left of my material, at first quite cheerily, sort of hoping that things would get better, hoping for the best, whatever that was, but in any event widening the gap between 'performer' and 'audience' to unbridgeable proportions.

Once this happened, it was only a short hop to becoming openly antagonistic, at which point the audience was united against me. They had me exactly where they wanted – on the back foot, helpless, feeble, compliant, utterly lost, completely alone.

'I'm going to tell you a joke now . . .' I snarled.

'About bloody time,' someone added.

'You are one,' a second added.

'A piss-poor one, though,' laughed another.

'I am going to tell you a joke,' I persisted, 'now.'

'Was that it?' came a response.

'You've already said that,' added his mate as they clinked glasses and cackled to one another.

'I'm. Going. To. Tell. You. A. Joke,' I said. Then the dam burst: 'But because you're all such ignorant cunts I doubt you'll understand it.'

'Ooooh!' hissed a fat girl in the third row.

'Language!' said someone to my left.

'Fuck off! You're not funny,' someone called from the back.

It had developed into a bit of a free-for-all, comments being shouted from all parts of the club, the audience acting as a unit, emboldened by the realisation that hostile fire would not be returned, the sense of disapproval rippling around me, isolating the stage.

Then I began to hear some of the pre-prepared put-downs: things like, 'This is what happens when cousins get married' and 'Do I come round to your place of work shouting "Give us a Big Mac"?' Most of this kind of thing isn't very good, merely adding to the general disquiet rather than generating hurt. Though above the clamour, I did hear someone say, 'What do you *want*?' which was, I admit, more effective.

I remember thinking, I must remember that.

I finished, or at least ground to a halt near the finish of what a week ago I had the nerve to call 'my routine', and sort of lolloped joylessly off stage.

No more of this, thank you very much.

Rhod saw me in the bar and placed a consoling hand on my shoulder. 'Never mind, mate. Happens to us all. We've all been there.' Then he turned back to a blonde girl with lipstick and teeth, a great deal of both, who was busy hanging on his every word.

Comes with the territory, I suppose.

Though, obviously, not for me.

Jane came over, still smiling, and said, 'They usually go for someone. I could tell things might get a little rough. They were looking at one another as soon as you got on stage. Checking if it was all right to have a go.'

'Yes.'

'And it was all right.'

'It was, rather.'

I told her in more detail about my comedic quest and how the experience, though not seeming too good at the moment, would actually be of help to me, breezily adding that I had held my own in Eastbourne less than a week ago. This was also my last ever gig.

'You'll get over it.'

I went outside for a breath of air. Since I'd gone into the club a couple of hours ago, things had moved on. People were wandering around drunk or nearly drunk, some singing, others shouting, a few even making no noise at all. Taxis and buses were offloading more people who squeezed into one or other of the large, busy bars on Creek Road or back towards Greenwich itself.

Pippa was away, so I phoned Max, just back from what he calls 'uni?' (how I hate that negative interrogative). I needed to tell someone about the disaster, share the hurt.

'No surprises there, then,' he said coolly.

'I'm glad you weren't there.'

'I wouldn't go that far.'

'Ho-ho.'

'It is, a bit.'

'Tell me I'm funny.'

'You're funny.'

'Not that way. Tell me I'm really funny.'

'You're really funny.'

'Funny ha ha?'

'Maybe.'

'Give me an example.'

'When you speak French.'

'This isn't going to work, is it?'

'No.'

'OK. What are you doing tomorrow? I thought we could meet for breakfast . . .'

'Sorry, I'm working at the gym. The early shift. Then putting details of the chromatic glasses in the post to you.'

'Thanks.'

'You're welcome.'

He's a good lad, is Max. Balanced, mature, responsible. Everything a proud father could wish for. When his mum and I separated, humour played an important part in helping to get through things. Actually, now I think about it, maybe not for her. Max was about fourteen when it happened, so it's difficult to gauge what sort of effect it had. Things have gone all right for him so far, so maybe we'll only find out when he hits a bad patch.

Then we'll find out about his sense of humour.

After Otto was born, Max picked us all up from the hospital in his car. 'There you are,' I remember saying, 'I always promised you wouldn't be brought up as an only child.'

'Fuck off, Dad,' he replied.

Chip off, I thought, chip off.

I tried to get back into the club to watch the other Canadian's act, but was stopped at the door.

'I'm one of the acts,' I said, though not much wanting to say it.

'I don't remember you,' said Doorman Number One.

'Yes you do,' said his mate, 'he's the one who, er, you know . . .'

'Oh, yes,' he snorted, 'I *do* remember you. In you go.'

Craig had already started and I couldn't bear the thought of walking past or through the two hundred or so people who had just given me such a hard time, so I found a seat at the back, actually directly behind the bloke Jane had pointed out to me, the man with the dent in his head.

The audience were obviously liking Craig. He took a swig of Volvic mineral water and said he wasn't drinking it because he liked the French but he was proud to do anything which might contribute to a national drought there. There was a lot of mugging, his features cartoonishly exaggerated by the cloth pulled tight over his hair, and I didn't think his material particularly strong, though he was soon causing waves of laughter to ripple through the audience. It was like Logan said – you can get away with anything, it's just fucking around; the trick is in getting the audience to allow you to fuck around.

Maybe I should have worn a sock on my head.

By this time, Craig was becoming semi-incoherent, sardonic observations about English traffic roundabouts and so on tumbling from his mouth. On the other hand, it seemed he only had to speak, though speak with plenty of jaw-jutting, eye-rolling menace, for the audience to roll over in hilarity. Dent Man wasn't really listening – you could tell as much from his glazed expression – though he was still doubled up with laughter. He was in his own giggle zone, merely using Craig as a prompt.

There's been plenty of stuff written about the beneficial, therapeutic nature of laughter. Jonathan Miller, for example, the medicinal comedian, thinks one of the functions of humour is to allow us to rehearse in our minds alternative categories and classifications of the world in which we find ourselves, laughter thus being a way of trying things out, imagining ourselves into other spaces. And the 1987 Annual Meeting of the British Association for the Advancement of Science devoted a series of lectures to humour, broadly concluding that we derive great biological benefit from comedy.

Undoubtedly, a bit of comedy does you a power of good, but everything in moderation. I like to think that Dent Man and maybe other members of the audience were determined to laugh, bent on it no matter what – as a safety valve, as a public display of having a good time, whatever. I'd seen a programme on TV the week before, about dads and husbands who slept with their au pairs. One of the girls, I think from Poland, had obviously set her cap at some chap from Surrey or somewhere, and even though she couldn't speak a word of English, she was guffawing heartily at his every witticism. If you have a good reason to laugh, you're unlikely to be put off by actually finding something unfunny.

Similarly, everyone was at Up the Creek to have a *bloody good laugh*. Afterwards, there'd be a disco. In between, there'd be lots of drink and ciggies and maybe a few drugs. They didn't want to merely smile. Smiling was wimpy. What they craved was what one psychophysiological study called 'an abrupt, strong expiration' followed by 'a series of expiratory-inspiratory microcycles superimposed upon the larger expiratory movements'.

A right good laugh, in other words.

And Craig had let people know it was absolutely OK to have one. So, they let rip, quaking away, relaxing nervous tension, expressing Freud's 'sum of psychic energy', heaving their shoulders, forgetting whatever it was that made them want to laugh in the first place, generally feeling cheered up. Besides, it's cheaper than booze and less dangerous than drugs.

And why not?

Well, you can have too much of a good thing. In the 1960s, a traveller to Africa observed pygmies fall on the ground and kick their legs in the air, possessed by paroxysms of breathless and apparently painful laughter. There have also been stories of people laughing themselves to death. It's not unheard of to hear of people literally pissing themselves with laughter. And in 1804, a 'grinning match' took place at Bridlington in Yorkshire. *The Times* reported on 11 June that 'There were three competitors for the prize, all of whom were speedily seized with the most painful symptoms, in consequence of their violent contortions, and two of them died in a few days; the third lies dangerously ill.'

Up the Creek, with its mood of Friday-night release, its tribal determination to have a cracking good time, was no place for me. The critic Max Beerbohm once observed, 'The mass of people, when it seeks pleasure, does not want to be elevated: it wants to laugh at something beneath its level.' Not that I sought to elevate people, though I hardly appealed to their baser desires. My fault, or rather my limitation, but there you go: simply, I wasn't able to supply this particular audience's demands.

On the other hand, they had still arrived at laughter through my presence, though admittedly by a more roundabout route, by taking the piss out of me. And that was fair enough, too. Eventually, they goaded me into becoming an object of fun, a lamentable plaything, something they could laugh at rather than with. Ah well. At least I served some purpose. And afterwards, I lived on – sort of – when Nick Wilty made further jokes about my non-performance, my name being received with pantomime boos and derisive giggling.

It really was the end for me. I felt if I persisted, worked very hard indeed, developing material and honing performance skills, denying myself a family or a social life, somehow making myself simultaneously thick- and thin-skinned, and becoming completely committed to the goal of making people laugh, then I could, given time, maybe four or five years, and in the right environment with the right audiences, have become a competent comedian. In its way, this was something of a triumph, though only in the qualified sense, say, of a non-swimmer envisaging his first unaided width. Logan was wrong. Not everyone could be a comedian. Though some could, and they deserve respect.

Standing up in front of people and trying to make them

laugh is a courageous thing to do. It's the most naked thing you can do while still wearing clothes. I have nothing but admiration for those who do it, though it doesn't necessarily follow that I always admire how they do it. But it wasn't for me. I was too set in my ways, too private, too introverted, too anti-social, too mean-spirited, too complicated, too comfortable with myself, too melancholy, too discreet, too wary, too self-conscious, too analytical, too sensitive and, finally, maybe not sensitive enough.

So, after all, I hadn't really discovered myself through comedy, though possibly I could say I'd consolidated myself. I was a white, middle-class, middle-aged, well-educated ironist with a passing taste for the unconventional, someone who had gained the not inconsiderable satisfaction of knowing he could occasionally step beyond his natural boundaries, though was most content when he was comfortably within them.

How exciting is that?

There is a character in an Iris Murdoch novel who profoundly distrusts music because he suspects it of giving him feelings he does not have. I feel much the same about doing stand-up.

By the time I'd thought all this, I'd left Up the Creek and had walked a couple of hundred yards to the *Cutty Sark*, the old tea clipper, dry-docked in the middle of a pedestrianised area abutting the Thames. It's an evocative place. Home, for example, to the Greenwich Observatory, and the place where the world's time is measured from. And once, long ago, great tea clippers, sails billowing in the wind like so much drying laundry, beat their way before the breeze along the river to the London docks. Not many years ago, a mile or so upriver, the docks at Wapping and Rotherhithe had big cargo ships at berth rather than upmarket grill-rooms, corporate headquarters and apartments for high earners. Nelson's body rested in the hospital just round the corner.

Up the Creek is a good name for a comedy club. Though it works well enough in a metaphorical kind of way, its genesis is more literal. It's on Creek Road, and I assume it's called Creek Road because it was actually a creek, maybe a small bay or inlet where boats and small ships were once moored before putting out to sea. Now there are buses, a 1970s retro shop, a chippy, a shop that sells CDs and bars. Lots of bars.

This was the sort of thing that would have irritated Michael Wharton, a controversial humorist in the 1950s and 60s, and author of the 'Peter Simple' column in the *Daily Telegraph*. He talked about the ruin of England's past, observing that all 'influence is almost gone' and asking, 'Is it all utterly Beyond a Joke?' His answer was that the way England was going, the only response possible to its ironic jumble of values was a desperate laugh – laughter as a kind of survival strategy.

Some writers and thinkers have observed that our sense of humour constantly tries to defuse life, rather than attempt to solve its problems. This habit, they argue, is in large measure a product of early twentieth-century war and depression. What can't be cured must be endured. 'Carrying on' is the British way, getting by, pressing on regardless. When German cities were being heavily bombed towards the end of the Second World War, Goebbels called on German citizens to display the same good-humoured, jovial fortitude of the English to see them through. He reminded them that Englanders were also a Teutonic people.

So, do we Brits need a laugh, and if so, how desperately? Well, if you believe the papers, we do. Over one-six day period, I collected articles from just a few broadsheets about national angst and modern Britain's dazed awfulness, a snapshot of self-flagellation. Eighty per cent of doctors admit to over-prescribing antidepressants; one in three GP appointments involve a patient reporting depression; modern Britain is a perplexed, post-imperial island floating nervously between Europe and America; 'The English identity crisis: who do you think you are?' asked the *Observer*; Britain is filled with people who are really proud of their stupidity; 'We're thick . . . Everybody else is a tosser,' suggested one magazine; the French don't understand the English people's obsessive identification with its national football team; 'Discontent, uncertainty, boredom and disillusionment are becoming an indelible feature of the English culture'; one survey revealed that fatherhood in Britain is becoming a form of depression for the modern-day man; 'Why we loathe Britons abroad,' announced the *Telegraph*; British tourists are ranked as the world's worst by an online travel service; and, finally, Britain is work-obsessed, work having overtaken us and invaded our consciousness creating new kinds of psychological hardships. Stress levels are rising on all fronts.

Nervous, depressed, lacking identity, puzzled, overworked, anxious, disliked and stupid. All that in a week, and I wasn't even looking particularly hard. So what's the answer? Maybe 'laughter yoga'? Madeleine Bunting's book, *Willing Slaves: How the Overwork Culture is Ruling Our Lives*, suggests that one answer is comedy, and cites David Brent from *The Office* who wants above all else to be seen as a 'good laugh'. In an otherwise generally grotesque caricature, it's his most redeeming feature. Apparently, one minute of laughter is equal to ten minutes on a rowing machine. Studies have shown that in the 1950s, people used to laugh an average of eighteen minutes a day. Now, that's down to six minutes a day.

There's plenty of evidence out there to support the notion of humour as a kind of commodity; of humour evolving into a service industry. A few years ago, Strathclyde University launched a comic-skills course designed to help budding comics deliver the perfect punchline. 'Keep staff laughing and the company profits,' one managing director has observed, and the same, he noted, could be said of UK plc. 'I try to get people to laugh,' said David Firth, a stage actor turned management consultant whose clients include Barclays, BA, and IPC magazines. 'Organisations would become better places if they could laugh.' One comedian I know has a seasonal job with the local council, directing and organising its Christmas talent show, teaching accountants how to structure a gag and showing personal secretaries how to gauge an audience.

I've read of an Academy of Juvenile Humor in America, set up for ten- and eleven-year-old comedians, churning out pint-sized deliverers of laughs. Like all things American, it's an idea which will, in all probability, end up over here. Shortly, they'll be schools for comedy, with their own league tables, punchline targets, comedy inspectors, clowning practicals, comedian profiles, laughter coursework, and all the rest of it. And that's the point at which we'll know how much trouble we're in – when humour arrives in prescribed, preferred packages of plastic, manufactured brilliance. And once business twigs the full potential of funniness, the burgeoning demand for it, then who's to say it won't muscle in on the independent clubs and standardise or control the humour in some way?

Don't laugh. Humour as commodity. As *mere* commodity. It could happen.

In some ways, it already has. A number of comedy clubs are mere links in a commercial chain of other similar comedy clubs. Most of the MCs I saw or worked with have a horribly equivalent style of patter which is blandly, pleasantly democratic. (And while we're about it, what in Christ's name are comedians doing in big stadiums? That's about as funny as a Nuremberg rally.)

Nostalgia isn't what it used to be, runs the old joke. Still, I don't see myself as another Grumpy Old Man, or the new Roger Scruton. Let me put it on record, for instance, how much I like motorways, body piercing, selected high street retailers, processed cheese, shopping at Waitrose, bottled water and probably many more of the grouchy brigade's shibboleths. On the other hand, there *is* an awful lot of comedy around these days and I suppose there has to be a reason for it, doubtless a supply-and-demand kind of reason.

Comedy, of course, is also a part of a collective memory. Today's comedians, whether they like it or not, are following a long line of other comedians. Howerd, Cooper, Monkhouse and so on have been reinvented and revived, brought back into the limelight.

Appreciating that we are probably aware of and conditioned by humour more completely than other countries has led to numerous attempts to account for English humour. In 1946, Harold Nicolson produced an academic, itemised list which included a propensity for high spirits and finding comedy in the dangerless misfortune of others. J.B. Priestley once remarked, 'There are good reasons why Englishness creates a climate in which true humour can flower. It is, so to speak, avoiding closed rational systems that encourage men to believe they know everything about everything. (This makes for pride, at once the enemy and victim of humour.)' And most recently, Peter Ackroyd's *The Origins of the English Imagination* has claimed the importance of the weather, the landscape, even the trees, in shaping a characteristic taciturnity, pragmatism, melancholy, dreaminess and comic irreverence.

Then there's Alan Bennett's contention that we are conceived in irony, floating about in it from the womb, which washes away 'guilt and purpose and responsibility'. In other words, allowing us to avoid feelings which might be painful, distance ourselves from our emotions. 'Joking but not joking. Caring but not caring.'

Maybe a pervasive sense of humour is a characteristic which helps us to deal with embarrassment – for what, exactly? For having had an empire? For having *lost* one? For assuming superiority? For managing the evidence of *inferiority*? – apparently a nineteenth-century sentiment and perhaps even a narrowly English one. It has always been part of the Englishman's objection to foreigners that they are 'brazen-faced', unembarrassable and therefore untrustworthy.

Especially the French.

How can you trust a people whose very language does its best to conceal the existence of the blush? '*Rougir*' does not in itself differentiate between a blush and a flush, though all good Englishmen, of course, know precisely what the difference is.

I sat down on a wall near to the *Cutty Sark*. Back at Up the Creek, they'd be gearing up for the disco. The pubs were emptying and there was jollity in the air, though not actually any of 'the disgraceful loutishness of yob culture' which had become such a feature in recent documentaries about badly behaved, incendiary Britain. A pity, really, I thought. At my age, a fight or even a public show of promiscuity might have been quite interesting.

This was definitely The End. I felt calm and relieved that I wouldn't be going back on stage. I'd recently learned that I hadn't made it through to the semi-finals of the Channel 4 comedy competition, though Rich, from the AmusedMoose course, appearing in a different heat from me, had. From what I'd heard, not many of them were doing much comedy. Julie had had her baby, a boy. Laurence had got enough material together for his Edinburgh show and would be previewing it in London next week. And a week after I'd appeared at Up the Creek, I heard that Nick Wilty had somehow injured his willy at Glastonbury, apparently skewering it with a tent pole.

Now *that's* funny.

Three other people, two blokes and a girl, came over and sat close to me, eating kebabs, chatting about a comedy club they'd been to, though not, thank God, Up the Creek. They seemed genuinely interested in what they'd witnessed, discussing jokes that worked, performers who didn't, that sort of thing. Then they stopped talking and slowly, more or less at the same time, we all looked towards the river, contemplating it, probably in different ways, maybe thinking of the ugliness spreading like gangrene across the body of the country, maybe of work, maybe of sex, maybe of history, whatever, though still doing broadly the same thing. Inevitably, we looked downriver, imagining what lay there as the waters thickened and eventually spilled into the North Sea and the English Channel. It was a pleasant feeling. Just to be here means to partake in the essence of the country. Even if England was a shithole there were times when it didn't seem like such a bad shithole. And if things got any worse, we could take comfort from Peter Cook's observation that Britain was sinking, sinking yes, but sinking giggling into the sea.

Appendix 1

This is the basic routine, occasionally modified. The joke which ends it changed most frequently, mainly because I never quite trusted it, yet could never think how to change it.

'Good evening ladies and gentlemen. My name is Steve Jacobi. You might be familiar with the name – that's because I'm the bastard son of the famous homosexual English actor Derek Jacobi. But it's OK. We see a bit of one another, he looks after me. For example, he pulled a few strings and got me this gig. Because that's what families do, isn't it? They look after you. No matter how strange or odd they might be, they get behind you. Take my grandfather, for instance. An odd man – but also an interesting one. A decorated war hero, but like all those old soldiers, he doesn't talk about his experiences. Actually, he can't. He's dead. But even when he was alive, he didn't. And I'm sure he would have had things to say – he led not a good war, but a colourful one: 1936 – joined the SS; 1941 – taken prisoner on the Russian Front. On the other hand, he may well have been talking about it and I'd never have known – he didn't speak English and I couldn't speak German. So when I thought he was saying vaguely German things like 'Could you please pass me another enormous slab of chocolate cake with a cherry on top', or 'Take my advice, son – get your towels down early', he could just as well have been saying, 'Why don't you get off your fat arse and do something useful like annexing the Sudetenland?' – and I'd never have known. One of my biggest regrets is not getting to know my grandfather very well. On the other hand, seeing him did mean we spent every summer in Germany. And for those two or three months every year, my mum put me in lederhosen; zips, harness, embossed hunting scene, the lot. I think she liked to do this because lederhosen didn't need washing – just a quick wipe down with a damp cloth and the occasional buffing with an appropriately hued dab of Kiwi shoe polish. It was, however, very difficult to go to the toilet while you were wearing them. So during daylight hours, my willy . . . my little willy, meine kleine Wilhelm, Helmut . . . lay curled up and undisturbed in his leathery cocoon. By mid-August, I smelt of piss. Well, piss and polish. But it was all right. We all did. It was the same for everyone in my gang – Günter, Heinz and poor, unfortunate little Adolf. Things only got nasty when we came back to England at the end of the holidays and Mum still insisted I wore the lederhosen. Now at that time in the 1970s, lederhosen hadn't quite caught on in Birmingham. And I was teased. People laughed at me. First it was 'Fritz', then 'Leather Knicks', and finally 'Plastic Pants'. But I didn't blame my mother. She was only doing her best, bringing me up the best way she knew. It's difficult bringing up children. I know this, because quite recently I've had one of my own. Before he was born, we went through the usual 'for' and 'against' arguments about having him. Against – more visits from the in-laws; more projectile vomiting; no sleep; no social life; no money; no holidays; no sex; no two-seater open-topped sports car. For . . . (*pause*) . . . his arrival was the final piece in our familial jigsaw puzzle; that, and not having to fork out four hundred quid to the clinic for a termination. So it was a close call. And even after he was born, the sense of uncertainty continued to rage. Was it right to bring a young, innocent child into a world full of terrorism, pollution and Ant and Dec? Still, in the long run, I don't think it's the big issues which affect you the most. It's the small things which most influence how you feel, and sway the decisions you make on a day-to-day basis. In my own case, things like running out of tea bags, a phobia of public toilets – and a concern for the niceties of the English language. I hate it, for example, when I hear people saying 'at the end of the day' or 'at this moment in time'; I hate people who say 'to be fair' or 'to be honest', thereby implying that for the rest of the time they're being neither fair nor honest; I hate people who say they've 'reinvented' themselves when what they really mean is that they've changed – a bit. But I'm not immune to this kind of abuse. I also have problems with language. With the word 'love', for example. I find it very easy to say, 'I love James Bond movies,' but far more difficult to say, 'I love my father.' Is this a fault of the word or a fault of my use of the word? If we follow Plato's advice on this – and, ladies and gentlemen, you look like the kind of audience which might – then Plato tells us that we should love people and things for their virtues. With James Bond, this is comparatively straightforward: I love James Bond movies for their style, their music, and the classic three-part structure which invariably ends with the impregnation of a techno-womb. But my father? Even once you get past the adultery, multiple bankruptcies, regular non-attendance on family holidays and the fact that he's a bit of a baldy? Well . . . he likes cats; and he's quite a good driver. Perhaps if he'd occasionally skydived into the back garden with a Union Jack parachute, or slept with a Chinese air hostess, or karate-chopped the milkman, things might have been different. On the other hand, he does have a wonderful sense of humour, my dad . . . which he's passed on to me. So I should be grateful. And I'd like to end with one of my dad's favourite jokes, and not just end with one of his favourite jokes, but end with one of his favourite jokes and a sentimental lump in my throat . . .

Appendix 2

What happened in New York. These are merely jottings which somehow ended up as a semi-coherent performance. The outline is more or less as it was scribbled in my notebook, but you probably get the general idea.

'Intro: probably tell I'm English from the accent, that and charm, wit, irony etc., bred into us from an early age . . . at public school I was sodomised on a regular basis by the headmaster (school colours for buggery?). At Cambridge, became homosexual for a while – we all did – and then took usual route into spying for the Soviets.

In New York to find out about comedy. Admit to not being a real stand-up? Proportion through distance etc. Guarantee that you can tell a good joke they won't find funny (e.g. Ken Dodd ventriloquism joke?) and present it as crucial piece of research: are Americans too conservative to laugh at ref to women's genitalia? (Expand?) I don't mind if you laugh or not – either response has validity for me (research/successful gag).

TELL JOKE – comment on response . . . maybe add something about having a president whose name is the equivalent of being called 'pubic hair' (too obvious?).

Cut to discussion about why different countries have different senses of humour. (By this time, for instance, audiences in England would be helpless with mirth . . . maybe tell them they're getting there – slowly but surely etc.) Number of things that makes us different is getting smaller – Americans exporting their way of life to whole world. Soon, we'll have no choice but to laugh at the same things. Colonising of laughter etc.

Is there such a thing as a universal joke?

LIST: Ways in which America is changing the world/taking over, therefore having effect on humour:

1. Hollywood (all endings are happy; good always triumphs over bad)
2. Cosmetic surgery (looking the same – jokes about ugly people)
3. Milky coffee
4. McDonald's (apart from quality of food, no joy in eating – time constraints etc.)
5. Being fat
6. Bad cars
7. Bad sports
8. Concept of choice (more is not better/spending time worrying about trivia is counter-productive . . . only illusion of choice)
9. Political correctness (dishonest? From now on, I want to be known as 'not disabled')
10. Mangling of English language (just kidding, better out than in, love you. 24/7 . . .)

Sources and Acknowledgements

Ackroyd, Peter. *Origins of the English Imagination*
Amis, Kingsley. *The Biographer's Moustache* and *Memoirs*
Amis, Martin. *Money*
Betjeman, John. *Collected Poems*
Bunting, Madeline. *Willing Slaves*
Burn, Gordon. *The North of England Home Service*
Carter, Angela. *Wise Children*
Crompton, Richamal. *William the Fourth*
Dawson, Les. *A Card for the Clubs*, *Well-fared My Lovely*, *Hitler Was My Mother-in-law* and *A Time Before Genesis*
DeLillo, Don. *White Noise*
Disher, Maurice Willson. *Fairs, Circuses and Music Hall*
Fry, C.B. *Life Worth Living*
Glanville, Brian. *The Comic*
Grigson, Geoffrey, ed. *About Britain No. 3*
Hardee, Malcolm. *I Stole Freddie Mercury's Birthday Cake*
Heller, Ted. *Funnymen*

Hicks, Bill. *Love all the People*
Huxley, Aldous. *The Island*
Koestler, Arthur. *Act of Creation*
Leith, William. *British Teeth*
Low, David. *British Cartoonists, Caricaturists and Comic Artists*
Monkhouse, Bob. *Crying with Laughter*
Morecambe, Eric. *Mr Lonely*
O'Farrell, John. *This is Your Life*
Orwell, George. *English People*
Phillips, Adam. *On Kissing, Tickled and Being Bored*
Priestly, J.B. *English Humour*
Shakespeare, William. 'Troilus and Criseyde'
Skinner, Frank. *Frank Skinner*
Taylor, D.J. *The Comedy Man*
Thompson, Ben. *Sunshine on Putty*
Trevor, William. *Children of Dynmouth*
Waugh, Evelyn. *Brideshead Revisited* and *Tactical Exercise from Complete Short Stories*
Wodehouse, P.G. *Summer Lightning* and *Heavy Weather*